Age Related Pension Expenditure and Fiscal Space

T0293225

This book explores the linkages between age related pension expenditures and the fiscal space needed to fund them as well as to organize the mix of financing methods with different risk-sharing arrangements. After critically assessing the existing models projecting age related expenditure in the literature, this book focuses on the case studies of these inter-linkages in four highly populated East Asian countries, namely China, Indonesia, India, and Japan. Nearly two-fifths of the global population live in these countries. Therefore, how these inter-linkages manifest themselves and the initiatives in these countries for finding fiscal space will have an impact on how the ageing issues are addressed globally.

This book has several distinguishing characteristics, including exploration of inter-linkages between age related expenditure and fiscal space, and application of country-specific methods to explore these linkages, rather than relying on the standard macroeconomic model. In the process, the studies also bring out the limitations of the standardized model used in the literature. Scholars and policymakers interested in the subject will definitely find the book of valuable use.

Mukul G. Asher is a Professorial Fellow at the Lee Kuan Yew School of Public Policy, National University of Singapore. He specializes in social security issues in Asia and in public financial management.

Fauziah Zen is an economist at the Economic Research Institute for ASEAN and East Asia (ERIA). She is also an associate professor at the Faculty of Economics, University of Indonesia. She has been working with the governments in ASEAN in the field of fiscal policy, infrastructure issues, disaster risk reduction, and social security. She also serves as an advisor to the Finance Minister of the Republic of Indonesia on the fiscal decentralization issue. She obtained her PhD from Hitotsubashi University, Japan.

Routledge-ERIA Studies in Development Economics

Age Related Pension Expenditure and Fiscal Space

Modelling techniques and
case studies from East Asia

**Edited by Mukul G. Asher
and Fauziah Zen**

LONDON AND NEW YORK

First published 2016
by Routledge

2 Park Square, Milton Park, Abingdon, Oxfordshire OX14 4RN
711 Third Avenue, New York, NY 10017

*Routledge is an imprint of the Taylor & Francis Group,
an informa business*

First issued in paperback 2018

British Library Cataloguing in Publication Data
A catalogue record for this book is available from the British Library

Library of Congress Cataloging-in-Publication Data
Names: Asher, Mukul G., editor. | Zen, Fauziah, 1970– editor.
Title: Age related pension expenditure and fiscal space:
   modelling techniques and case studies from East Asia / edited
   by Mukul G. Asher and Fauziah Zen.
Description: Abingdon, Oxon ; New York, NY : Routledge,
   2015. | Includes index.
Identifiers: LCCN 2015035173
Subjects: LCSH: Pensions—East Asia. | Social security—
   East Asia. | Fiscal policy—East Asia.
Classification: LCC HD7226 .A435 2015 | DDC
   331.25/24095—dc23
LC record available at http://lccn.loc.gov/2015035173

ISBN: 978-1-138-82579-6 (hbk)
ISBN: 978-1-138-31797-0 (pbk)

Typeset in Galliard
by Apex CoVantage, LLC

Contents

Figures

Tables

Contributors

Mukul G. Asher is a Professorial Fellow at the Lee Kuan Yew School of Public Policy, National University of Singapore. He specializes in social security issues in Asia and in public financial management.

Bambang P. S. Brodjonegoro is currently serving as Finance Minister of the Republic of Indonesia. His previous public services include Vice Finance Minister and Head of Fiscal Policy Office, both in Indonesia, Director General of IRTI of Islamic Development Bank, and Dean of Faculty of Economics, University of Indonesia. He has extensive working experience in regional economics and fiscal policy. He also has authored several publications in the fields of urban and regional economics, fiscal decentralization, and fiscal policy. He received his PhD from the University of Illinois at Urbana-Champaign. He is also Professor at the Faculty of Economics, University of Indonesia.

Qin Chen is affiliated with the Post-Doctoral Faculty in Department of Economics, Fudan University. He has worked on the issues of Chinese demographics and economies, particularly related to urbanization and pension. Qin obtained his PhD from Fudan University, and was a visiting scholar in the Department of Demography at the University of California, Berkeley.

Astrid Dita is an independent researcher working on issues related to public finance, fiscal decentralization, public-private partnership, and social protection in Indonesia. She is a consultant to various multilateral organizations such as the Asian Development Bank, World Bank, and AusAID. She obtained her Master's degree in Economics from the University of Indonesia.

Jin Feng is Professor of Economics at Fudan University and the Associated Dean of Faculty of Economics. She is also a researcher at the Employment and Social Security Research Center of Fudan University and Fudan Development Institute. Her publications and research interests focus on social security reforms, health insurance, health care, and elderly care in China. She has papers published in various economics journals. She is serving on the boards of the Gerontological Society of Shanghai and the Chinese Women Economists Society.

Hefrizal Handra is Senior Lecturer at Faculty of Economics, Andalas University, Indonesia. He specializes in public finance. He received his PhD from Flinders University of South Australia. He has also served as a member of the advisory team to Indonesia's Finance Minister for fiscal decentralization since 2006.

Suahasil Nazara is Chief of the Fiscal Policy Office in the Ministry of Finance, Republic of Indonesia. Before his present position, he had been extensively supporting the Government of Indonesia in various roles. He was member of the National Economic Council and the Policy Group Coordinator of the National Team for the Acceleration of Poverty Reduction (TNP2K), Office of the Vice President of the Republic of Indonesia. He obtained his PhD from the University of Illinois at Urbana-Champaign. He is also a professor at the Faculty of Economics, University of Indonesia, and former head of the Economics Department. During his professional career he has authored several publications.

Junichiro Takahata is Lecturer of Economics at the Faculty of Economics, Department of Economics on Sustainability, Dokkyo University. He received his PhD in Economics from Hitotsubashi University. He specializes in public economics and has published articles on public finance issues. His recent publications include "Child benefit and fiscal burden in the endogenous fertility setting," *Economic Modelling*, 2015.

Yutika Vora is an independent researcher working on issues related to social protection, public sector governance, and public finance in Asia. She is a consultant to multilateral organizations and non-governmental organizations. She has been working on examining challenges in implementing rural development programs and on improving public service delivery. She has a Global Public Policy Network dual degree, with a Master's degree in International Affairs from Columbia University and a Master's degree in Public Policy from the National University of Singapore. She has a Bachelor's degree in International Political Economy from University of California, Berkeley.

Fauziah Zen is an economist at the Economic Research Institute for ASEAN and East Asia (ERIA). She is also an Associate Professor at the Faculty of Economics, University of Indonesia. She has been working with the governments in ASEAN in the field of fiscal policy, infrastructure issues, disaster risk reduction, and social security. She also serves as an advisor to the Finance Minister of the Republic of Indonesia on the fiscal decentralization issue. She obtained her PhD from Hitotsubashi University, Japan.

Preface

Social protection for the people is a quintessential element in building the ASEAN Community. The envisioned ASEAN Community is a people-centred one, where prosperity of the people becomes the foundation of development measures. The Cha-am Hua Hin Declaration on the Roadmap for the ASEAN Community recognized the role of social protection in enhancing the well-being and livelihood of the people of ASEAN. Furthermore, strengthening social protection has been a priority for ASEAN since its declaration of adoption by ASEAN Leaders during October 2013.

Indeed, one of the key issues in empowering individuals in the economy – thus to create a robust society – is the various risks that can be pooled and addressed by instruments of social protection, both contributory (i.e. social security) and non-contributory (i.e. social safety net). Social security is a component of provision to meet the basic needs and contingencies of life in order to maintain an adequate standard of living. It is not only a part of basic human rights, but it is also a fundamental measure to reduce poverty, vulnerability, and social exclusion, as well as to enhance social cohesion, equity, and sustainable development.

Faced with a situation of increasing life expectancy and rising population growth, the need for social security planning has become more crucial than ever before. Recalling the experience of developed East Asia economies such as Japan, ageing has been recognized as one of the profound risks which will eventually arrive and which can heavily influence an economy. Managing the age-related expenditures, such as pension benefits expenditure, is a foreseeable challenge for any country, which calls for early preparation.

The goal of a prosperous and sustainable ASEAN Community may be achieved with specific mind sets, in which social security is not only an important tool with employment and work, but is also an effective tool for economic growth. It is not a cost for the system, but is an investment for the people, the country, and the region. However, to find a balance between economic development and social sustainability is a very crucial and daunting task for each country.

Although it is fundamental for development, only few countries have achieved the universal coverage of which some populations can enjoy access to comprehensive social security systems, while most of them are covered partially or not at all. The need to extend social security coverage is becoming a contemporary issue. The extension of protection is not concerning only domestic workers, but migrant workers as well. With this important task, there are some issues which are worth mentioning: migrant workers from the measures to facilitate the flow of labour, and informal workers as the biggest labour group. The latter is becoming common theme in the developing countries in this region.

This volume shows that the East Asian experiences in developing and implementing social security systems have been different. The chapters in this volume provide estimates of pension expenditures, lessons learned, and recommendations on the pension policies in the countries with big populations in East Asia (India, China, Indonesia, and Japan). It also looks at the fiscal policies adopted in these countries and how they respond to the future needs of age-related spending.

This edited volume is a product of ERIA's project in Fiscal Year 2012 "SSN (Social Safety Net) in East Asia", with the aim to estimate the fiscal need of social security expenditures and the link with fiscal policies in East Asia. ERIA would like to thank the contributing authors, and especially the editors, for their efforts to materialize the project.

Fukunari Kimura

Acknowledgements

This edited volume focuses on age-related expenditure and its implications on fiscal space for four highly populated countries in East Asia. The editors would like to express sincere gratitude to the Economic Research Institute for ASEAN and East Asia (ERIA) for organizing and funding this research project, and to the ERIA leadership for intellectual support. The contributors to this volume have been immensely cooperative as a group in bringing the research project to the final publication stage. They richly deserve our special thanks. The editors and the contributors received strong cooperation and support from relevant government agencies in respective countries, and from many researchers from academic institutions and think tanks.

We owe a special debt of gratitude and are pleased to mention special thanks to Shujiro Urata, who was instrumental in facilitating the publication with Routledge. We appreciate the thorough professionalism with which Batari Saraswati and Ma'rifatul Amalia assisted in preparing the typescript. This volume is therefore a collective effort, and we have been privileged to be a part of this effort.

Mukul G. Asher and Fauziah Zen
February 2015

1 Age related pension expenditure and fiscal space

An overview

Mukul G. Asher and Fauziah Zen

1. Introduction

This book constitutes the third publication arising from the project on Social Security Systems by the Economic Research Institute for ASEAN and East Asia (ERIA).[1] The primary motivation for this book arises from the need to better understand linkages between age related pension expenditures and the fiscal space needed to fund and finance them. In addressing growing anxiety concerning the credibility of pension promises among policymakers and populations in Asia, deeper understanding of these linkages is essential. This book, however, focuses on pension expenditure requirements intermediated through the fiscal system and not on total resources of the society to meet retirement income security.

After critically assessing the models commonly used by researchers in projecting age related expenditure in the literature, this book focuses on the case studies of age related pension expenditure and fiscal space in four highly populated East Asian countries, namely China, Indonesia, India, and Japan. These four countries account for nearly two-fifths of the global population. As these countries exhibit different per capita income levels and are at different stages in the demographic cycles – with Japan and China exhibiting much more rapid ageing than Indonesia and India – these case studies may be instructive for other middle- and high-income countries in Asia and elsewhere.

Among the four countries, only Japan is a high-income country, while the others are middle-income countries. Japan is also a member of the OECD[2] (Organization of Economic Co-operation and Development), which was set up in 1960. Japan's policymakers face the challenge of declining population, whereas the other three countries will need to cope with rapid ageing and increasing share of aged population at relatively lower levels of income as they strive to move up from middle-income to high-income economies.

The United Nations (2013a) has projected a more rapid pace of ageing over the next several decades. To quote: *"World population ageing is about to start a phase of acceleration. During the past 30 years, between 1980 and 2010, the proportion of the population that is aged 60 years or over increased by 2.4 percentage points in the world as a whole, from 8.6 per cent to 11 per cent. The absolute change in this proportion was much greater in the more developed regions (6.3 percentage points) than in the less developed regions (2.3 percentage points). But these changes pale in comparison to the 7.6 percentage-point increase that is about to occur on average in the next 30 years. . . . Both the less and the more developed regions will experience large changes, of 7.9 per cent and 8.8 per cent, respectively. By comparison, the least developed countries will experience a significant, though much smaller increase of 2.9 percentage points."* (p. 13).

Both the pace of ageing and the number of aged populations – particularly those above 80 years old, who require large support from society as their savings and other assets get depleted – represent policy challenges for these countries. The pace of ageing is relevant, as rapid ageing reduces the time available for all stakeholders to adjust to rapid ageing.

This book explores age related expenditure projections to finding avenues for fiscal space. The country studies in this volume demonstrate how characteristics of the fiscal system and institutional capabilities in each country impact the avenues that may be relevant. Thus, in both India and Indonesia reforming formal systems of pensions is essential for finding fiscal space. Enhancing capabilities to use non-conventional avenues, such as utilization of state assets to generate revenue, is also relevant for India and Indonesia. China has been using the National Social Security Fund (NSSF) and revenue from divestment of public enterprises as non-conventional avenues to help finance age related pension expenditure. One of the major issues in China, however, is to address the pension needs of the substantial number of migrants from rural to urban areas – an issue of not significant relevance to India and Indonesia. For Japan, improving the returns from the Government Pension Fund (GPF) has become essential, and so has the political management of rationalizing pension benefits and increasing the consumption taxes.

2. Funding and financing distinction

There is a distinction between funding age related expenditure and the mix of financing methods and instruments used to fund the expenditure needs of each cohort of population. The funding concerns the society's resources that are devoted to the needs of the elderly. As the proportion of aged in a total population and the longevity of the successive population increases, a greater share of society's resources – which may be drawn from both the public and private sectors – will be required to address the needs of the elderly population. This process is facilitated if a high core rate of economic growth, sustained over a longer period, is exhibited by a country and if appropriate consumption smoothing arrangements – such as increasing retirement savings and channelling them to productive growth-enhancing uses – are effectively implemented.[3] Intergenerational smoothing of nation's wealth through such instruments as Sovereign Wealth Funds (SWFs), commodity stabilization, and other such reserve funds, may also represent an avenue for funding age related pension expenditure.

The financing-mix on the other hand concerns various financing methods and instruments used for funding. A defined contribution (DC) method of retirement financing, whether mandatory or voluntary, specifies the contributions made by the members, employees, and governments; but leaves the monetary benefits to be generated from contributions and investment income during the retirement period undefined. In contrast, the defined benefit (DB) method specifies the benefits to be provided during retirement, but leaves contribution and investment income undefined. A distinction is also made in using the social insurance method, in which participation is compulsory and contributions rates are uniform up to the covered wages. In the commercial insurance method, in contrast, participation could be voluntary or mandatory, but insurance premiums may vary by age and, where not prohibited by law, by gender, as well as by other characteristics of the insured.

The financing-mix instruments may include in varying proportions tax or budgetary allocations for pensions; private saving, whether mandatory or voluntary for retirement; conversion of housing and other assets into retirement income streams; family and community support; and others. With increasing levels of income, growing urbanization, and a higher female labour force participation rate, the need for intermediation of retirement financing through formal state-intermediated institutions increases, while the role of family and community support diminishes.

The weight given to financing methods DB and DC may vary among countries. Their relative importance may also vary in the same country at different stages of economic development and pension objectives and structures. This is also the case with the financing-mix used by a country. This suggests that pension reform is a dynamic context-specific process, and therefore a quest for the 'best' pension structure system and financing method is unwarranted.

3. Demographic projections and their limitations

In estimating age related pension expenditure, demographic projections are essential. The standard internationally comparable data source for demographic projection is the Population Division of the Department of Economic and Social Affairs of the United Nations (UNDESA). The most recent projections available when the chapters in this volume were written (and this is still the case as of February 2015) were the UNDESA's 2012 Revision of the World Population Prospects (UNDESA, 2013b).[4]

The UNDESA (2013b) projections are undertaken for low, medium, high, and constant fertility assumptions, with the medium variant most commonly used. According to the medium variant projections, the global population is projected to increase from 7.2 billion in mid-2013 to 8.1 billion in 2025, and to 9.6 billion in 2050. This represents a nearly one-third increase in only 37 years.

The differences in population projections between the fertility variants are significant. Under the high fertility variant,[5] the projected global population in 2050 is 10.9 billion, 1.3 billion persons more than under the medium variant. At the other end, under the low fertility variant, the global population in 2050 will be 8.3 billion, lower by 2.6 billion as compared to the high variant. In 2050, the population is even higher if the constant rather than the declining fertility rate is assumed.

The UN projections, which focus on the chronological age of the population, are conventionally used for analysing ageing trends. Sanderson and Scherbov (2007), however, argue that as individuals live longer, both the traditional chronological concept of ageing, which they term 'retrospective age', and the forward-looking concept termed 'prospective age' should be used for policy formulation and analysis. While the traditional concept measures how many years a person has lived, the 'prospective age' measures the number of expected years an individual has left to live. With increasing longevity, a fifty-year-old person, who currently has a much longer life expectancy than a same aged person in 1990, may well make different saving, investment, labour force participation, and other relevant economic and personal decisions. The differing behavioural decisions in turn have different implications for public policies and social attitudes towards ageing. The data on 'prospective age' are, however, not published by the UN and other international agencies. The country studies therefore also use projections based on 'retrospective age'.

The above discussion of demographic projections has at least three major implications for projections of age related expenditure for the country studies in this book. First, relatively small errors in fertility rate projections can lead to disproportionately large variations in population projections for a country, as well as for regions in a country. This would impact the projections of age related expenditure and the needed funding by the society and fiscal space. Regular monitoring of fertility and longevity trends and their implications for population projections are therefore essential.

The second implication is that in countries with large populations and land mass – such as China, India and, Indonesia – national and regional fertility variations would have significant implications for regional migration patterns and for the location of individuals and businesses. This in turn would differentially impact the fiscal capacities in different regions. Aggregate national fiscal space needed to manage age related expenditure may thus need to be complemented by the analysis of regional funding and fiscal capacities. This extension of national-level analysis has not been undertaken in the country studies in this book, as this would have significantly expanded the scope of the project. This issue has been deferred for future research. As devolving fiscal and other powers and responsibilities to lower levels of government progresses, such a disaggregated analysis will become even more essential.

The third implication is that projections based on 'retrospective age' used in the individual chapters in the book would alone be not sufficient to fully understand the economic and social behaviour of the elderly, as 'prospective age' considerations will also need to be taken into account. This is, however, left as an area of future research.

4. The concept of fiscal space

The country studies in this book strongly suggest that substantial fiscal space will be needed to fund age related pension expenditure. There is, however, considerable ambiguity in the manner in which fiscal space is defined in the literature. As a result, several definitions co-exist (Heller, 2005; World Bank Group, 2015; Roy *et al.*, 2009).

Heller (2005) defined fiscal space as "the availability of budgetary room that allows government to provide resources for a desired purpose without any prejudice to the sustainability of government's financial position" (p. 3). This is a broad and rather vague definition. The key elements emerging from the brief survey on fiscal space literature are that additional fiscal revenue or expenditure should not unduly hamper government's financial or fiscal sustainability, usually measured by flow indicators, such as budget deficits, and by stock measures, such as public debt and an estimate of contingent liabilities on the government or constraints to broad-based growth. Both generation of additional fiscal space and its use are emphasized. Those focusing on short-term stabilization measures emphasize the sustainability aspects, involving gaps in available resources.

Thus, the World Bank Group (2015, Chapter 3), in their discussion of how to generate fiscal space and use it in the developing countries, adopts the definition of fiscal space of Ley (2009). Fiscal space is defined as the "availability of budgetary resources for a specific purpose . . . without jeopardizing the sustainability of the government's financial position or sustainability of the economy" (p. 122). The focus of the World Bank Group (2015, Chapter 3) study is on fiscal space generation and is used among a cross-section of countries for short-term counter cyclical fiscal policy to cope with macro-economic shocks, such as those generated by the 1997–98 East Asian Financial Crisis and by the 2008 Global Crisis.

The above study identifies fiscal rules imposing specified numerical targets on budgetary aggregates; stabilization and reserve funds which involve setting aside revenue from commodity booms or fiscal balance of payments surpluses; and medium term expenditure frameworks (MTEFs) designed to link budgetary plans and allocations on the one hand, and growth and other strategic objectives on the other hand, in a multi-year flexible framework.

Analysts focusing on broader development issues, however, focus on how additional fiscal revenue and expenditure can be generated from such avenues as reprioritization and efficiency enhancing of and effectiveness of expenditures, domestic revenue mobilization, and budgetary deficits – and in selected countries in the short run, from development assistant. These analysts also emphasize how these additional resources are used for enhancing broad-based economic growth.

Thus, Roy *et al.* (2009) adopt the following definition of fiscal space: "Fiscal space is the financing that is available to government as a result of concrete policy actions for enhancing resource mobilization, and the reforms necessary to secure the enabling governance, institutional and economic environments for these policy actions to be effective, for a specified set of development objectives" (p. 2).

Some analysts, such as Asher (2005), have argued that greater competence and willingness in generating non-conventional revenue resources can help generate fiscal space. Such sources include using state assets, both physical and financial, more productively;[6] revenue from state-created property rights in a transparent and economically desirable manner; and willingness to use non-tax revenue, including appropriate cost recovery and user charges, and surpluses of regulatory bodies.

In analysing fiscal space generated for use in any one area, such as age related expenditure, the opportunities foregone for using the space for other purposes should also be considered in public policy discussions. Tanzi (2006) has argued that addressing the curbing of activities that result in a collection of benefits from government programs by those not targeted by the government programs could also help improve fiscal space.

The above discussion suggests that specific instruments and avenues for generating and using fiscal space will vary among countries, and among regions within the same country. It also suggests that both government income and expenditure flows and its assets represented in the balance sheet will need to contribute to generating fiscal space. This is also evidenced by the country studies in this book.

5. Organization of the book and main findings

This overview chapter has so far provided the rationale for the book, has clarified the distinction between funding and financing of pensions, briefly discussed demographic projections and the need to interpret and use them in a nuanced manner, and explained the concept of fiscal space. This section focuses on the organization of the book and the main findings in each chapter.

In Chapter 2, Junichiro Takahata examines selected methods and studies used to project age related pension expenditure in the literature. This chapter thus represents a summary of what is currently state of the art in age related long-term pension expenditure modelling.

Takahata examines three types of pension-expenditure projection techniques. The first is the arithmetical method. It is based on estimating future social security expenditure from structural details of the existing programs. This method does not incorporate behavioural responses. The IMF (2011) study uses this method. The second method uses micro-simulation from the household panel survey data to replicate the real economy. This method can incorporate behavioural responses of economic agents and dynamic situations. This method can provide the impact of policies in income and wealth distribution in the economy. The third method discussed is the dynamic general equilibrium method. It is more suited to analysing macro-economic rather than micro-economic issues, which are of relevance in pension analysis.

Takahata reports that most studies in this area have been focused on high-income, often called advanced, economies. Only a few have been conducted for emerging economies. However, there exist two projections focusing on emerging economies, including China, India, and Indonesia. The first is by IMF (2011), and the second is by Standard and Poor's (2010).

IMF (2011) focuses on public expenditure and not total pension expenditure. It projects that for China the public pension expenditure will increase from 3.4 percent of GDP in 2010 to 9.2 percent of GDP in 2050, an increase of 5.8 percent of GDP (Table 2.4 in this book). But Standard and Poor's Study (2010) projects pension spending in China to be only about 30 percent of the IMF estimate for 2050, with a projected increase of only 0.4 percent between 2010 and 2050 (Table 2.5) There is also gross inconsistency between Standard and Poor's 2010 and 2013 studies on age related total expenditure, which also include health expenditure, in China (Tables 2.7 and 2.8 in this book). The 2013 study projects such expenditure at 15.1 percent of GDP, more than twice the 7.0 percent projected in the 2010 study.

Estimates for pension expenditure in India curiously project a sharp decline in public pension expenditure between 2010 and 2050 in both the IMF (2011) and Standard and Poor's (2010) studies. The projected expenditure of 0.7 percent of GDP by IMF (2011), and 0.9 percent of GDP by Standard and Poor's (2010) is sharply lower than the actual expenditure on civil service pensions of 2.14 percent of GDP reported by Asher and Vora in this book.

In the case of Indonesia, IMF (2011) projects public pension expenditure increasing from 0.7 percent of GDP in 2010 to 1/6 percent of GDP in 2050; while the corresponding figures for Standard and Poor's (2010) are 0.9 percent and 2.1 percent respectively. The 2004 SJSN Law aiming for universal pension and healthcare coverage by adopting the social insurance method (see Chapters 5 and 6 in this book) has witnessed implementation since 2014. Such a major systemic change makes projections of the above studies not policy relevant.

In the case of Japan, projections of the public pension expenditure by IMF (2011) and by Standard and Poor's (2010) are fairly close, from around 10 percent of GDP in 2010 to 11 percent in 2050. Relatively constant fiscal burden for pensions between 2010 and 2050 are not consistent with the anxieties being exhibited by Japanese policymakers and the Japanese population about credibility of pension promises.

There is a large differential of 5.4 percent of GDP for 2050 in the projections for total age related expenditure, which include health care, for Japan between the Standard and Poor's (2010) (Table 2.7 in this book), and the Standard and Poor's (2013) (Table 2.8 in this book) studies. This suggests a high degree of sensitivity to data and methods applied in the projections, greatly diminishing their policy relevance.

Chapter 3 by Feng Jin and Qin Chen analyses the public pension system in China and the fiscal policy response to meet the challenges of age related expenditure. China is about to achieve universal coverage in its public pension system. The authors argue that there are four schemes within the system intended to cover the entire eligible population, but the Basic Old Age Insurance system (BOAI) for employees in enterprises and other private sectors is the most important scheme in China in terms of pension expenditure and potential future reform.

The authors indicate that the BOAI in 2014 covered about 15 percent of migrant workers and 60 percent of total urban employees. So if pension coverage is extended to these groups, BOAI will receive larger cash flows in the short and medium term, but will have greater pension liability in the future. Inclusion of migrants will also help lower the Urban Old Age Dependency Ratio (OADR) in China (Figure 3.10 in this volume), and will thus improve sustainability of the BOAI. The authors estimate OADR under various scenarios involving combinations of fertility trends, migration rates, coverage ratio, and retirement age (Figure 3.12 in this book).

The authors then simulate the financial outcomes arising out of several reform scenarios; these include increasing the retirement age, reducing the contribution rate, and changing the indexation of pension benefits. They also estimate the fiscal subsidies required in order to keep the reform proposals manageable.

There is a clear trend that the number of pensioners is increasing over time, while the number of contributors is declining – suggesting that the current arrangement of the BOAI is unsustainable. The authors project that share of BOAI pension expenditure will increase from around 3.5 percent of GDP to between 6 and 8 percent of GDP in 2030 (depending on the scenario assumed), and to around 9.5 percent of GDP in 2050. This suggests a need to generate about 6 percent of additional fiscal space for BOAI alone.

The authors suggest that feasible avenues for generating the fiscal space necessary to meet public pension liabilities in China include reforming the BOAI system, including increasing retirement age and changing pension indexation provisions; expanding resources of the National Social Security Fund (NSSF), including improving investment returns; increasing reliance on dividends from state enterprises; enhancing returns obtained from foreign exchange reserves; and improving labour productivity.

In Chapter 4, Asher and Vora estimate age related pension expenditure in the context of India's complex but fragmented social security system. The challenges of designing and implementing pension policies in India's federal political structure, in which responsibilities for pension delivery and financing are shared between the Union government and 29 states, are evident from their chapter.

They characterize India as exhibiting moderately rapid ageing trends. The number of persons 60 years and above is projected to increase by more than three times, from 93 million in 2010 to 296 million in 2050 (UNDESA, 2013a). When combined with increasing feminization of the elderly a and large informal labour force, a shift from the current fragmented national pension system to a unified national system does not appear to be a public policy priority in India.

The authors also note that projections for India by IMF (2011) and Standard and Poor's (2010) show declining pension expenditure between 2010 and 2050, making them not policy relevant. The authors adopt a disaggregated approach, estimating age related pension expenditure for major components of India's pension system using context specific assumptions and judgments. Poor database on pensions, demographic profiles under various schemes, and unfunded and contingent liabilities preclude data-intensive projection methods. The pension expenditure estimates are therefore to a more-than-usual degree based on the best judgment of the authors. They are therefore only indicative of the fiscal space which may be needed to finance age related expenditure.

The authors focus on examining four components of India's pension system: First the Civil Service Pension schemes of the Union (Central) Government and the states (each state has its own pension design). This applies to those in the Union government who were employed before January 1, 2004. Those employed after that are under a defined contribution scheme of the National Pension System (NPS). Similar provisions apply in each State (only two have not adopted NPS). The main rationale for introducing the NPS was to limit future pension liabilities of the government.

The second component is the NPS, which has mandatory and voluntary membership. The government has been co-contributing for those who voluntarily join the NPS. The fiscal burden would thus depend on the pace at which individuals join NPS, and on the time period and level of co-contributions.

The third component is the Employees' Provident Fund Organization (EPFO), which administers provident fund and pension schemes for private sector employees. The government does contribute a small percentage to its pension scheme. But this scheme has large but unfunded liabilities, which will ultimately have to be met from the government budget, requiring fiscal space.

The fourth component is the National Social Assistance Program (NSAP). It is a non-contributory, budget-financed, means-tested assistance to the elderly. It is financed by the Union and respective state governments, but administered by State governments. These features result in large variations in coverage, benefit levels, effectiveness, and fiscal costs of this program across the country. The actual NSAP costs were only 0.07 percent of GDP around 2010. The authors cite estimates which suggest that additional fiscal space of between 0.5 percent and 1.7 percent of GDP will be needed by 2030, depending on the assumptions. The authors note that political pressures on implementing the One Rank One Pension (OROP) arrangements for current and former military personnel is strong. Under this system, the armed forces personnel would receive the same pension if they hold the same rank at retirement regardless of the years of service and date of retirement. While no reliable estimates of the fiscal costs of OROP are available, the judgement of the authors is that fiscal space of between 0.8 and 1.2 percent of GDP may be needed.

The authors estimate that under realistic progress in coverage and benefit levels, between 2 and 4 percent of additional fiscal space will be needed by 2030 to finance pensions. They then analyse India's fiscal system and conclude that while there is some room for finding fiscal space from conventional tax sources, a more complex and systemic approach is needed. This will involve measures to enhance economic growth rate and to widen its reach among regions and sectors; rationalization of fees and charges for public amenities and services; non-conventional resource generation such as the auctioning state assets; and better expenditure management. Their analysis suggests that many of the new pension reform initiatives are likely to create contingent liabilities which will need to be taken into account in an overall fiscal cost of the pension arrangements.

They also suggest the following avenues: Greater professionalism by EPFO and other formal social security organizations; better expenditure management, particularly in the use of technology to reduce transaction costs of subsidies, including curbing expenditures accruing to unintended beneficiaries; greater proficiency in generating revenue from non-conventional sources of revenue, such as auctions; and the more productive use of state assets.

In Chapter 5, Handra and Dita observe that Indonesia will face the challenge of coping with an increasing life expectancy and old-age dependency ratio in the near future. They note that details of pension provisions of the 2004 SJSN Law were still not available when their research was completed in late 2014.

The authors therefore chose to project public pension expenditure under three scenarios: (a) the central government will be liable to pay the basic pension benefit for the poor pensioners, (b) the central government will be responsible to pay the basic pension benefit for those who have never been working in the formal sector, (c) the central government will pay the basic pension benefit for all populations at pension age (other than civil servants). Depending on the scenario chosen, the age related expenditure in 2030 (assuming current retirement age of 55 years remains constant) ranges from 1 percent to 2.6 percent of GDP. The projected expenditure decreases significantly if the retirement age of 65 years is assumed. Thus, the authors suggest higher retirement age as an important initiative to manage pension costs and to find fiscal space. They also suggest several other initiatives: First, reforms in tax design, tax administration, and improved compliance to increase the tax-to-GDP ratio. Second, initiative concerns adjusting contributions form pension beneficiaries in all sectors to help reduce fiscal contribution towards pensions. Third, greater competence by pension fund organizations in improving pension funds returns. Fourth, a re-examination of the current imbalance in civil service pension expenditure, under which local government does not contribute significantly.

In Chapter 6, Bambang P.S. Brodjonegoro, Suahasil Nazara, and Fauziah Zen provide policymakers' perspective on policy challenges facing Indonesia in implementing the SJSN Law of 2004, which aims to use the social insurance method to provide pensions and health care on universal basis. It therefore nicely complements Chapter 5 by Handra and Dita.

Brodjonegoro *et al.* observe that with improving standards of living, government must manage to mitigate risks and at the same time provide better coverage, benefits, and an amount of social protection. Since 2014, in aiming to achieve universal coverage in 2019, the government has started implementing reform to its national social security system through two BPJS institutions (BPJS Healthcare and BPJS Labour) while still administering scattered social safety net programs under different frameworks. By June 2014, BPJS Healthcare has succeeded in covering around 50 percent of the population through several healthcare insurance schemes. On the other hand, Jamsostek – the informal private sector mandatory social security scheme – has been transformed into a foundation for BPJS Labour, which will later see the migration of public sector pension schemes of Taspen and Asabri. There are challenges in the implementation of the new national social security system, e.g. fiscal policy strategy and transformation of the fragmented and often overlapping programs into an integrated and sustainable system. For example, the healthcare programs for the poor and vulnerable, called Jamkesnas and Jamkesda, were essentially reimbursement programs under the Ministry of Health and local governments, respectively, with no avenue to accumulate the unspent funds. Integration of Jamkesnas and Jamkesda under BPJS Healthcare will enhance efficiency and enable the funds to accumulate. With low tax ratio and compliance, the government is very limited on financial resources to finance the system, thus only the poor and vulnerable (35 percent of the population) is eligible for the healthcare premium waiver. On the other hand, BPJS Labour, entrusted with administering Workers Accident, Death Benefit, Old-Age Saving, and Pension programs, is seeking to cover all workers in Indonesia, both in formal and informal sectors. Database integration with the BPJS Healthcare and other social assistance programs is crucial to minimizing exclusion and inclusion errors.

The 2004 SJSN Law also aims to unify civil services, military pensions, and their healthcare programs with that of the rest of the population by 2029.

This chapter argues that the two biggest challenges from the perspective of the policymakers has been transitioning from several existing agencies to only two newly established agencies, BPJS Healthcare and BPJS Labour (for pensions) and finding fiscal resources to make the SJSN promises credible.

The trade-offs facing the policymakers involve coverage (the law promises universal coverage), fiscal costs (complicated by the provision that the state will bear the insurance premium costs of those who are deemed to not be able to afford it, and by the absence of actuarial projections before the law was enacted), benefit levels under health care, and pensions programs. Harmonizing differential benefits for health care (particularly relatively generous Jamkesnas and Jamkesda programs primarily financed from the government budget) and for pensions (differing benefits for private sector workers, military personnel, and civil servants) is also proving to be a major challenge. Another major challenge identified in the chapter is to professionally manage assets and liabilities of the two agencies over a longer term, with due weight given to the fiduciary responsibility.

Indonesia's ambitious experiment in transitioning from a fragmented system with limited coverage to universal pension and health care using the social insurance approach will be keenly watched by other middle-income countries with large populations and fragmented systems with low coverage.

In Chapter 7, the final chapter, Junichoro Takahata analyses the extent to which the macro-economy indexation system introduced in 2004 can help manage Japan's expenditure dynamics. This chapter also reviews fiscal initiatives, which could help finance future pension expenditure liabilities.

The chapter examines how macro-economy indexation performs under several scenarios, and projects the likely future trend of pension expenditure GDP ratio. The chapter employs a simplified model where the macro-economy

indexation might be executed any time so that it could be easily observed whether the indexation works as intended or not. It is shown that the macro-economy indexation fully works only when the growth rate is higher than about 2 percent. The chapter project that, assuming the Japanese economy grows at 2 percent over a long period, the public pension expenditure to GDP ratio will increase from 5.8 percent in 2010 to 11.7 percent in 2060. Takahata suggests considering the incorporation of negative revision rates in the current pension indexation and increasing the pension eligibility age as policy initiatives to help Japan cope with future pension burden.

6. Concluding remarks

The first distinguishing characteristic of this book is that it takes initial steps to explore linkages between age-related expenditure and generation of fiscal space, a relatively unexplored area in Asia, in a country-specific demographic, fiscal, and pension system context, rather than relying on standard models applied in cross-country studies.

One of the strong general conclusions emerging from the book is that the country context-specific disaggregated projections of age related pension expenditure are more likely to be of policy relevance in the emerging economies than the projections from standardized models, which usually are mechanically applied.

The second distinguishing characteristic of this book is its focus on countries with large populations and uneven development across various regions of each country. Globally, there is relatively little experience with the middle-income countries, with the 2014 population size of China (1.37 billion), India (1.27 billion), and Indonesia (0.25 billion) aiming to progress towards near universal coverage of pensions in a relatively short period of time. So the country case studies of these countries with large populations would be instructive for other countries with relatively large populations and wide regional variations, who are grappling with similar issues.

This book is likely to be of relevance to researchers in multilateral institutions and elsewhere concerned with fiscal risk management at policy and operational levels, and to those specializing in sub-disciplines of pensions, public financial management, and demography, who may be interested in understanding linkages among these sub-disciplines.

A rich research agenda – specialized as well as inter-disciplinary – can be derived from the contents of this book. It is hoped that this book will make a contribution to stimulating interest in rigorous, empirical evidence–based, policy-relevant research efforts in Asia.

Notes

1   The first publication is Asher, Mukul G., Sothea Oum and Friska Parulian (Eds.) (2009), *Social Protection in East Asia: Current State and Challenges*, Jakarta, IDN: ERIA Research Project Report. The second publication is Asher, Mukul G. and Fukunari Kimura (2015), *Selected Issues in Strengthening Social Protection in East Asia*, London, UK: Routledge.

2 As of April 2015, OECD had 34 members, most of them high-income countries, although it also engages in dialogue with others, including the three middle-income countries covered in this book (www.oecd.org).
3 The economic and social security of the elderly ultimately depends on their access to and affordability of a bundle of goods and services, rather than in a given amount of pension and other benefits specified in nominal monetary terms. The conventional analysis, however, also followed in this book, focuses on monetary benefits, whether in nominal or in inflation adjusted terms, rather than on a bundle of services accessed from a variety of sources.
4 United Nations, Department of Economics and Social Affairs, Population Division (2013). World Population Prospects: The 2012 Revision, Key Findings and Advance Tables. Working Paper No. ESA/P/WP.227.
5 The high variant assumes half a child more per women than the medium variant, while the low fertility variant assumes half a child less than the medium variant. The constant variant assumes no change in the fertility rate during the projection period.
6 State assets involve such areas as land owned by the state, mining, the telecommunication spectrum, and other rights such as airspace above and the area within and below public sector properties, including railways and bus stations, and accumulated balances in various funds, including pension funds.

References

Asher, M. G. (2005). Mobilizing non-conventional budgetary resources in Asia in the 21st century. *The Journal of Asian Economics* **16**: 947–955.
Heller, P. (2005). *Understanding fiscal space*. IMF Policy Discussion Paper PDP/05/04, Washington, DC: International Monetary Fund, https://www.imf.org/external/pubs/ft/pdp/2005/pdp04.pdf
IMF (International Monetary Fund). (2011). The challenge of public pension reform in advanced and emerging economies. http://www.imf.org/external/np/pp/eng/2011/122811.pdf
Ley, E. (2009). Fiscal policy for growth. PREM (Poverty Reduction and Economic Management) Network, Note 131, Washington, DC: World Bank.
Roy, R., Heuty, A., & Letouze, E. (2009). Fiscal space for what? Analytical issues from a human development perspective. In R. Roy & A. Heuty (Eds.), *Fiscal space: Policy options for financing human development* (pp. 31–66). London, UK: Earthscan.
Sanderson, C. W. & Scherbov, S. (2007). A new perspective on population ageing. *Demographic Research, Max Planck Institute for Demographic Research* **16**: 27–58.
Tanzi, V. (2006). *Corruption and economic activity*. Distinguished Lecture Series 26, Cairo, Egypt: Egyptian Center for Economic Studies.
United Nations, Department of Economics and Social Affairs, Population Division (UNDESA). (2013a). *World population ageing 201*. New York, United Nations., http://www.un.org/en/development/desa/population/publications/pdf/ageing/WorldPopulationAgeing2013.pdf
United Nations, Department of Economics and Social Affairs, Population Division (UNDESA). (2013b). *World population prospects: The 2012 revision, key findings and advance tables*. Working Paper No. ESA/P/WP.227, http://esa.un.org/unpd/wpp/index.htm
World Bank Group. (2015). *Global economic prospects, January 2015: Having fiscal space and using it*. Washington, DC: World Bank, Chapter 3.

Table 2.1 Overview of reports in the 12 OECD member countries surveyed

Country	Most recent report title	Responsibility	First/Most Recent Release	Most recent time horizon	Frequency produced
Australia	Intergenerational Report 2010	Department of the Treasury	2002/2010	40 years	At least every 3 years
Canada	Economic and Fiscal Implications of Canada's Aging Population	Department of Finance	2000/2012	40 years	Ad hoc
Denmark	Convergence Programme Denmark 2012	Ministry of Finance	1997/2012	Until 2070	Annually
Germany	Third Report on the Sustainability of Public Finances	Federal Ministry of Finance	2005/2011	Until 2050	At least every 4 years
Korea	Vision 2030	Joint Task Force Team	2006/2006	25 years	Ad hoc
Netherlands	Ageing and the Sustainability of Dutch Public Finances	Central Planning Bureau	2000/2006	Until 2100	Ad hoc
New Zealand	New Zealand's Long-Term Fiscal Position	New Zealand Treasury	1993/2006	40 years	At least every 4 years
Norway	Long-Term Perspectives for the Norwegian Economy	Ministry of Finance	1993/2009	50 years	At least every 4 years
Sweden	Sweden's Economy (Budget Bill)	Ministry of Finance	1999/2009	Until 2060	Annually
Switzerland	Long-Term Sustainability of Public Finances in Switzerland	Federal Finance Administration	2008/2012	50 years	At least every 4 years
United Kingdom	Long-Term Public Finance Report	HM Treasury	1999/2009	50 years	Annually
United States	Analytical Perspectives (long-run budget outlook)	Office of Management and Budget	1997/2013	75 years	Annually
	The Long-Term Budget Outlook	Congressional Budget Office	1991/2012	75 years	Approx. every 2 years
	The Nation's Long-Term Fiscal Outlook	Government Accountability Office	1992/2013	75 years	3 times per year

Source: Author's update on Table 4 of Anderson and Sheppard (2010)

of construction. Studies which use this type of modelling strategy includes IMF (2011), Dang *et al.* (2001), OMB (Office of Management and Budget, 2012) for the United States, Hatta and Oguchi (1999) and MHLW (Ministry of Health, Labour and Welfare, 2009) for Japan, and the Directorate-General for Economic and Financial Affairs and the Economic Policy Committee (DG-ECFIN and AWG, 2012) for the EU, to name a few.

OMB (2012) reports the future budget balance projection of the United States with a long-term budget outlook (for 75 years) including age-related expenditure. The report focuses just on the budget balance by calculating revenue and expenditure, and there are no micro-economic foundations such as individual behavioural responses to changes in income or other factors. For computational purposes, a variety of assumptions on variables on demographic trends, GDP growth, inflation rate, and so on are incorporated into the model.

On the assumption of demographic changes, it is pointed out that "the key assumptions for projecting long-run demographic developments are fertility, immigration and mortality" (OMB 2012, p. 62). Thus, they assume that TFR is equal to 2.0 for the baseline case, and for the alternatives that the figures in the latest Social Security Trustees' report (1.7 and 2.3) are employed. With regards to immigration, a baseline inflow of around 1 million is assumed, with the alternatives set at 1.3 and 0.8 million.

For mortality, it is assumed that the longevity will be 80.5 in 2010 to 86.7 in 2085 for women, and 75.8 to 83.3 for men. In this case, two alternatives from the latest Trustees' report are also examined, where average female and male life expectancy reaching 83.2 and 79.4 in the short life expectancy scenario, and 90.3 and 87.6 in the long life expectancy scenario. Moreover, for computing the future budget balance, they assume that, after 2020, real GDP growth rate is 2.5 percent, inflation rate is 2.1 percent, unemployment rate is 5.4 percent, and so on.

In OMB (2012), it is mentioned that there exist other projections for the United States done by Congressional Budget Office (CBO), Federal Reserve Open Market Committee, and Blue Chip Consensus. However, only CBO carries out a long-term projection, where our interest lies, so the exercise by CBO will be focused on more in the following subsection.

For the case of Japan, MHLW reports long-term budget outlook for the public pension system every five years, where revenue and expenditure of the public pension system are calculated until 2105 under various assumptions. The latest one is MHLW (2009), where the underlying assumptions and programming code are publicly provided. According to this most recent model, demographic trends are computed for each group of four schemes of the public pension system based on the population projection done by the National Institute of Population and Social Security (IPSS).[1] TFR is assumed to be 1.26 in 2050 for the baseline case, which was the figure as of 2005. Alternative TFRs of 1.55 and 1.06 are used for other scenarios. The baseline long-term economic environment and reform scenarios were assumed as inflation rate at 1.0 percent, wage growth rate at 2.5 percent, and rate of investment return at 4.1 percent.

Based on these assumptions, the revenue and expenditure components are calculated to see the balance of the system.

As the model by MHLW was not publicly available prior to 2009,[2] Hatta and Oguchi (1999) developed the OSU model (Osaka University and Senshu University Pension Projection Model) for the purpose of stimulating policy debates on the public pension in Japan. The OSU model displays three key features: the first is that the model is constructed so that the simulation result is the same as that of MHLW; the second feature is that the model is made publicly available with the relevant data files uploaded onto the website:[3] and the third feature is that the model takes account of the detail structure of the actual public pension system in Japan.[4]

Besides single-country studies, there are also several multi-country studies present. DG-ECFIN and AWF (2012) provide long-term expenditure projection from 2010 to 2060 for the case of EU member states in "The 2012 Ageing Report". This paper covers the 27 EU member states and reports a variety of estimates apart from just pension expenditure. Other expenditures such as unemployment benefits, health care, and long-term care are also covered in the report. The chart for the report's projection system is shown in Figure 2.1.

They adopt EUROPOP2010, which is the latest population projections done by Eurostat, for the demographic data in the model. Generally the key factors which have an impact on demography are fertility, longevity, and migration, where it was documented that EUROPOP adopted a "convergence hypothesis" over the very long-term, i.e. fertility and mortality rates converge to those of the forerunners in EU member states, such as Sweden, Spain, and France. Furthermore, taking account of the age structure of the member states, they assume immigration and emigration also to converge and equalize across member states.

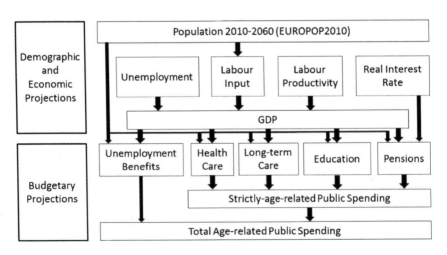

Figure 2.1 Overview of the 2012 long-term budgetary projections

Source: Reconstructed from the figure of ECFIN and AWF (2012), p. 22.

The cohort simulation model, initially developed by OECD (see Burniaux *et al.*, 2003), is used to project labour participation rates by gender and single age. Since the labour force projection is important both for contributions and benefits, it is considered in this age-related expenditure projection. Using this projection, it is thus possible to calculate economic OADR – the ratio between the inactive elderly (over 65) and total employment (20 to 64 or 20 to 74). Potential GDP is derived from a Cobb-Douglas production function assuming several parameters, such as total factor productivity (TFP) development.

Since pension systems differ across member countries, using national models for individual member states was allowed in contrast to computing costs and expenditures for other programs such as health care, where a common model is adapted. In addition, both public and private pensions are covered in the projection. Member states were asked to fill in the sheet shown in Annex 6.1 to report their absolute levels of pension costs. This mitigated the issue of differing pension systems; they could therefore report figures.[5]

The assumptions for the member states are shown in the Statistical Annex in the end of the report. Demographic projections include fertility, longevity, migration, and population. As the convergence hypothesis implies that fertility rates will converge to that of the forerunner states, changes to TFR are not uniform and are country dependent.[6]

For longevity, both life expectancy at birth and at 65 are shown in the paper. In 2060, the longest life expectancy at birth for males is 85.5 years (Italy and Sweden), and for females is 90.0 years (France), and the shortest for males is 80.6 years (Lithuania), and for females is 86.6 years (Bulgaria). The longest life expectancy at 65 for males is 22.9 years (Spain) and for females is 26.6 years (France), and the shortest for males is 20.4 years (Lithuania) and for females is 23.6 years (Bulgaria), respectively.

In addition, migration is to fluctuate between 0.0 percent (Bulgaria and Lithuania) and 0.4 percent (Cyprus). Incorporating the above factors, the total population for each country is projected, disaggregated into individual cohort populations, such as for children (0–14), working age (15–64), and elderly (65 and over), which are shown together in the table found in the report. The ratio of the elderly population to the total is expected to range from 21.9 (Ireland) to 35.6 (Latvia) in 2060.

For macro-economic assumptions, the range of average potential GDP growth rate during 2010–60 among the EU's 27 member states varies from 0.8 percent (Ireland) to 2.1 percent (Germany). Labour force assumptions for an average EU member state were also set for the labour participation rate, unemployment rate, etc. The unemployment rate for 15–64 is assumed to decline from 10.1 percent in 2010 to 6.7 percent in 2060.

Using the mentioned assumptions, expenditure ratios for all programs to GDP are calculated in the Statistical Annex of DG-ECFIN and AWF (2012). While the average rate of public pensions to GDP of the member states in 2010 stood at 11.3 percent, this is projected to grow gradually to 12.9 percent in 2060. The report also provides projection results for: (1) a higher life

Table 2.2 Funded pension benefits projection by CSIS (2010) (percentage of GDP)

	Netherlands	Australia	US	Sweden	UK	Brazil	Japan	Russia	China	India
2007	5.2	3.4	5.6	2.7	4	0.9	2	0	0	0.2
2040	10.8	9.1	8	6.3	5	3.2	2.7	1.4	1.2	1.1

Source: Figure 4 of CSIS (2010)

expectancy scenario, (2) a higher labour productivity, (3) lower migration, (4) a higher employment rate, and (5) a higher employment rate of older workers. The results range from 12.6 percent to 13.1 percent for the corresponding case in 2060.

Karam *et al.* (2011), which is based on the result of IMF (2010), reported how much the ratio of public pension expenditure to GDP will increase by 2030 for advanced and emerging economies. According to the results, the increase will be 1.1 percent for advanced economies and 1.0 percent for emerging economies on average. Asian countries especially (China, India, and Indonesia) will have a small increase at less than 0.5 percent.

CSIS (2010) derived the Global Aging Preparedness (GAP) Index to provide a comprehensive and realistic assessment of government policy reform to aging. The study generally focuses on age-related expenditures, but it also provides the ratio of funded pension benefits for the old to GDP by 2040. The results show that the Netherlands has the highest benefits at 10.8 percent of GDP in 2040, followed by Australia and the United States (See Table 2.2). China and India are shown in the table as well, the percentages of which are 1.2 percent and 1.1 percent, respectively. Since the model was not described in detail in the paper, it is difficult to know how the figures were calculated.

With the development of information technology, improvements in computing power made it easier to implement more complicated projection models, models which may be considered to incorporate more realistic settings and assumptions. We review two methods which have been developed over the last decade and made possible by better computing capabilities below.

2.2. Micro-simulation model

The micro-simulation model is based on information obtained from household panel survey data to replicate the real economy. This type of projection is classified into two types: an arithmetical model and a behavioural model. As the differences in nomenclature may suggest, the former does not take into account household reactions to an environmental change, while the latter does consider their behavioural change, such as labour supply.

It is possible to further classify this class of models into a static and dynamic micro-simulation model. The dynamic model can deal with an inter-temporal change and is suitable for analyses on social security systems. Since we will calculate age-related expenditure of three Asian countries in this project, the dynamic micro-simulation model is more related to our interests.

Table 2.3 lists the dynamic micro-simulation models in existence (63 in total) surveyed in Li and O'Donoghue (2012). The key advantage of this approach is that since the model considers change for all agents, it can report the effect of policies to income distribution or wealth distribution in the model (CBO, 2009).

As an illustration, CBO (2012) has long-term projections (up to 75 years) for public revenue and expenditure, including pension system, using a model called CBO-LT. The report was started in 2003 to provide objective evidence in terms of budget expenditure to Congress and is reported every two years. Besides the usual macro-economic and social variables, other more micro-level details, such as even marriage matching, are taken into account, leaving the detailed model as rather complicated.

Table 2.3 The number of studies using dynamic micro-simulation model for each country

Country	Dynamic microsimulation model
USA (11)	CBO-LT, CORSIM, DYNASIM I/II/III, FEM, MINT, PENSIM, POLISIM, PRISM, PSG
UK (8)	IFS Model, INFORM, LIFEMOD, Long Term Care Model, PENSIM, PENSIM2, SAGE, SimBritain
Italy (8)	ANAC, CAPP_DYN, DYNAMIC TUSCAN, DYNAMITE, Italian Cohort, LABORsim, MIND, Tdymm
Sweden (6)	IFSIM, MICROHUS, MiMESIS, SESIM, SVERIGE, Swedish Cohort
Australia (6)	APPSIM, DYNAMOD I/II, Harding, HouseMod, Melbourne Cohort
Canada (5)	DEMOGEN, DYNACAN, LifePaths, POHEM, XEcon
France (3)	DESTINIE I/II, GAMEO
Ireland (3)	Dynamic Model, LIAM, SMILE
Japan (3)	INAHSIM, Japanese Cohort, PENMOD
Norway (3)	MOSART 1/2/3
Netherlands (2)	NEDYMAS, SADNAP
Germany (2)	MICSIM, Sfb3
Multi (2)	MIDAS, SustainCity
Austria (1)	FAMSIM
Brazil (1)	BRALAMMO
New Zealand (1)	MIDAS
Belgium (1)	Pensions Model
Slovenia (1)	SIPEMM

Edited by the author, referring to Li and O'Donoghue (2012)

The study reports that key parameters for CBO's long-term model are both assumptions and policy levers. There exist 11 key parameters for assumptions, i.e. (1) fertility, (2) mortality, (3) immigration, (4) disability incidence and termination rates, (5) total factor productivity, (6) inflation (consumer price index), (7) difference between growth rates of the price index for GDP and the consumer price index, (8) unemployment, (9) government and corporate bond rates, (10) return on equities, and (11) health care cost growth. On the other hand, there exist mainly 8 parameters for policy levers, i.e. (1) replacement rates and (2) "bend points" (or amounts of earnings used in conjunction with replacement rates in calculating benefits), (3) statutory retirement ages, (4) delayed retirement credits, (5) actuarial adjustments for early claiming, (6) tax rates, (7) maximum taxable earnings, (8) parameters for individual accounts, and so on. All of these parameters are certainly important in any kind of pension projections, and these should be kept in mind when interpreting the result of projection.

In a different attempt, Shiraishi (2009) exercises a case study for Japan by PENMOD and calculates pension revenue and expenditure required until 2100. In the model, with individual records of pension contributions being kept, transition in the labour market is explicitly considered in order to derive the pension contribution revenue and benefit necessary for each scheme; namely the National Pension, Private Employees' Pension, and Public Servants' Pension for the old, disabled, and widows.[7] Since the amounts of contribution and benefit for three pensions are rather different, it is important to replicate the numbers of contributors and benefit recipients.

Despite its promise, implementing a micro-simulation model requires the availability of longitudinal panel data for calibrating household behaviour parameters specified in the model. While this method has been applied to various advanced economies, the extent of it usefulness is somewhat doubtful in the context of an emerging economy, where the timespan of existing data collected is too short.

2.3. Dynamic general equilibrium model

The third method, a dynamic general equilibrium model, has the advantage that general equilibrium effects are taken into account in the model. This class of models has been often applied for quantitative exercises when it is hard to give an answer to some theoretical economic problem. For example, if a proposed policy is known to have two opposing and offsetting effects, it becomes analytically difficult to conclude which effect dominates. In such a situation, a general equilibrium model, able to incorporate a richer set of economic dynamics of the real economy, is helpful to providing some form of a numerical solution. However, the main outputs of such models are often of a more aggregative macro-economic nature than micro-economic, which are what pensions policies are likely to fall under. Nevertheless, there exist several papers on public pension reforms that have been done using this method.

De Nardi *et al.* (1999) apply a dynamic general equilibrium model to future projection for a case of the United States. They found that additional 12.7 percent of payroll tax is necessary to sustain the social security system compared to the result derived by Goss (1998), Deputy Chief Actuary of the Social Security Administration, from the official model, where it was found that 4.7 percent immediate increase was necessary in order to sustain the social security system.

For Japan, RIETI (The Research Institute of Economy, Trade and Industry) provided a dynamic general equilibrium model by Fukao *et al.* (2007), who computed a future public pension balance for various scenarios until 2100. Moreover, Ihori and Bessho (2008) computed a future payroll tax rate in an environment with 1 percent of technological growth in a report from the Ministry of Finance, Japan. According to the result, the National Burden Ratio will be 50 percent in 2020.[8] If reform is taken place to reduce the replacement rate, the National Burden Ratio will be 50 percent around 2040.

A third study explores the effect where population growth rate is determined in the model. In this type of model, households choose their number of births maximizing their utility level, which affects the population growth rate of the economy. The population growth rate matters for public pension financed by a pay-as-you-go method, since a higher population growth rate means a higher rate of return in such a method, and low population growth rate may affect the sustainability of a public pension system. Oguro *et al.* (2011) used such a model to point out the possibility that a child benefit increase financed by government bonds may improve the welfare of future generation, but thus far there exists no pension projection which uses such a model.

The methods introduced here are just a subset of the choices available, and it should be noted that all projection methods carry their own inherent advantages and shortcomings. In the next section, we take a detailed look at some individual model specifications which are useful with respect to the conditions of emerging economies.

3. Age-related expenditure projection for Asian countries

There exist two major projections, OECD's *Economic Outlook* and IMF's *World Economic Outlook*. These projections do not focus on age-related pension expenditure; rather, economic growth is emphasized more.[9] As both the economic outlook forecasts provided by IMF and OECD calculate future economic growth based on assumptions such as population projection, including several emerging economies, it would be helpful to see how some of the assumptions and forecasts they provide may be useful for age-related pension expenditure projections.

In this section, we will discuss these issues along with some related studies which have used them to make projections of age-related expenditure.

3.1. The World Economic Outlook

The World Economic Outlook (WEO), released in April and September/October each year, includes past economic data together with economic forecasts for advanced and emerging economies provided by IMF. The WEO contains no age-related expenditure projection, but public finance projections are shown. The availability of historical data and population projections in the WEO suggests that parts of the survey might be useful for age-related expenditure projections in emerging economies.

As stated, the source of the WEO for its data is described as follows: "national statistical agencies are the ultimate providers of historical data and definitions".[10] This is supplemented with historical data and projections with information obtained by individual IMF country offices and missions.

In the 2012 edition of the outlook, the IMF provides 5-year projections up to 2017. However, not all countries are covered because of issues of data availability.[11] As such, there also appears to be no uniform method in how projections are done given the country-specific nature of the reports – these done by country desk officers in each country, and there appears to be no clear expositions of the assumptions and methodology used. Unfortunately, this severely limits the usefulness of the WEO for making pension expenditure projections.

Instead, using projected results by other studies, IMF (2011) shows the projection results for pension expenditure,[12] and also decomposing future social security expenditure into several factors for advanced and emerging economies, including the three Asian countries which are part of our project. The study reviews the long-term changes in public expenditure from 1970 to 2050 with a variety of datasets used in the analysis.[13]

Data sources for future pension spending projections are given in the Appendix, Table 7, of IMF (2011). For example, ECFIN2011 is the referred source for European countries for data of 2030 and 2050. Sources for other advanced economies are similarly documented. It should be noted, however, that while there is data on past social security expenditure, there are no projections made for emerging economies.

Instead, pension expenditure is decomposed according to the following equation:

$$\frac{PE}{GDP} = \frac{population\ 65+}{population\ 15-64} * \frac{pensioners}{population\ 65+} * \frac{average\ pension}{average\ wage} * \frac{population\ 15-64}{workers} * \frac{compensation}{GDP} \quad (2.1)$$

where pension spending as a share of GDP is the product of old-age dependency ratio (O), eligibility ratio (E), replacement rate (G), inverse of employment ratio (L), and compensation share in GDP (assumed to be constant).

Thus, so long as we have an access to these figures, it is possible to derive the ratio of pension to GDP. In the absence of any, or information about, pension reforms, it may be assumed that coverage ratio and replacement rate are constant and that changes are driven only by employment ratio and old-age dependency ratio.

Historical data and information for demographic projections is available from the United Nations' *World Population Prospects*. The factors which influence demography changes can then subsequently be calculated. The 'workers' number shown in the previous equation is defined as the population aged 15 and older who are economically active (EA). The ILO's *Economically Active Population* database provides the past figures for projecting future trends. Data for 2025–2050 are projected using a fixed-effects regression on a 5-year cohort (c) for every 5-year period (t) over 1950–2020. The regression is done for all countries following the equation:

$$EA_{c,t} = \alpha EA_{c-1,t} + \beta EA_{c,t-1} + \gamma EA_{c,t-2} + \delta EA_{c,t-a} + \rho YEAR \qquad (2.2)$$

where α, β, γ, δ, and ρ are parameters. It means that the economic active of cohort c in 2020 is regressed on the 5 years younger than the cohort and on the observed economic active rate of cohort c in 2015, 2010, and 2005.

The number of pensioners comes from analogy of the preceding calculation. Once previous data are known, it is necessary to substitute these numbers into the equation to obtain the future number. If individuals below the statutory retirement age are no more economically active, they are considered as 'retired'. Data of labour compensation to GDP is taken from United Nations System of National Accounts 1993.[14]

There is no data available on China and Indonesia about any type of pension reforms; thus a scenario with constant variables is applied that changes are attributed to employment ratio and old-age dependency ratio:

$$\frac{PE}{GDP}(t_2) = \frac{PE}{GDP}(t_1) * \frac{O(t_2) * L(t_2)}{O(t_1) * L(t_1)} \qquad (2.3)$$

It needs to be noted that for China especially the system is still very much a work in progress, and several of the assumptions included in the analysis may be controversial. For instance, the generosity of the basic pension is maintained at its current level in the baseline scenario. This is close to that of Oksanen (2010), where pension spending during 2010–30 substantially increases in the projection.[15]

For advanced economies, the results show that countries whose pension spending is below the average level in 2010 (such as Korea, New Zealand, and the United States) will increase their age-related spending rapidly. Furthermore, to ensure the continuation of a sustainable pension provision at current revenue collections, a trade-off exists between raising the retirement age by 1 year and reducing benefits by 6 percent. If this trade-off is to be avoided, government revenue needs to increase over the years.

For emerging economies, the situation differs greatly among countries. For India and Indonesia, replacement rates and eligibility ratios are projected to stay low (the latter will be about 20 to 25 percent),[16] and it is pointed that expanding their retirement systems in a fiscally sustainable manner will be the main challenge. Tables 2.4 and 2.5 summarizes the projection results for the selected economies of China, India, Indonesia, and Japan from IMF (2011).

Table 2.4 Public pension expenditure of three Asian countries with Japan (percentage of GDP)

	2010	2020	2030	2040	2050
China	3.4	4.7	6.7	7.9	9.2
India	1.0	1.0	1.0	0.9	0.7
Indonesia	0.7	0.9	1.1	1.4	1.6
Japan	10.0	10.3	9.8	10.4	10.7

Source: Appendix Table 4 of IMF (2011). The figure of 2010 is from the actual number

Table 2.5 Decomposition of pension spending growth, 2010–2030 (percentage of GDP)

	Old-age dependency ratio	Inverse of labour force participation rate	Eligibility rate	Replacement Rate
China	3.5	0.0	−0.2	0.0
India	0.5	0.0	−0.1	−0.3
Indonesia	0.5	0.0	0.0	0.0
Japan	4.3	−1.0	−1.6	−1.9

Source: Appendix Table 3 of IMF (2011)

3.2. OECD Economic Outlook

The OECD Economic Outlook is an economic forecast focused primarily on the OECD economies, but which also includes several emerging economies. The survey has economic growth projections over a 2 to 3 year horizon. These projections are "produced by its country experts interacting with its topic specialists, taking into account current and prospective developments, officially mandated policies, historical relationships between key variables and new information and indicators related to domestic and global conditions" (http://www.oecd.org/eco/economicoutlookfaq.htm). In this outlook, macro-economic policies are typically assumed to be unchanged over the projection period and performed on the basis of current existing fiscal and monetary policies.

In a separate study, the OECD made some long-term projections in *Looking to 2060: Long-term global growth prospects,* the short-term results of which are consistent with the short-term projections of the Economic Outlook. In this study, GDP growth rate is projected for advanced economies and major emerging economies using a baseline long-term (BLT) model up to 2060 (details in Johansson *et al.* 2013). The demographic assumptions are obtained from EUROSTAT population statistics for European countries, whereas data from the United Nations Population Database was used for non-European countries.

Note that the above projections do not deal with age-related pension expenditure explicitly. These are more comprehensively covered in the OECD working paper by Dang *et al.* (2001), where age-related spending, including old-age pension health care, child-related programs, etc. are projected up until 2050.

In the study, assumptions are made on demography, labour supply, and government policy. The demographic assumptions are based on the middle variant (median?) of Eurostat population projections for the member states of the EU, and national projections for the others. Going by these assumptions, total fertility rates (TFR) will rise by 8 percent, and longevity will grow 4.5 years on average amongst OECD economies.

The participation rates are assumed to be constant for men aged 20–54 and 55–64. The participation rates for women aged 20–54 and 55–64 rise progressively towards a ceiling at the end of the period equal to 5 percent below those of men in countries with widely subsidized childcare and 10 percentage points below elsewhere. All individuals aged over 65 and below 20 are assumed to have constant participation rates. For unemployment rates, most countries are assumed to converge to the same rate as that of 2005. Labour productivity growth, measured as per capita GDP growth, is assumed to be 1.96 percent, while GDP growth is projected to be 1.91 percent on average.

The projection results show that Italy will have the highest rate of public pension spending to GDP in 2000 (around 14 percent), but that Spain and Germany will increase to 17 percent as the ceiling in 2050.

As an OECD paper, long-term age-related expenditure projections of emerging economies are documented in *OECD Pensions Outlook 2012*. The projection results for emerging economies come from Standard and Poor's (2010a). According to the study, the total age-related spending is projected by 2050 for major economies in the world. It is documented that two assumptions are set throughout the calculation for various scenarios. The first assumption is the 'fiscal autopilot', in which the primary balance in 2012 sets the level of total revenues and non-age related expenditure as constant for the projection period. The second assumption is the 'surplus ceiling', where maintaining a certain level of budget surplus (more than 2 percent of GDP) would be politically infeasible in the countries covered in the sample. It is assumed that if the surplus exceeded 2 percent, taxes would be cut.[17] In addition, the real interest rate would be 3 percent uniformly as of 2020, and the inflation rate 2 percent, similarly.[18] The projection results show that a share of public pension spending to GDP in China, India, and Indonesia will be 2.6 percent, 0.9 percent, and 2.1 percent in 2050, while those of 2010 are 2.2 percent, 1.7 percent, and 0.9 percent, respectively (See Table 2.6).[19]

Table 2.6 Pension spending of three Asian countries with Japan (percentage of GDP)

	2010	*2050*
China	2.2	2.6
India	1.7	0.9
Indonesia	0.9	2.1
Japan	10.3	11.0

Source: Table 8 of Standard and Poor's (2010). The figure of 2010 is from the actual number.

4. Assessment and robustness

When we see the results of age-related pension expenditure projections, it should be noted that those are crucially depending on the assumptions underpinning the models. However, it is evidently impossible to know future economic and demographic variables; thus the necessity for assumptions to derive the shares of pension expenditure to GDP. In order to calculate the total amount of pension benefit and GDP level of the whole economy, it is required to have working age population, retirement age population, wage level, and macro-economic variables such as growth rate and inflation rate. We will discuss several major points which can significantly affect projection results below. The importance of robustness checks is also illustrated concurrently.

Most crucially, demography is the key importance for the accuracy of pension projections. Therefore, the necessity for multiple scenarios of demographic changes cannot be over emphasized.

Japan provides a very illustrative example. It is a well-documented fact that Japan's TFR has been declining continually over the past half a century. The solid line in Figure 2.2 shows the projected TFR up to 2020 based on the median scenarios drawn in various years starting from 1992. In contrast, the actual TFR trend (shown by the broken line) is consistently below that of the projected value. There are several reasons this may have happened.[20] As the actual fertility rate has consistently been lower than the forecast, contribution

Table 2.7 Total age-related spending (including public pension, health care, long-term care, and unemployment benefits) of three Asian countries with Japan (percentage of GDP)

	2010	2020	2030	2040	2050
China	4.4	4.9	5.5	6.3	7.0
India	2.6	3.2	3.4	3.2	2.7
Indonesia	2.2	2.7	3.2	3.9	4.7
Japan	18.8	20.8	22.1	24.4	26.7

Source: Table 1 of Standard and Poor's (2010). The figure of 2010 is from the actual number.

Table 2.8 Total age-related spending (including public pension, health care, long-term care and unemployment benefits) of three Asian countries with Japan (percentage of GDP)

	2010	2020	2030	2040	2050
China	5.4	7.6	10.5	12.7	15.1
India	2.2	2.7	3.3	3.9	4.4
Indonesia	2.0	2.7	3.5	4.6	5.5
Japan	18.2	19.1	19.3	20.4	21.3

Source: Table 3 of Standard and Poor's (2013). The figure of 2010 is from the actual number.

Solid line: Projection
Broken line: Actual Record

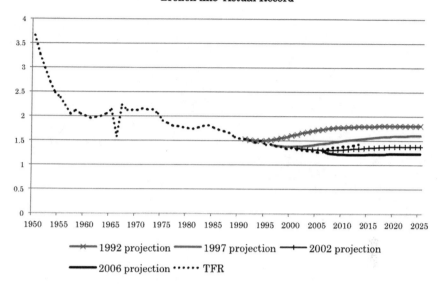

Figure 2.2 A comparison between the actual and projected TFR in Japan from 1992
to 2006

Source: Reconstructed from the figure of IPSS (Institute of Population and Social Security)
http://www.mhlw.go.jp/stf/shingi/2r9852000001rt29-att/2r9852000001rtmt.pdf

rates towards the pension system had to be revised upwards regularly. This has
led to some doubts about the sustainability of the pension system itself.

Yet, this is not the only case. It has typically been shown that the past projections for several countries have tended to be relatively optimistic (See p. 15 of
IMF, 2011). All of these underscore the importance of sensitivity analysis and
scenario variations for making fertility rate projections rather than relying on a
single case.

The next factor to consider is mortality rates. Some of the previously cited
studies assume mortality rates to be converged to that of the forerunner. However, it is historically known that life expectancy, even in the most optimistic of
cases, increases linearly (see Figure 2.3). As shown in Figure 2.3, life expectancy
is getting longer in the world. If 'convergence hypothesis' is adopted, it means
that all follower countries may not exceed the forerunner forever. However,
empirically the forerunner has been changing. If assuming this convergence
hypothesis, life expectancy would not grow linearly as a whole. Even if it is
impossible to know which country would be the forerunner, it is better to have
another scenario for longer life expectancy.

Next, projection results are made on the basis of aggregated macro-economic
data and assumptions. These are generally historical and time dependent, and
it is thus possible to overlook or omit structural changes in the economy. For

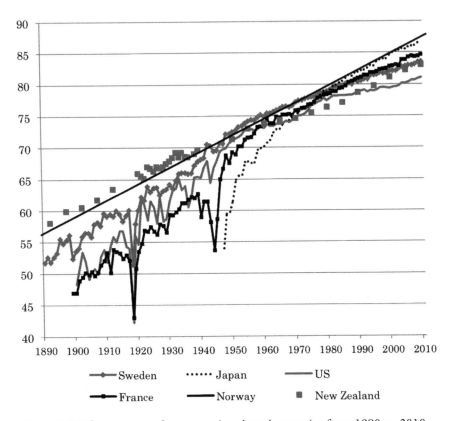

90
85
80
75
70
65
60
55
50
45
40

1890 1900 1910 1920 1930 1940 1950 1960 1970 1980 1990 2000 2010

◆ Sweden   •••••• Japan   US
■ France   Norway   ■ New Zealand

Figure 2.3 Life expectancy for women in selected countries from 1890 to 2010

Source: Reconstructed from the data of Oeppen and Vaupel (2002) and the following websites

The Berkeley Mortality Database (for the United States, Japan, France, and Sweden);
http://demog.berkeley.edu/~bmd/index.html

Centers for Disease Control and Prevention (for the United States);
http://www.cdc.gov/nchs/data/hus/hus13.pdf#018

National Institute of Statistics and Economic Studies (for France);
http://www.insee.fr/en/themes/detail.asp?ref_id=bilan-demo&page=donnees-detaillees/
bilan-demo/pop_age3d.htm

Statistics Sweden (for Sweden);
http://www.scb.se/en_/Finding-statistics/Statistics-by-subject-area/Population/Population-
projections/Population-projections/Aktuell-Pong/14505/Current-forecast/The-future-
population-of-Sweden-20132060/273436/

Norwegian Institute of Public Health (for Norway);;
http://www.fhi.no/eway/default.aspx?pid=240&trg=MainContent_6898&Main_6664=6898:
0:25,7524:1:0:0:::0:0&MainContent_6898=6706:0:25,7525:1:0:0:::0:0&List_6673=6674:0:25,
7528:1:0:0:::0:0

Statistics New Zealand (for New Zealand);
http://www.stats.govt.nz/browse_for_stats/snapshots-of-nz/nz-social-indicators/Home/
Health/life-expectancy.aspx

example, variables such as GDP growth and inflation rates are taken as largely constant in the existing projections. However, the results would not hold true anymore when realized rates differ from the baseline scenarios. As with the case of demographic assumptions, any changes may lead to wide-ranging differences in projections.

The third factor to consider is the continuation of current government pension policy into the future. While one cannot predict the direction of change of government pension policies and regulations, sensitivity analysis of any projections are very necessary to provide a range of plausible forecasts and scenarios of what may come. To place this in context, emerging economies are currently still enlarging the coverage of their pension systems. It is thus difficult to even suggest when an objective of, say, full coverage may be achieved. Considering a variation of scenarios on timing alone will provide greater scope in planning and preparing for future pension expenditure.

Fourth, pension expenditure is a part of governments' budgets. Even if pension expenditure is cut and the pension system is reformed by narrowing the coverage or by raising the retirement age, the government fiscal soundness might not be improved since such a reform costs for other policies, such as social safety net provisions for the people who are not covered. Since the government is ultimately responsible for the pension system, a pension system is no longer sustainable when the government cannot finance itself. Hence, it seems important to consider not only pension expenditure but also the whole government's budget balance.

Finally, a regularly omitted issue in comparing and evaluating across results is simply that the accounts and/or the methods of accounting differ. For example, IMF (2011) focuses on pension spending, while Standard and Poor's (2010a, 2010b) estimates focus on the total age-related spending, which includes pension spending. Since the figures used in the former is a subset of the latter's, the latter figure must be greater than the former's. Any comparison between the two is thus neither possible nor valid.

5. Conclusion

We have covered a number of long-term pension projections studies in existence for both advanced and emerging economies in this chapter. Unsurprisingly, a majority of the literature in existence pertains to advanced economies, as they enacted public pension systems from an earlier period, and over time this has become a stable fixture in public policy planning. Subsequently, coupled with the availability of a longer time span of data, it is thus easier for these economies to study and make long-term projections, even if demographic trends continue to change.

However, our interest is in the three emerging Asian economies of China, India, and Indonesia. Their pension systems are still growing, and it is likely that there will be further reforms undertaken. Not surprisingly, there are also very few studies and projections available for these economies.

Yet this does not mean there is nothing of relevance from the literature on developed economies for application. Several facets are very clear. First, results strongly depend on the assumptions or the definition of variables set in the studies. When we have simulation studies for future pension expenditure projection, robustness checks and sensitivity analyses are important in order provide sufficient width for consideration and planning purposes.

Second, variation in scenarios should be incorporated, even if some scenarios may be considered unrealistic or impractical for implementation. It is often true that governments do not consider unpopular scenarios, as they may be difficult to implement against strong opposition considering the political economy. Here one of the roles of simulation studies is to provide a set of concrete numbers that policymakers may compare among a list of possible choices and judge which may be the most plausible reform option.

Finally, data matters. The more recent the information a simulation study can incorporate, the greater the likelihood of realism in the future pathways the model projects. A key advantage of performing simulations in the three Asian countries in this project is that there is recent and up-to-date data available. As such, it appears possible to have a somewhat reliable set of pension expenditure projections which reflect the potential economic and demographic situations of these countries.

In summary, there is much value that can be drawn from the existing literature and promise in applying that knowledge to these countries in structuring and resolving the current state of pension systems in these countries.

Notes

1 In Japan, the public pension system is mainly classified into four schemes: the national pension (universal), the private employee's pension, private school workers' pension, and public servant employee's pension. These schemes have different benefit formulas depending on the record of contributors. See Takayama and Kitamura (2009).
2 MHLW projection methods and assessment are explained in detail in MHLW (2011).
3 Refer to the following for the revised OSU 2007 model: http://www.geocities. jp/kqsmr859/OSUnew.html
4 Thus far the OSU model has been further developed by Horioka *et al.* (2007) as the OSU 2007 model. Refer to the following website for details: http:// www.geocities.jp/kqsmr859/OSUnew.html
5 Since national models are allowed to be used, they can surely report their numbers in some form. If a common model is adopted, some might not be filled out since they have different systems. For example, if country A has pension X and Y, but country B has pension Z: If common pension is adopted and only pension X is shown in the answer sheet, only country A can answer partially, but country B cannot.
6 Some have their fertility rate raised, such as Spain, Italy, Germany, Latvia, Hungary, Poland, Portugal, Romania, and Slovak Republic, while others' fertility rates have dropped, such as Ireland, France, Sweden, and the United Kingdom.
7 MHLW(2009) classified the public pension system into four by regarding Public Servants' Pension containing two groups; namely, actual public servants and private school workers. See MHLW (2009) for more detail.

8 National Burden Ratio is defined as the rate of tax and social security to national income.
9 In addition, two more related studies are provided by international organizations; a medium-term outlook, Global Economic Prospects 2013, by World Bank, and the Long-Term Projections of Asian GDP and Trade 2011 by Asian Development Bank. These do not have age-related expenditure projections, however.
10 Refer to https://www.imf.org/external/pubs/ft/weo/data/assump.htm
11 Asked about long- and/or medium-term forecasts in WEO, IMF answers that they publish 5-year forecasts for many but not all indicators and country groups in the database, and that for some indicators and country groups they publish only 2 years of forecast data.
12 The IMF has developed a DSGE model as known as GIMF (The Global Integrated Monetary and Fiscal Model) for fiscal and monetary policy evaluation. As this model is not able to set precise demographic assumptions, long-term projection for age-related expenditure is not well considered in this model. See Kumhof *et al.* (2010) for the detailed structure of GIMF.
13 Historical data for OECD economies used in this study was taken from the *OECD Social Expenditure Statistics Database* for 1980–2007, Holzmann, R. (1988). Ageing and social-security costs. European Journal of Population/Revue européenne de Démographie, **3(3–4)**: 411–437, or imputed data based on ILO's *The Cost of Social Security* for 1970–79. For several other European countries, ESSPROS (European System of Integrated Social Protection Statistics) from EUROSTAT was used for 1990–2008, while for 1970–89 the imputed data based on data from ILO's *The Cost of Social Security* was adopted. The past data for the emerging economies are from IMF documents, countries' authority, or ILO's *The Cost of Social Security*.
14 This is available at the following website: http://data.un.org/Data.aspx?q=com pensation+of+employees&d=SNA&f=group_code%3a401%3bitem_code%3a9
15 Sin (2005) assumes that the second pillar is implemented fully.
16 The eligibility rate of China will be around 30 to 35 percent.
17 There exist two exceptions for the reason for resource revenue: Norway and Saudi Arabia.
18 The detail assumptions for sovereign ratings are shown in Standard and Poor's (2010b).
19 Standard and Poor's (2013) recently updated the total age-related spending for these countries. See Tables 2.7 and 2.8.
20 One possible reason for this happening is a structural change in the economy, such as an increase in female labour participation rate. Before the change, it was hard for women to get jobs, and for survival it was necessary to get married and to have children. However, it has became easier for women to get jobs. Some have chosen to work but not to get married and have children.

References

Anderson, B. & Sheppard, J. (2010). Fiscal futures, institutional budget, reforms, and their effects: What can be learned? *OECD Journal on Budgeting* **9**(3): 7–117.
Burniaux, J.-M., Duval, R., & Jaumotte, F. (2003). Coping with ageing: A dynamic approach to quantify the impact of alternative policy options on future labour supply in OECD countries. OECD Economics Department Working Papers No. 371, OECD Publishing.
CBO (Congressional Budget Office). (2009). *CBO's long-term model: An overview (June)*. Washington, DC: CBO.

CBO (Congressional Budget Office, Congress of the United States). (2012). *The 2012 long-term budget outlook.* Washington, DC: CBO.

Census of India. (2011). *Office of the registrar general and census commissioner,* http://www.censusindia.gov.in/2011census/hlo/PCA_Highlights/pca_high lights_file/India/Chapter-1.pdf

CSIS (Center for Strategic and International Studies). (2010). *The global aging preparedness index.* London, UK: CSIS.

Dang, T. T., Antolin, P., & Oxley, H. (2001). The fiscal implications of ageing: Projections of age-related spending. OECD Economics Department Working Papers, OECD Publishing.

De Nardi, M., Imrohoroglu, S., & Sargent, T. J. (1999). Projected U.S. demographics and social security. *Review of Economic Dynamics* 2: 575–615.

DG-ECFIN and AWG (Directorate-General for Economic and Financial Affairs and the Economic Policy Committee). (2012). *The 2012 ageing report: Economic and budgetary projections for the27 EU member states (2010–2060).* Brussels, Belgium: European Union.

Fukao, M., Hasumi, R., & Nakata, D. (2007). Declining fertility and aging of society, lifecycle, and public pension finance. Discussion Papers 07019, Research Institute of Economy, Trade and Industry (RIETI). (In Japanese)

Goss, S. C. (1998). *Measuring solvency in the social security system.* Manuscript Presented at the 1997 Pension Research Council Symposium at the Wharton School of the University of Pennsylvania, Social Security Administration, Baltimore.

Hatta, T. & Oguchi, N. (1999). *The theory of pension reform: Switch to a funded system* [Nenkin Kaikaku-ron: Tsumitate Hoshiki e Iko Seyo]. Tokyo, Japan: Nihon Keizai Shinbunsha.

Horioka, C. Y., Suzuki, W., & Hatta, T. (2007). Aging, savings, and public pensions in Japan. *Asian Economic Policy Review* 2: 303–319.

Ihori, T. & Bessho, S. (2008). *Impacts of demographic change to macro-economy and public finance.* Mimeo. (In Japanese)

IMF (International Monetary Fund). (2010). From stimulus to consolidation: Revenue and expenditure policies in advanced and emerging economies. Departmental Paper 10/03. Washington, DC.

IMF (International Monetary Fund). (2011). *The challenge of public pension reform in advanced and emerging economies,* http://www.imf.org/external/np/pp/eng/2011/122811.pdf

Johansson, A., et al. (2013). Long-term growth scenarios. OECD Economics Department Working Papers, No. 1000. Paris, France: OECD Publishing.

Karam, P., Muir, D., Pereira, J. & Tuladhar A. (2011). Cost of aging: Beyond retirees. *Finance & Development* **48**: 12–15.

Kumhof, M., Muir, D., Mursula, S. & Laxton, D. (2010). The global integrated monetary and fiscal model (GIMF)—Theoretical structure. IMF Working Paper 10/34, Washington, DC: International Monetary Fund.

Li, J. & O'Donoghue, C. (2012). A methodological survey of dynamic microsimulation models. UNU-MERIT Working Paper Series 002, United Nations University, Maastricht Economic and Social Research and Training Centre on Innovation and Technology Maastricht, Netherlands.

MHLW. (2009). *Long-term fiscal projections.* Tokyo, Japan: Ministry of Health, Labour and Welfare. (In Japanese)

MHLW. (2011). *Future population projection methods and assessment*, http://www.mhlw.go.jp/stf/shingi/2r9852000001rt29-att/2r9852000001rtmt.pdf

National Bureau of Statistics of China. (2013). China's Economy achieved a stabilized and accelerated development in the year of 2012 [Press release]. Retrieved on January 18, 2013, from http://www.stats.gov.cn/english/pressrelease/t20130118_402867147.htm

OECD. (2012). *OECD pensions outlook 2012*. Paris, France: OECD Publishing.

Oeppen, J. & Vaupel, J. W. (2002). Broken limits to life expectancy. *Science* **296**: 1029–1031.

Oguro, K., Takahata, J., & Shimasawa, M. (2011). Child benefit and fiscal burden: OLG model with endogenous fertility. *Modern Economy* **2**: 602–613.

Oksanen, H. (2010). The Chinese pension system—First results on assessing the reform options. Economic Papers 412, European Economy.

OMB (Office of Management and Budget). (2012). *Fiscal year 2013 analytical perspectives*. Washington, DC: Budget of the U.S. Government.

Shiraishi, K. (2009). *Policy options for the pension reform in Japan*, http://takayama-online.net/pie/stage3/Japanese/d_p/dp2008/dp421/text.pdf (In Japanese).

Sin, Y. (2005). China pension liabilities and reform options for old age insurance. Working Paper 2005-1.Washington, DC: World Bank.

Standard and Poor's. (2010a). *Global aging 2010: An irreversible truth*, http://www2.standardandpoors.com/spf/pdf/media/global_aging_100710.pdf

Standard and Poor's. (2010b). *Global aging 2010: An irreversible truth: Methodological and data supplement*, http://www.standardandpoors.com/en_EU/web/guest/article/-/view/sourceId/6245230

Standard and Poor's. (2013). *Global aging 2013: Rising to the challenge*, http://www.standardandpoors.com/about-sp/articles/en/us/?articleType=HTML&assetID=1245349076851

Statistics Indonesia. (2010). *Population census 2010*, http://www.bps.go.id/eng/tab_sub/view.php?kat=1&tabel=1&daftar=1&id_subyek=12&notab=1

Takayama, N. & Kitamura, Y. (2009). How to make the Japanese public pension system reliable and workable. *Asian Economic Policy Review* **4**: 97–116.

3 Public pension system and fiscal policy response in China

Jin Feng and Qin Chen

1. Introduction

China is about to achieve universal coverage in its public pension system. There are four schemes within the system intended to cover the entire eligible population: (i) Basic Old Age Insurance system (BOAI) for employees in enterprises and other private sectors; (ii) Public Employee Pension system (PEP) for civil servants and employees in public sectors; (iii) Urban Resident Pension scheme (URP); and (iv) New Rural Resident Pension scheme (NRP) for residents 16 and over without a formal non-agricultural job. Up to the end of 2012, the number of participants in the public pension system has exceeded 800 million people, and total public pension expenditure was at 3.4 percent of GDP.[1] Of the four, the BOAI system is the most important scheme in China in terms of pension expenditure and future reform.

Similar to many other countries, the pension system in China will have to face the challenges of a dwindling labour force and a rapidly aging population. Meanwhile, the present system is barely maintaining its financial balance with the help of government subsidies. The fiscal subsidy for the BOAI system currently stands at 265 billion RMB in 2012, or about 0.5 percent of GDP, and this is likely to exhibit a dramatic increase if there are no reforms to it in the near future.[2] Fiscal sustainability will become a key concern in ensuring the continuation of a viable and sustainable public pension system, and in particular the BOAI system, which we focus on in this chapter.

There are several studies simulating the outcomes of various reform options for the BOAI system over the next few decades (e.g. Herd *et al.*, 2010; Oksanen, 2012; Sin, 2005; Wang *et al.*, 2004) (Table A3.1 in the Appendix). The literature presents some common findings. First, expanding coverage and raising the retirement age are necessary policy options to reduce future pension liabilities. Currently, the BOAI system covers about 15 percent of migrant workers and 60 percent of total urban employees, so there is the potential gain of more cash flows with an increase in coverage. Second, pension benefits will need to be adapted in response to demographic changes. Notional account system is a possible choice for China to adopt for this purpose, where the notional interest rate for individual accounts will be adjusted according to the rates of economic growth and population aging. Third, more fiscal subsidies will be needed to finance the transition costs during the reform period. Under conditions of an extension of coverage, higher retirement age legislation, and more fiscal subsidies, it may even be possible to achieve a reduction of the required contribution rate.

It is worth noting that the possible opportunity provided by urbanization with an aging population in China has not been adequately studied in the literature. Expanding coverage in the process of urbanization combined with a gradual increase of retirement age and a relatively non-substantial fiscal subsidy will help to maintain financial balance of the pension system.

In this chapter, we address the following research questions: what will be the projected size of future pension expenditures and deficits? What are the opportunities for reform? And what alternative fiscal spaces are available to finance public pension expenditures? Our focus is primarily on uncovering what opportunities are available to counteract the negative effects of a population aging over the course of urbanization and exploring the potential fiscal spaces for the pension system.

In this chapter, we first show the old-age dependency ratio of BOAI under urbanization when expanding pension coverage to migrant workers. We then simulate the financial outcomes arising out of several reform scenarios. These include increasing the retirement age, reducing the contribution rate, and changing the indexation of pension benefits. We also show the fiscal subsidies required in order to keep the reform proposals manageable. Finally, we discuss some feasible avenues of fiscal space necessary to finance the provision of public pensions in China.

The rest of the chapter is structured as follows. Section 2 briefly summarizes the background of public pension system in China. Section 3 calibrates the urbanization process and projects demographics of both urban and rural China. Old-age dependency ratios for the pension system are simulated under various cases of coverage and TFR assumptions. Section 4 describes the benchmark model and assumptions in simulating financial outcomes of the pension system, and reports the pension expenditure under current policy. Future reform proposals and outcomes of simulation are also reported. Section 5 briefly introduces the key characteristics of the fiscal system in China. Section 6 proposes feasible fiscal options to maintain a sustainable public pension system. Section 7 concludes the chapter.

2. Current public pension system in China

2.1. Schemes

The four schemes in the public pension system – BOAI, PEP, URP, and NRP – are aimed at covering different groups of the population and workforce, and they vary in contribution and benefit rules. Table 3.1 summarizes the key features of the four pension schemes. These schemes were established by the State Council and are regulated by Ministry of Human Resources and Social

Table 3.1 Key features of the different pension schemes

Scheme	Basic Old Age Insurance system (BOAI)	Public Employee Pension (PEP)	Resident Pension	
			2011 Urban Resident Pension Scheme (URP)	2009 New Rural Resident Pension Scheme (NRP)
Establishment	1951; Current Practices Finalized in 1997	1953; Current Practices Finalized in1978	2011 Urban Resident Pension Scheme (URP)	2009 New Rural Resident Pension Scheme (NRP)
Participants	Urban employees in enterprises	Urban employees in public sectors	Urban non-employed 16 years or above	Rural residents 16 years or above
Contribution	Individual accounts: 8% of individual wage Social pooling: 20% of payroll (depending on locality)	No contribution required	Individual accounts: Individual contribution + Government subsidy	Individual accounts: Individual contribution + Government subsidy
Benefit	Individual accounts: Replacement ratio: 24.2%Total replacement ratio from both: 59.2% Social pooling: Minimum 15 years of contribution. 1 year accrual rate 1%; 35% based on 35 years of contribution	Average Replacement ratio: 80–90%	Basic Pension + Individual account pension	Basic Pension + Individual account pension
Mandatory	Yes	Yes	No	No

Sources: from relevant State Council Documents by authors. State Council Document #26 and #38 mandated the policy framework of BOAI.

Security (MOHSS) of China.³ Local governments are responsible for managing these schemes.

The Basic Old Age Insurance system (BOAI) is the most important public pension scheme. It was established in 1951 for urban employees in enterprises and reformed into a multi-pillar system in 1997. The first pillar of BOAI is a compulsory-defined benefit scheme, with employers obligated to pay 20 percent of employees' wage bill as contribution. Employees with a contribution history of 15 years or more are entitled to the pension benefits. The replacement ratio (pension benefit as a percentage of wage before retirement) is determined by the number of years of contribution. For example, a retiree after 35 years of contribution will have a pension replacement ratio of 35 percent. The second pillar of BOAI is the individual account, with the individual contributing 8 percent of his wage. In 2005, the Ministry of Human Resource and Social Security published the target replacement ratio of 59.2 percent for a person who worked for 35 years with average earning, 35 percent from the pooling account (basic pension) and 24.2 percent from the individual account.⁴

The Public Employee Pension (PEP) was established in 1953. It is more generous than the other schemes. Public employees have an average pension replacement ratio of 80–90 percent of wage before retirement. The participants comprise two types. The first type is civil servants. The second type is the employees in public sectors. Expenditure of the PEP system is included in both central and local government fiscal budgets.

The New Rural Resident Pension Scheme (NRP) was established in 2009 to cover rural residents, and the Urban Resident Pension Scheme (URP) was established in 2011 to cover urban non-employed residents. NRP and URP are voluntary schemes funded in conjunction with government subsidies. Individual contributions are put into individual accounts. Also, the amount of contribution depends on local economic conditions. So there is a clear variance both across regions and between the urban-rural population. There benefit is composed of two parts: a basic pension and the individual account pension. Participants with 15 years (or more) history of contribution are entitled to receive 55 RMB a month (in most regions) of basic pension upon reaching 60 years old. The basic pension is provided entirely by the central government in the middle and western provinces. In the eastern provinces, both the central government and the local government pays half of the basic pension. Local governments have the autonomy to the raise basic pension benefit according to situations on the ground and are responsible for the outstanding financial needs. On a nationwide average, the replacement ratio is at 20 percent of rural per capita net income. At the beginning of 2014, the State Council announced that the two schemes are to be merged into a uniform Resident Pension.

For rural migrant workers, the Social Insurance Law, which was enacted in 2010, specifies that rural migrant workers are entitled to the same treatment given to urban workers. However, the compliance with the policy by both employers and migrant workers is poor.

2.2. Coverage and OADR

Coverage of the BOAI system has been increasing steadily in recent decades (Figure 3.1). At the end of 2011, BOAI covered 284 million people (215 million employees and 68 million retirees), with 35 million being rural migrant workers. This amounts to 60 percent of urban employees (including rural migrant workers) and 14 percent of rural migrant workers.

In 2009, the pilot NRP started in 27 provinces, autonomous regions, and 4 municipalities. In 2011, the URP was introduced. There are 364 million participants in NRP and URP, among which are about 100 million retirees up to the end of 2011. The participation rate is 79.7 percent in the pilot regions.[5]

The OADR in BOAI has risen from 18.6 percent in 1990 to 32.5 percent in 2010, i.e. a reduction from 5.4 workers supporting a retiree to 3 workers supporting a retiree. The main reason is the shift in the age distribution of the Chinese population. The old-age dependency ratio (elderly/working age) has risen over time (Figure 3.2). From 1950 to 2010, the number of people over 60 increased threefold to 165 million, rising from 7.5 percent of the total population to 12.3 percent. The proportion of 65-year-olds and above has risen from 4.5 percent to 8.2 percent. The proportion of people in the 15–59 age group has risen 58.3 percent in 1950 to 68.2 percent in 2010; and the proportion in the 15–64 age group has risen from 61.3 percent to 72.4 percent. The rise in the population shares of both the aged group and the working age group reflected the rapid decline in China's fertility rate, which lowered the population share of the 0–14 age group from 34.2 percent to 19.5 percent.

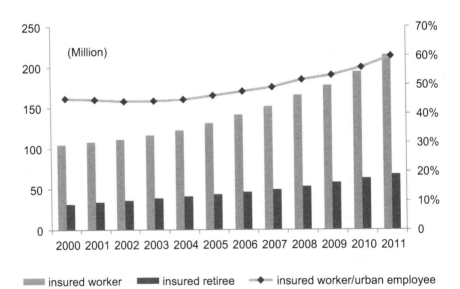

Figure 3.1 Coverage of BOAI 2000–2011

Sources: China Statistics Yearbooks

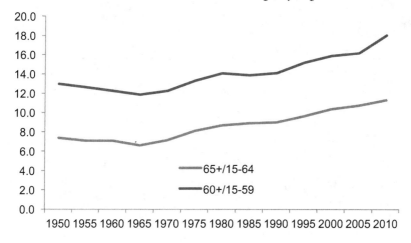

Figure 3.2 Old-age dependency ratio of whole population 1950–2010

Sources: United Nations World Population Prospects: The 2012 Revision (Medium variant)

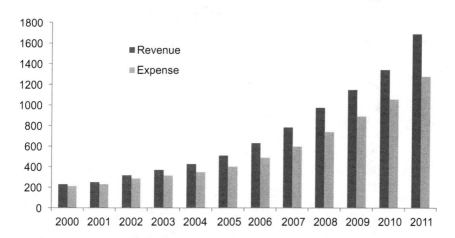

Figure 3.3 Revenue and expense of BOAI (billion, RMB)

Sources: China Statistics Yearbooks

2.3. Pension fund and fiscal subsidy

The pension fund in the BOAI has been maintained an annual surplus for many years. In 2011, revenue of the BOAI fund was 1.69 trillion RMB, and the expenditure was 1.28 trillion (Figure 3.3). The main reason for the surplus of the BOAI is the steady expansion of coverage, i.e. the expansion increased the number of participants, far exceeding the increase in the number of retirees. Furthermore, BOAI also receives government subsidies, 195.4 billion in 2010

Table 3.2 Fiscal subsidy in BOAI (billion, RMB)

	2002	2003	2004	2005	2006	2007	2008	2009	2010	2011
Subsidy	45.5	53.0	61.4	65.1	97.1	115.7	143.7	164.6	195.4	227.2
As % of fiscal revenue	2.41%	2.44%	2.33%	2.06%	2.51%	2.25%	2.34%	2.40%	2.35%	2.19%

Sources: China Pension Report (Zheng, 2012).

for instance, representing a fourfold increase over ten years (Table 3.2). If the government subsidies were discounted from the accounting, BOAI funds in 14 provinces (including Shanghai, Jiangsu, Hubei, and Hunan) are likely to been in a deficit. In this case, the BOAI accounts would have reported a total deficit, possibly as large as 67.9 billion in 2010, instead of the surplus that was observed.

In NRP and URP, the revenue was 183 billion RMB in by end of 2012, among which about 40 percent was from individual contribution; the rest was from government subsidy, both national and subnational. The total expense was 115 billion. So there is an accumulated surplus of 230 billion in the two schemes. Most of them belong to funds accumulated in individual accounts.[6]

3. Demographic and labour market trends

3.1. Rural urban migration in China

In this section, we aim to estimate the size and age-gender structures of rural-urban migration. In order to do so, we compare the simulated and actual population age structures in 2010. The idea is simple. If the (adjusted) birth and mortality rates in the 2000 census are reliable and these rates remain stable from 2000 to 2010, we can simulate 'natural' 2010 urban/rural population age structures where no migration takes place over the period. The 2010 urban/rural population survey incorporates all individuals living in urban/rural areas. Therefore, the difference between simulated age structures and survey data can reveal the size and age structures of rural-urban migrants (Chen and Song, 2013).[7]

Johnson (2003) is perhaps the first to estimate China's migration population using natural population growth rates. Our approach is different from Johnson's work in two aspects. First, his focus is on migration across provinces, while we estimate the size of rural-urban migration. Second, Johnson estimates population of certain provinces, while we back out the migration age structure which is needed for the later analysis on social security. Therefore, our simulation of natural population growth involves the use of far more detailed information of age/gender-specific birth and mortality rates.

A major concern about the methodology used is if the natural population can well be approximated by the use of projections. Goodkind (2004) provides some evidence that it can. He finds that total population projection for China based on the 1990 census produces an excellent match with the 2000 census data (a part for children in the under-9 age group). Although some minor discrepancies are observed among adults, the positive spikes are typically counterbalanced by negative spikes at adjacent ages, suggesting that these discrepancies would largely disappear with the use of age smoothing. We will conduct the same exercise by comparing total population projection based on the 2000 census with the 2010 census data.

We first introduce the following notations for expositional ease.

The superscripts $h \in \{u, r\}$, $i \in \{f, m\}$, and $j \in \{0, 1, 2, \cdots 100\}$ stand for urban/rural, gender, and age, respectively.

$p_t^{h,i,j}$ represents (adjusted) population in the period-t census. For instance, $p_{2000}^{u,f,10}$ stands for the population of urban females of age 10 in the 2000 census.

$\hat{p}_t^{h,i,j}$ represents simulated natural population in period t according to the equation:

$$\hat{p}_t^{h,i,0} = \sum_h \sum_{j \in [15,49]} \theta_{t-1}^{h,i} b_{t-1}^{h,j-1} \hat{p}_{t-1}^{h,f,j-1}, \tag{3.1}$$

$$\hat{p}_t^{h,i,j} = \sum_h \left(1 - m_{t-1}^{h,i,j-1}\right) \hat{p}_{t-1}^{h,i,j-1}, j > 0, \tag{3.2}$$

where $b_t^{h,j}$, $m_t^{h,i,j}$, and $\theta_t^{h,i}$ represent birth rates, mortality rates, and sex ratios at birth in the period-t census, respectively, where $\hat{p}_t^{h,i,0} = p_t^{h,i,0}$.

We make the following assumptions. Birth rates are adjusted upwards to correct the potentially under-reported birth rates in the 2000 census. We multiply $b_{2000}^{h,j}$ by an adjustment coefficient of 1.2. This was chosen because the 2000 census reveals a total fertility rate of 1.2, while the actual TFR suggested in the literature is often believed to be above 1.4 (see e.g. Morgan *et al.*, 2009). In addition, using primary school enrolment data, there is some literature to suggest that birth rates were under-reported by 16 percent in the 2000 census (Zhang and Cui, 2003; Zhang and Zhao, 2006). So 1.2 seems to be a reasonable adjustment parameter to use. It should be noted that the following results are also robust to alternative values of the adjustment coefficient.[8]

Figure 3.4 and Figure 3.5 respectively report the simulation and actual census data of the rural/urban population for 2010. The difference between the solid line and the dotted line is the rural-urban migration of gender *i* and age *j* during 2000 and 2010, i.e. $M^{i,j}$.

We can back out rural-urban migration by using either urban or rural population in the following formulas:

$$p_{2010}^{u,i,j} = p_{2010}^{u,i,j} + M^{i,j} \tag{3.3}$$

$$p_{2010}^{r,i,j} = p_{2010}^{r,i,j} - M^{i,j} \tag{3.4}$$

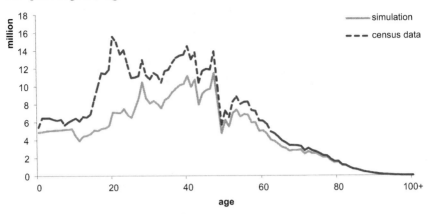

Figure 3.4 Simulation and census data of the 2010 rural population

Simulation results/author's calculation

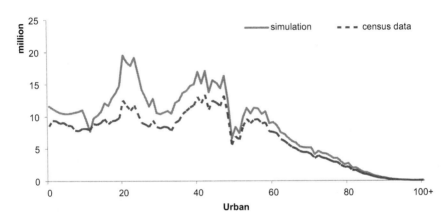

Figure 3.5 Simulation and census data of 2010 urban population

Simulation results/author's calculation

Where $M^{i,j}$ denotes the net flow of migration from rural to urban areas, we can thus back out $M^{i,j}$. The results are reported in Figure 3.6.

Migration rate from rural to urban is defined as the net flow of migration per hundred rural population of a certain age. The migration rate of each age group satisfies the condition:

$$p_{2010}^{r,i,j} = \hat{p}_{2010}^{r,i,j} \cdot \prod_{k=1}^{10}\left(1 - r^{i,j-k}\right), j \geq 10 \tag{3.5}$$

where $r^{i,j}$ denotes the migration rate of gender i and age j. We can calculate $r^{i,j}(j \geq 10)$ by solving (1.5), in which j ranges from 10 to 100. We set $r^{i,j}(j < 10)$

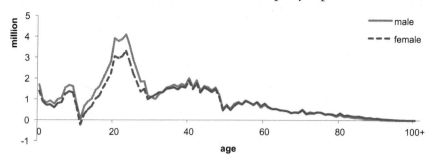

Figure 3.6 Number of migrants

Simulation results/author's calculation

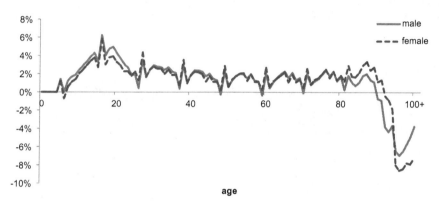

Figure 3.7 Age-specific migration rate

Simulation results/author's calculation

as 0. Age-gender annual migration rates $r^{i,j}$ are presented in Figure 3.7. These peak at 6 percent for age 16 and then fall to the level below 3 percent after age 25. Quantitatively, migration after age 50 is not important for measuring the size of migration population.

3.2. Demographic projection for urban and rural population

Using (3.1) and (3.2), together with population, birth rates, mortality rates, and sex ratios at birth in the 2010 census, we can project future population and age structures by assuming

$$b_t^{h,j} = 1.2 \cdot b_{2010}^{h,j}, \quad m_t^{h,i,j} = m_{2010}^{h,i,j}, \quad \theta_t^{h,i} = \theta_{2010}^{h,i} \qquad (3.6)$$

Figure 3.8 plots total population projection from 2010 to 2100. The total population peaks around 2022, reaching the level of 1.4 billion, and then declines over time. Our estimation is comparable to the projections performed

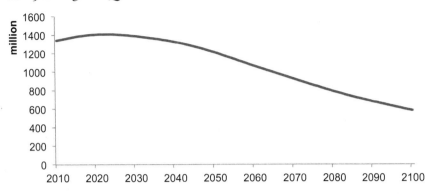

Figure 3.8 Population projection

Simulation results/author's calculation

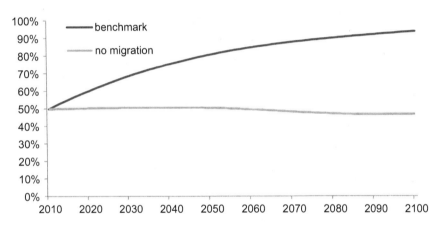

Figure 3.9 Urban and rural population projection

Panel A: Urbanization rate

under the scope of several projects of the United Nations (See Appendix, Figure A3.1).

Our focus is on BOAI system, which covers employees in non-agricultural sectors. To incorporate rural-urban migration, we assume that in the benchmark case the annual migration flow is determined by age-specific migration rates, illustrated in Figure 3.7.

Figure 3.9 plots urban and rural population projection in the benchmark case (solid lines) and the case without migration (dotted lines). The benchmark

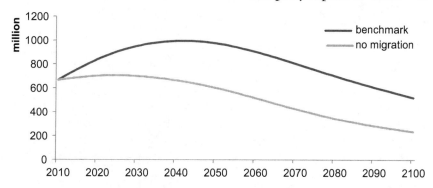

Figure 3.9b

Panel B: Urban

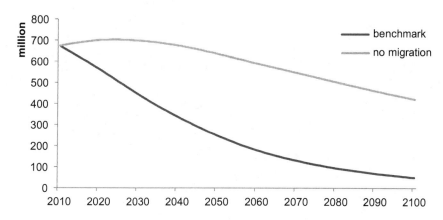

Figure 3.9c

Panel C: Rural
Simulation results/author's calculation

urban population features a hump-shape, while rural population is decreasing over time. The urban population share is 50% in 2010 and will rise to 80% in 2051 according the benchmark projection. If no migration takes place, urban population would slightly increase until 2018 and decline afterwards, resulting in an urban population share of 48% in 2051 (2 percentage points lower than the current level). This sharp comparison highlights the importance of rural-urban migration for the change of the urban and rural population.

3.3. Projected OADR

We can further compute the OADR of the urban and rural population: the number of individuals above retirement age per hundred individuals of working age. In China, the official retirement age is 55 for females and 60 for males. Working age is thus defined as from 16 to 55 for females and 16 to 60 for males. The projected urban and rural OADRs are plotted in Figure 3.10. The difference between the dotted and solid lines in Panel A shows the contribution of rural-urban migration in lowering urban OADRs. For instance, the urban OADR without migration would reach 91 percent in 2056, whereas it would be 71 percent if rural migrants are included.

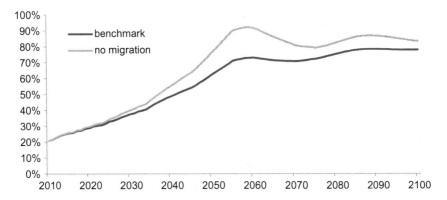

Figure 3.10 Old-age dependency ratios

Panel A: Urban

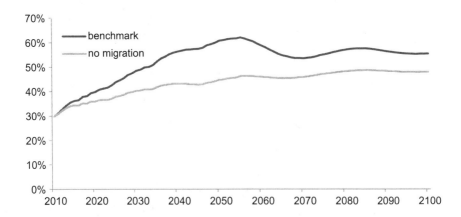

Figure 3.10b

Panel B: Rural
Simulation results/author's calculation

Accordingly, the rural population will be aging faster during urbanization, as observed from the earlier peaking of the OADR in Panel B of Figure 3.10, but it still remains about 10 percentage points lower as compared to the OADR of the urban population. The higher rural OADR also implies that the absolute number of people is declining more rapidly, leaving more room for government subsidy of the pension system for farmers.

3.3.1. OADR in BOAI

We use data from year 2010 to calibrate labour participation rates, and 2010 is the starting year for simulation. Age-related labour participation rates are employed to estimate the number of future employees (Figure 3.11). The coverage rate is used to determine the number of contributors. Calculation of the total number of contributors follows equation 3.7, comprising three determinants: the absolute number of the working age population, the labour participation rate (LPR), and the coverage rate. The coverage rates for local employees in 2010 was 80 percent and 20 percent for migrant workers.

$$Contributors = Working\ Age\ Population * LPR * Coverage\ Rate \qquad (3.7)$$

We assume there is no return to labour participation after workers' retirement at the statutory age.[9] If the retirement age is increased, the labour participation rate of elderly workers will be adjusted correspondingly.[10] Each year, the number of pensioners is the population above retirement age multiplied by a given coverage rate. Because retirees comprise retired employees, the coverage rate of retirees can be approximated by a linear combination of the lagged coverage rate for employees. We calibrate the coverage for retirees in BOAI system. The coverage

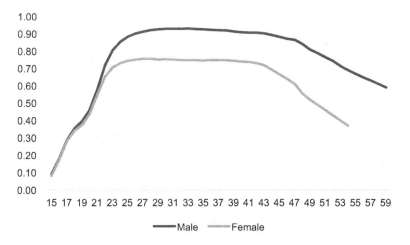

Figure 3.11 Labour participation rate

Simulation results/author's calculation

rate for retirees in 2010 is about 65 percent, which is consistent with what was obtained from a large sample survey by the China Household Financial Survey (CHFS) in 2011.[11] Equation 3.8 is used to calculate the number of pensioners.

$$Pensioners = Population\ above\ retirement\ age \times coverage\ rate \qquad (3.8)$$

Demographic dynamics and the urbanization process will have different effects on the OADR of the BOAI. With an aging population, the increase of retirees is greater than that of employee-contributors. Hence a rising OADR is unavoidable if the current statutory retirement age remains unchanged. But urbanization leads to more young people migrating to the urban sectors, which has a counterveiling effect on the OADR of the BOAI if those people are covered. Therefore, future OADRs depend on the interactions between the said demographic dynamics and urbanization, the pension coverage rate, the retirement age, and the total fertility rate. We simulate the OADR for the BOAI system under the following four possible cases, with the assumption that urban migration rates are as estimated in the section 'Rural urban migration in China'.

Case 1: Current coverage, i.e. 80 percent for local employees and 20 percent for migrant workers.

Case 2: Expanding coverage to 80 percent of all urban employees from 2010 to 2030.

Case 3: Case 2 combined with a higher total fertility rate of 1.44 increasing in 30 years from 2014.

Case 4: Case 3 combined with an increase of retirement age by 5 years in 20 years from 2014.

The results are presented in Figure 3.12.

Figure 3.12 shows in the benchmark projection (Case 1) that if the BOAI's coverage is not going to be expanded, any potential gains of lowing the OADR

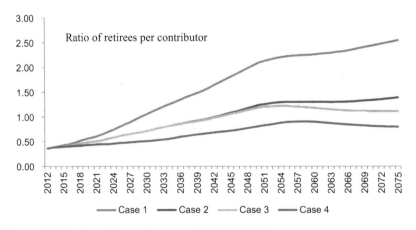

Figure 3.12 Projected dependency ratio in BOAI (%)

Simulation results/author's calculation

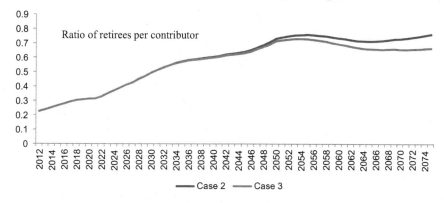

Figure 3.13 Projected dependency ratio in URP and NRP (%)
Simulation results/author's calculation

as a result of urbanization is limited. The projected ratio of retirees per employee may well be as high as 2.09 in 2050. In Case 2, expanding the coverage will reduce the ratio dramatically to 1.19 in 2050. The effect of TFR is less immediate. Its impact on the OADR begins after 2040. A higher TFR of 1.44 will result in the OADR reducing only after 2055.[12] In contrast, simply increasing retirement age by 5 years over a 20-year time frame has very significant effects on the OADR. As shown in the projections for Case 4, this is reduced to 0.81 by 2050.

3.3.2. In URP and NRP schemes

The coverage of URP and NRP is expanding quickly these years. The number of participants was 364 million in 2011 and 484 million in 2012, or about 65 percent of the rural population plus the urban population who are not in BOAI system. We consider a future situation of full coverage by URP and NRP of rural residents and urban residents outside that of the BOAI.

We simulate the results corresponding to the previous Case 3, with expanded coverage of BOAI and with a higher total fertility rate of 1.44 increasing in 30 years from 2010. When we simulate the outcome of increasing retirement age, we use the above Case 4.

The results illustrated in Figure 3.13 suggest that the OADR for NRP and URP will reach 0.7 in 2050. The higher TFR will moderately reduce the OADR after 2040. But the overall OADR is lower than that of the BOAI system.

4. Age-related pension expenditure projections and analysis

4.1. Model and assumptions

Though the BOAI has a DB pension and an individual account, the individual accounts in most cities are empty, and there is no real investment return for the individual accounts. To a large extent, the individual account is a notional account in China. Official data of the annual pension expenditures do not distinguish between the DB pension and the individual account pension.[13] In more practical terms, the BOAI system actually operates as a pay-as-you-go (PAYG) system. As such, we will treat the BOAI system a pure PAYG system in the following simulation, with a total contribution rate of 28 percent of wages paid jointly by the employer and employee.

The model for simulating pension expenditure and contribution involves three steps. In the first step, we need to calibrate the average replacement rate (average pension/social average wage of the year), the first year replacement rate after retirement (entry replacement rate, first year pension/average wage of the same year) and the collection rate (contributions collected/contributions due).[14] Pension expenditures, revenues and balances for 2010 are used as the initial conditions. We use information of average pension benefits and average wages to obtain the average replacement rate for 2010. According to the transitional arrangement in the reform, entry replacement rate will be reduced to 50 percent gradually in next 30 years. If retirement age is increased by 5 years, the figure will be 62 percent. This policy rule will be used to obtain the entry replacement rate of new retirees for each year. The collection rate is found by comparing the actual contribution as a percentage of wage and the institutional contribution rate (see Table 3.3).

In the second step, we make assumptions for the parameters necessary for the projections. These are the wage growth rate, GDP growth rate, inflation rate, and interest rate (Table 3.4). The interest rate, which can be treated as an

Table 3.3 Calibration results

	Entry replacement rate	Average replacement rate	Collection rate	Coverage rate for employees	Coverage rate for retirees
2010	71%	45%	57.5%	80% (local) 20% (migrant)	70%

Notes: average replacement rate = average pension/social average wage of the year; entry replacement rate = first year pension/average wage of the same year; collection rate = contribution collected/contribution due

Table 3.4 Assumption of parameters

	2011–2015	2016–2020	2021–2025	2026–2030
GDP annual growth (%)	8.6	7.0	5.9	5.0
Wage annual growth (%)	8.3	7.1	6.2	5.5
Inflation rate (annual, %)	5	5	5	5
Interest rate (annual, %)	5	5	5	5

Source: GDP growth rate and wage growth rate are real values, from "China 2030: Building a Modern Harmonious, and Creative High-Income Society. The World Bank, DRC, 2012". The discount rate is used to make the values of different years comparable. GDP growth and wage growth are in real terms.

investment rate or discount rate, is used to calculate the future value of accumulative assets or the present value of accumulative deficit.

In the third step, we compute pension expenditure and contribution for each
year using equations (3.3) and (3.4). *i* is the age of the beneficiary. *T* is the
maximum age.

$$Pension\ expenditure = \sum_{i=retirement\ age}^{T} beneficiaries_i * average\ wage$$

$$* replacement\ rate_i \qquad (3.9)$$

$$Pension\ Revenue = Contributors * Average\ wage * Contribution\ Rate \qquad (3.10)$$

4.2. Pension expenditure in BOAI

We simulate pension expenditure in the BOAI system according to the current
policy rule listed in Table 3.1 for all participants and retirees, and we keep the
coverage rate as in Case 1, i.e. 80 percent for local employees and 20 percent
for migrant workers. We could then obtain the number of pensioners, the pension expenditure, the number of contributors, the revenue of pension funds,
and the financial balance. These are reported in Table 3.5.

There is a clear trend that the number of pensioners is increasing over time,
while the number of contributors is declining. The pension expenditure would
have increased by 18.7 times between 2012 and 2030. Already for 2012, there
is the incurrence of an annual deficit in the absence of any government subsidies.
Annual deficit as a percentage of GDP will be 5.03 percent in 2030. The accumulated deficit in 2030 will be 20 trillion and 31.78 percent of GDP. It is
obvious that the current arrangement of the BOAI is unsustainable.

Table 3.5 Pension expenditure in BOAI

	2012	2015	2020	2025	2030
Pensioners (million)	78.93	96.56	132.57	178.99	222.95
Contributors (million)	215.35	216.99	212.41	200.83	188.21
Pension Revenue (billion)	1641.5	2437.6	4435.6	7432.5	11898.4
Pension Expenditure (billion)	1717.7	2912.6	6851.5	15604.3	32226.5
Balance (billion)	–76.3	–475.0	–2415.9	–8171.8	–20328.1
Balance as a percentage of current GDP	–0.14%	–0.61%	–1.70%	–3.36%	–5.03%
Accumulated deficit to current GDP	2.35%	0.56%	–5.06%	–15.52%	–31.78%

Sources: Simulation results

4.3. Pension expenditure in URP and NRP

Due to the lack of data of contributors, we will only discuss the provision of government subsidies in the URP and NRP systems. The government provides a basic pension of 55 RMB per month to all participants who are more than 60 years old, i.e. 660 RMB per year to participants in either system. We should also note that 55 RMB per month is the minimum guaranteed basic URP and NRP pension. For the coastal provinces, where the living cost is higher and fiscal revenue is more sufficient, the provincial governments undertake more responsibility to provide extra pension to the participants. For instance, Shanghai provides a 500 RMB per month pension for the participants. However, given the amount of variation present, it is difficult to determine an average level of pension benefits across provinces.

Therefore, the calculation below should be treated as an estimation of the base provision. We assume that the basic pension of URP and NRP has the same adjustment rate with BOAI in the future, i.e. it accumulates with the real wage growth rate and inflation rate according to the different scenarios. From Table 3.6 we find that the combined expense of the URP and NRP systems is about 5 percent that of the BOAI. The URP and NRP will cost less in subsidies to maintain relative to the pension deficit in BOAI. In 2030, a fiscal expenditure of about 1.6 percent of the GDP in 2030 will be enough to cover the total subsidies of URP and NRP from 2010 to 2030 (Table 3.6).

The better situation in URP and NRP is guaranteed by two reasons. One is that the initial pension benefit is rather low in these two schemes, which is about 3 percent of the level of BOAI. The other reason is that the expanding coverage of BOAI leads to a slower increase of pensioners.

4.4. Scenarios for reform

Four reform scenarios for the BOAI system are proposed, with the purpose of simulating the effects of increasing retirement age and reducing contribution rates, and estimating the total amount of government subsidies required

Table 3.6 Pension expenditure in URP and NRP

	2012	*2015*	*2020*	*2025*	*2030*
Pensioners (million)	136.56	149.71	157.21	169.78	180.14
Subsidy (billion)	99.37	132.4	187.5	268.4	373.2
Subsidy as a percentage of current GDP	0.19%	0.17%	0.13%	0.11%	0.09%
Accumulated subsidy to current GDP	0.53%	0.90%	1.28%	1.47%	1.58%

Sources: Simulation results

Table 3.7 Proposed reform scenarios

	Contribution rate	Coverage	Collection rate	Retirement age	Indexation	Fiscal subsidy
Baseline	28%	80% for local; 20% for migrant	60%	60 for male; 55 for female	(Wage growth rate + inflation rate)/2	0
Scenario 1	28%	80%	60%	60 for male; 55 for female	(Wage growth rate + inflation rate)/2	0
Scenario 2	Reduced to 20%	80%	Increased to 80%	60 for male; 55 for female	(Wage growth rate + inflation rate)/2	0
Scenario 3	Reduced to 20%	80%	Increased to 80%	Increased by 5 years	(Wage growth rate + inflation rate)/2	1% GDP
Scenario 4	Reduced to 20%	80%	Increased to 80%	Increased by 5 years	Inflation rate	1% GDP

Notes: If changing, retirement age, collection rate, and contribution rate change from 2014 gradually to the target value in a 20-year period.

(Table 3.7). Reducing contribution rates has been suggested in the literature (ILO, 2010; Feldstein, 2008), but concerns about its negative effects on the pension system's financial situation makes it a doubtful choice. We argue that a higher contribution rate acts as a pullback for participation in the BOAI, so the negative effects of reducing contribution rates on the pension fund's financial balances will be offset by expanding coverage and increasing collection rates (Feng and He, 2012). Furthermore, the financial considerations of the reform will be facilitated by increasing the retirement age and financing part of the transition cost through fiscal revenue.

4.5. Simulation results

From Figure 3.14, the baseline scenario is clearly unsustainable. The pension fund is in deficit very early on, and this keeps increasing until it reaches a trough of 7.22 percent of the GDP in 2050. Figure 3.15 is the percentage of accumulated surplus/deficits to the current nominal GDP, and the accumulated surplus/deficits are calculated after discounting, which, for the baseline scenario, is set at 5 percent. In this case, the accumulated asset comes to 94.5 percent of the GDP in 2050 (Figure 3.15).

Compared to the baseline results, increasing coverage in Scenario 1 improves the potential deficit situation to the pension's finances. If retirement age is increased as per Scenario 2, the financial situation will be further improved. The qualitative results from Scenario 2 are similar to Scenario 1, which shows that

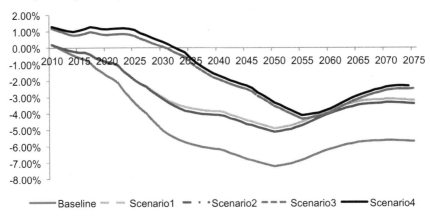

Figure 3.14 Contributions minus expenditures, percentage of GDP

Simulation results/author's calculation

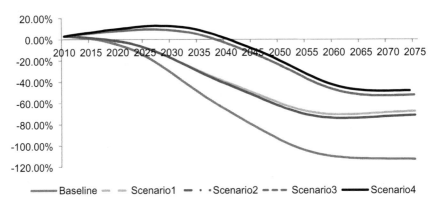

Figure 3.15 Accumulative balance, percentage of GDP (2010–2075)

Simulation results/author's calculation

cutting contribution rates can be offset by giving incentives for participating and inputting a larger government subsidy. Simulations of Scenario 3 indicate that the BOAI system will run a surplus until 2030 (Figure 3.14), and its accumulated surplus then just exceeds 8.6 percent of the GDP in 2030 (Figure 3.15). Changing the indexation rule to inflation rate in Scenario 4 will further contribute towards making the deficit more manageable over the next 60 years.

Figure 3.16 shows the sensitivity of the accumulative surplus/deficits to a variety of discount rates. A low discount rate guarantees a relatively smooth accumulation of surplus/deficits, but it will ultimately not affect the overall annual deficit outcome.

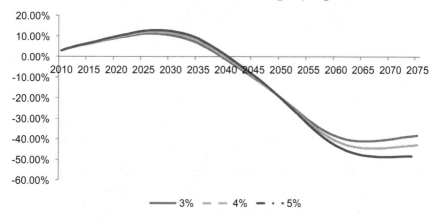

Figure 3.16 Accumulative balances with various discount rates, percentage of GDP (2010–2075)

Simulation results/author's calculation

5. Key characteristics of the fiscal system

We have shown that regardless of the scenarios hypothesized, a fiscal subsidy will be necessary to improve the financial balance of the BOAI system in the long run. In this and the following section we address the question on where the fiscal space could be found to finance public pensions in China.

Over the past two decades, China has reformed its fiscal system significantly. A new tax system with a value added tax at its core laid the foundations for a significant increase in the ratio of revenue to GDP since 1994, and China has succeeded in raising sufficient revenues to maintain sound public finances. Public deficits are low and tax revenues have risen steadily in relation to GDP. Central government enhanced its ability in revenue mobilization after 1994. The central government's share of total fiscal revenue increased from less than 30 percent to around 50 percent in 2012. A financial transfer payment system is employed to subsidize local governments, comprising provinces, municipalities, and counties. The other characteristic of local governments who are mobilizing fiscal resources is that revenue collection through the selling of land is done locally and there is the presence of a large amount of off-budget borrowing.

Thus, China can be considered as among the most decentralized countries in the world in the aspect of government expenditure. The subnational governments account for 80 percent of total budgetary expenditures and bear responsibility for the provision of vital public services, including health care and education, pensions subsidies, unemployment insurance, disability, housing, infrastructure maintenance, and minimum income support. The central government finances about 40–50 percent of total local expenditure in the form of inter-government fiscal transfers (The World Bank, 2012).

5.1. Fiscal revenue and expenditure trends in China

Fiscal revenue in China has been increasing at a remarkable rate. The average annual growth rate of revenue collection has been 19.7 percent since 2000, twice as much as the GDP growth rate. Besides normal fiscal revenue, there is also a so-termed 'land public finance', where local governments seek to increase revenues by selling land. It is estimated that land sale revenues contribute as much as 40 percent of local fiscal revenue on average. Bank loans are another source of revenue for local governments. The loans are partly collateralized by land and other local government assets (Hemming, 2012). Compared to the regular fiscal revenue, which is mostly used to sustain the basic government operations and education/health/social security system expenditures, land sales revenue are mostly used in infrastructure constructions. Local governments have also become increasingly reliant on central government transfers. But these transfers mainly cover public service spending. In order to finance local infrastructure, an off-budget borrowing mechanism was created. The local government could create a company or trust entity, allowing it to borrow from banks and financial markets.

Correspondingly, spending of central government has increased by 44 percent since 2007. Local government spending has increased by 142 percent, an increase far greater than that of the central government. The central government is mainly responsible for expenditure on diplomacy/national defence and treasury interest payments. Local governments are now undertaking more responsibilities for the welfare expenditures, such as education/social security and employment, than they were just 5 years ago.

As we can see from Figure 3.17b, all categories of the fiscal expenditure have been expanding over the last 5 years. Besides normal fiscal revenue in Figure 3.17a, there is also a so-termed "land public finance" where local governments seek to increase revenues by selling land. The fastest expanding category in the last 5 years was in the transportation and health category, whose share grew from 3.85 percent to 6.86 percent and from 4.00 percent to 5.89 percent respectively. Though still having increased in absolute value, the share of expenditure on social security and employment changed little, from 10.9 percent to 10.2 percent.

5.2. Fiscal risks

China's fiscal position has shown a general improvement in recent years. The official gross debt ratio to GDP in China was only about 17 percent, and total debt ratio was 47 percent in 2010 (Table 3.8), both of which are much lower than most industrialized countries and emerging countries in Asia. However, there is a growing concern about China's fiscal risks, especially on the contingent liabilities of local governments in recent years.[15] A slowing down of the economic

Domestic VAT
Domestic consumption tax
Import VAT and consumption tax
Export rebate tax, consumption tax
Business tax
CIT
Personal Income Tax
Resource tax
Urban maintenance and construction tax
Property Tax
Stamp
Stamp duty on securities transactions
Urban Land Use Tax
LAT
Travel tax
Tonnage tax
Vehicle purchase tax
Tariff
Arable land occupation tax
Deed
Tobacco tax
Other tax revenues
Special revenue
Administrative charges
Confiscation of income
Other income
20000 16000 12000 8000 4000 0 4000 8000 12000 16000 20000 24000
Central 2007
Local 2007
Central 2011
Local 2011

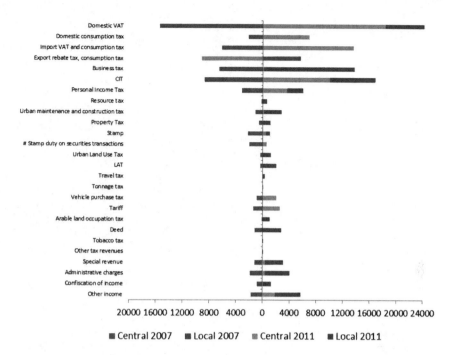

Figure 3.17a Fiscal revenue (million)

Source: China statistics yearbook, 2012.

General public services
Diplomacy
National defense
Public Safety
Education
Science and Technology
Culture, Sport and Media
Social security and employment
Health
Environmental Protection
Urban and Rural Community Affairs
Forestry and Water Affairs
Transportation
Treasury interest expense
Industrial commercial and financial affairs
Earthquake reconstruction spending
Other expenses
10000 6000 2000 2000 6000 10000 14000 18000
Central 2007
Local 2007
Central 2011
Local 2011

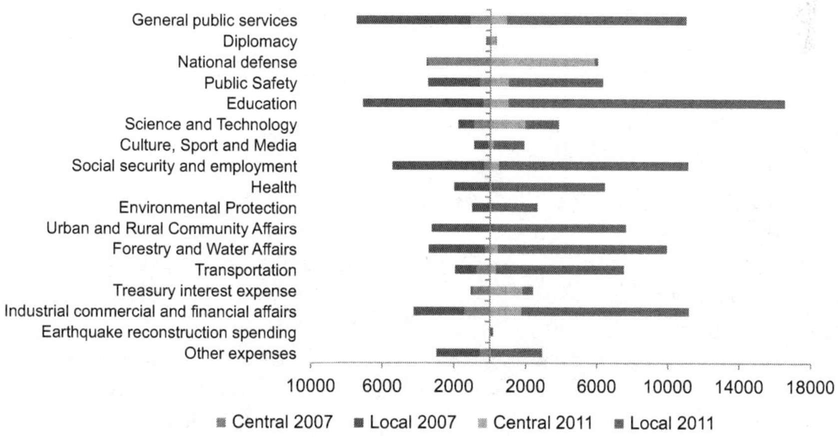

Figure 3.17b Fiscal expenditure (million)

Source: China statistics yearbook, 2012.

Table 3.8 Total government debt 2010 (percentage of GDP)

Debt	2010
Official government debt	17.0%
Local government debt	26.9%
Ministry of Railways liabilities	4.8%
Total government debt	48.7%

Source: Hemming (2012). Data from IMF World Economic Outlook database; National Audit Agency; and Ministry of Railways.

growth rate, an aging population, and financial repression are all factors indicating that conditions will not always be so supportive towards maintaining a respectable fiscal position (Kawai and Morgan, 2013). Hemming (2012) pointed out that contingent liabilities in China are one of the reasons for the lower government debt ratio in emerging Asian countries, and China is a notable example. Various contingent liabilities in China will raise the potential total debt ratio to as high as 113 percent. The risks posed by contingent liabilities will challenge the sustainability of the fiscal system when growth slows down.[16]

Nevertheless, the Chinese government has taken various initiatives to contain local government fiscal risks. Studies by IMF pointed out that debt sustainability analysis and stress tests illustrate that the augmented fiscal debt is still at a manageable level (Zhang and Barnett, 2014). Overall, with contingent liabilities, Chinese fiscal position is weaker than suggested by on-budget revenue and expenditure, but there is still room to use fiscal policy to support demand for public services as needed. Preventing and controlling local government debt will be among the major tasks for the new leadership group. It is believed that the central government will look at fiscal sustainability, with a specific focus on local government risk prevention and control.

5.3. Fiscal expenditure on social security

It is worth noting that as a program of social insurance, contribution and expenditure of the BOAI system is not included in the statistical collection of the fiscal system in China. But the subsidy to the BOAI system for covering its deficits is included in both local and central fiscal expenditure records. In most provinces, contribution and expenditure of BOAI are pooled at the city level or county level. The labour bureau of the local government takes charge of the program and pension expenditure, but the central government will provide the required subsidies if the local government has difficulties in financing the pension deficit. One aspect of the reform of the BOAI system is to pool funds at higher levels of administrative aggregation over time, first at the provincial level and then ultimately at the national level.[17]

The expenditure on social security reported in the statistics of the official fiscal system contains two main parts: the Public Employee Pension (PEP) and

Table 3.9 Fiscal expenditure in social security (0.1 billion yuan)

Year	GDP	Fiscal expenditure	Expenditure on social security			% of BOAI subsidies in fiscal expenditure	% of BOAI subsidies in GDP	% of Social security expenditure in fiscal expenditure
			ALL	PEP	BOAI subsidies			
1997	78,061	9,234	339	197				3.67%
1998	83,024	10,798	617	297				5.72%
1999	88,479	13,188	934	396				7.08%
2000	98,000	15,887	1,300	479				8.18%
2001	108,068	18,903	1,710	626				9.05%
2002	119,096	22,053	2,179	789	455	2.06%	0.38%	9.88%
2003	134,977	24,650	2,656	895	530	2.15%	0.40%	10.77%
2004	159,454	28,487	3,116	1,028	614	2.16%	0.36%	10.94%
2005	183,617	33,930	3,699	1,165	651	1.92%	0.35%	10.90%
2006	215,904	40,423	4,362	1,330	971	2.40%	0.44%	10.79%
2007	266,422	49,781	5,447		1157	2.32%	0.41%	10.94%
2008	316,030	62,593	6,804	1,874	1437	2.30%	0.42%	10.87%
2009	340,320	76,300	7,607	2,141	1646	2.16%	0.45%	9.97%
2010	399,760	89,874	9,131	2,285	1954	2.17%	0.48%	10.16%
2011	468,562	109,248	11,109	2,641	2272	2.08%	0.47%	10.17%

Notes: Social insurance expenditure for employees in private sectors, including pension, health care, and unemployment benefits, is not included in fiscal expenditure. Off-budget borrowing by local government is not included.

Sources: China statistic yearbook (2000–2012)

BOAI subsidies (Table 3.9). We focus on the subsidy to BOAI. With continued aging as discussed in last section, subsidies to the BOAI system will dominate future expenditure on social security. The share of BOAI subsidies in total fiscal expenditure remained at 2 percent in the last 10 years, while the share of social security expenditure in total fiscal expenditure was about 10 percent. The share of BOAI subsidies in GDP increased from 0.38 percent to 0.47 percent over the same period. Since 1997, the share of fiscal revenue as a percentage of GDP had increased from 11 percent to 22 percent, providing a strong premise for the continued financing of social security. In the future, it is inevitable that the central and local fiscal revenue will be one of the key sources of financing the BOAI system. The reason for the government subsidy is that the transition cost caused by public pension reform during the middle of the 1990s should be financed partly by fiscal revenue.

However, there are also reform options available by which to control the level of fiscal subsidies that the central government must provide for the BOAI system in order for it to continue being viable. These have been discussed earlier.

We are going to discuss fiscal subsidies required under various scenarios and the fiscal spaces in the next section.

6. Fiscal space options including future pension liabilities

In this section we compute and show that the share of BOAI pension expenditure stands at 6–8 percent of GDP in 2030, increasing to about 9.5 percent in 2050. Total fiscal subsidy will account for 5–22 percent of total fiscal expenditure. To finance the increase in expenditure, however, there appears limited prospects in increasing the usual range of taxes – consumption taxes, income taxes, corporate taxes, and tariffs, etc., as the domestic tax burden is already high in China. From 1995 to 2010, per capita fiscal revenue has increased by 8 times, and the annual growth of tax revenue has exceeded the GDP growth rate for 18 consecutive years since 1994. If levies and fees are included with taxes, the overall tax burden currently stands at 32 percent of GDP.[18] This is higher than 6 of the 8 OECD member countries bordering the Pacific Ocean. Thus, there is a need to focus on alternative fiscal resources to finance the pension subsidy. Some possible options include the Nation Social Security Fund, dividends from state-owned enterprises, and investment returns of foreign exchange reserves.

6.1. Future pension liabilities

As we saw in the last section, the deficit of the BOAI pension system will grow rapidly without any reform being undertaken. However, it is clear from the scenarios proposed in Table 3.7 that this could be improved upon, depending on the reform options taken. We will estimate the fiscal subsidies needed in Scenarios 1 and 4 in Figure 3.15. Scenario 1 is a scenario which only expands the coverage of migrant workers, but without any other reform to the BOAI system. In Scenario 4, we postpone the retirement age and change the indexation of pension to the inflation rate. In the test we will fix the share of fiscal expenditure at 20 percent of the GDP. We do not consider the effects of the NRP and URP systems, as they account for only a small share (less than 1 percent) of fiscal expenditure. We also assume that the accumulated surplus will be expended first in the event of a deficit, and we set the interest and inflation rates at 5 percent.

In Scenario 1, the accumulated surplus is fully expended within 5 years before required subsidies for the BOAI pensions began to increase (Table 3.10). By 2020, an extra 3.4 percent of fiscal expenditure is required to sustain the BOAI system. This share quickly increases to 15 percent in 2030 and reaches a peak of 24.5 percent in 2050, rendering it to be a heavy burden for fiscal expenditure. In Scenario 4, a constant annual contribution of 1 percent of GDP to the BOAI revenue ensures that the accumulated surplus will not be fully expended before 2040, thereby avoiding the situation in Scenario 1. The extra subsidies required

Table 3.10 Fiscal space of required subsidies for BOAI

Year	Scenario 1		Scenario 4	
	Pension expenditure as % of GDP	Required subsidies for BOAI as % of fiscal expenditure	Pension expenditure as % of GDP	Required subsidies for BOAI as % of fiscal expenditure
2015	3.7%	0.0%	3.4%	5.0%
2020	4.8%	3.4%	3.9%	5.0%
2025	6.4%	9.8%	4.7%	5.0%
2030	8.0%	15.0%	6.1%	5.0%
2035	8.7%	18.2%	7.1%	5.0%
2040	8.8%	19.2%	8.1%	7.6%
2045	9.3%	22.1%	8.7%	16.4%
2050	9.6%	24.5%	9.5%	21.7%
2055	9.1%	22.5%	10.1%	25.5%
2060	8.4%	18.8%	9.6%	23.6%
2065	7.9%	16.3%	8.8%	19.5%
2070	7.6%	15.6%	8.3%	16.9%
2075	7.6%	15.9%	8.1%	16.4%

Sources: Simulation results

in Scenario 4 reach the peak of 20.5 percent in 2050. It should be noted that relative to Scenario 1, the cost to the government for 2050 to 2070 is actually higher in Scenario 4 since a postponed retirement age increases the replacement rate of the current working generation before they retire.

6.2. National Social Security Fund (NSSF)

The National Social Security Fund (NSSF) of China was established in 2000 as a strategic reserve fund to cope with future pension needs. This fund is financed in four ways: (1) funds allocated from the central government's budget; (2) capital and equity assets derived from state-owned enterprise share sales (state-owned enterprises are required to send 10 percent of their IPO funds to NSSF); (3) other ways approved by the State Council, such as state lottery license fees, as well as funds obtained through a securities repo program; and (4) investment returns. NSSF assets have increased rapidly, so much so that by the end of 2012 total assets managed by the NSSF stood at 176 billion USD, half of which are funded from fiscal resources.

The NSSF has broad channels for investment, including bank savings (not less than 10 percent of total assets), treasury bonds (not lower than 50 percent), business bonds (not higher than 10 percent), financial bonds (not higher than

Table 3.11 National Social Security Fund assets and investment return rate

	2005	2006	2007	2008	2009	2010	2011	2012
Assets (billion RMB)	195	272	414	480	693	781	773	893
Investment return (%)	3.12	9.34	38.93	–6.79	16.12	4.23	0.84	7.01

Source: NSSF Board of Managers

10 percent), securities investment funds (not higher than 40 percent) and stocks (no more than 40 percent). Some of these funds are invested in foreign venture capital funds and other financial instruments. Between 2001 and 2012, the NSSF has achieved annual return rates of more than 8 percent, a rate much higher than inflation, which stands at around 4 percent. But it should be noted that the NSSF invests nearly 40 percent of the fund in the Chinese stock market, and therefore fluctuations in investment returns are likely to be correlated with the volatility of the domestic stock market (Table 3.11).[19] The fund is now allowing investments to private equity and foreign equity and is beginning to invest in both emerging and European markets.

6.3. Dividends from state-owned enterprises (SOEs)

State-owned enterprises in China have assets currently valued at 33.8 trillion yuan. SOE profits, as a share of China's GDP, rose from 1.7 percent in 2001 to 3.7 percent in 2007. SOEs were also exempted from paying dividends through much of the 1990s and 2000s, which gave these firms an advantage over current and potential competitors by keeping their cost of capital low. At same time, it also reduced the government revenue that could have been spent on pensions, education, and other social services. This changed in 2007 when the State Council mandated central SOEs to begin paying dividends, 10 percent in highly profitable industries, 5 percent in the industries where SOEs were less profitable, and 0 percent for protected firms like military armaments manufacturers. The rates were increased by 5 percent across the board to 15, 10, and 5 percent in 2011. In 2012, SOEs in China made a net profit of 1.1 trillion yuan, in which only 82.3 billion, about 7.4 percent of the net profit, was submitted to central and local governments.[20]

As the World Bank pointed out, Chinese SOEs practiced far from normal dividend payout ratios.[21] The average dividend payout for mature and established industrial firms in the United States is 50 to 60 percent. SOEs in Demark, Norway, Finland, and Sweden set multi-year payout targets, from 33 percent to 67 percent of earnings. Chinese SOEs that are listed in Hong Kong pay an average dividend of 23 percent. So even the top rate of 15 percent set by the State Council is still quite a bit lower than what Chinese SOEs themselves pay to shareholders in Hong Kong.

China will moderately increase the ratio of dividends paid out by state-owned enterprises by increasing the number of centrally administered SOEs and locally administered SOEs that are required to pay dividends to the state. SOE dividends have been regarded as a key building block in funding the social security system by the central government. Further reform also calls for the changing of management of SOE dividends. In the past, these funds have not been included in the general budget to pay for public expenditures. It has now been decided that the Ministry of Finance will collect the dividends and place them into a 'State Capital Management Budget'.

Hypothetically, if the dividend rate SOEs are subject to can be increased to 20 percent, this translates to an extra 140 billion yuan which can be used to finance the BOAI pension deficit. Notice too that under Scenario 1 the simulated deficit stood at 24 and 90 billion for 2012 and 2013 respectively. An extra 140 billion thus implies that contributions from the net profits of SOEs can certainly help to sustain the BOAI, at least in the short term.

6.4. Investment return from foreign exchange reserves

Foreign exchange reserves offer another resource to help sustain China's pension system. Until the first quarter of 2013, China recorded about $3.44 trillion in foreign exchange reserves. China's foreign exchange reserves account for one third of the world's total and 50 percent of China's GDP. Like many other governments, China invests most of its reserves in Treasury bills issued by the US government due to the safety and high liquidity of these bills. However, given the extremely low return, there is great potential for this investment strategy to be adjusted for higher returns.

The question is, how can one make use of these accumulated foreign reserves to help improve the financial viability and sustainability of China's pension system?

One option is the establishment of a sovereign wealth fund (SWF) using revenues from natural resources or foreign exchange reserves. Examples include the SWF of Norway, the Superannuation Fund of New Zealand, and the Future Fund in Australia. In 2007, Chinese authorities established the China Investment Corporation (CIC), a type of sovereign wealth fund (SWF). Similar to the sovereign wealth fund in other countries, the CIC fund is responsible for managing part of China's foreign exchange reserves. Depending on the performance of the fund, it is possible that more foreign exchange reserves could be allocated to the CIC fund, and the investment returns be used to finance the deficit of the BOAI system.

However, because continued pension funding requires a more stable investment cash flow, a more complicated question implicit here is how one reconciles between a robust investment strategy for the needs of the pension fund against an investment strategy which entails greater risk-exposure to meet some other investment target concurrently. The CIC is currently making efforts to improve its governance and investment strategy to better manage these (potentially) conflicting objectives.

6.5. Improving productivity

The key to sustaining a pension system lies in the enhancement of labour productivity. If productivity is rising, the wealth created by the younger generation can in effect support a larger group of old people. With growing output (and thereby income), the PAYG system remains in balance without the need for either a reduction in pensions or an increase in contributions. An increase in output is also possibly the best solution for funded schemes, since it will help control inflation in the goods market and deflation in the asset market (Barr, 2000).

Table 3.12 reports the World Bank's estimates of the growth in China's labour productivity in the next two decades. Here labour productivity is measured by the amount of real GDP produced by an employee. While China's labour productivity growth rate is expected to drop in tandem with the GDP growth rate, it will still continue to grow at a relatively high level of approximately 5.5 percent annually from 2026 to 2030. Improving labour productivity will thus increase the amount of effective labour and offset the negative influence of population aging.

It should be pointed out that future productivity increases are dependent on some crucial factors: first, on the quality of the labour force. The educational level of China's labour force has been rising. The average number of years of schooling received by workers as of the 1964 census was only 2.34 years. This figure increased to 9.07 years in 2010. The enrolment in higher education increased from 45.7 (per ten thousand individuals) in 1995 to 218.8 in 2010.[22] Faced with an aging population, expanding investment in human capital is likely to be an effective strategy to raise productivity. Secondly, the change in labour productivity growth is also dependent on economic restructuring. Labour productivity in the agricultural sector is typically lower than industries, leaving room for rural labourers to shift to non-agricultural sectors. This lowers the proportion

Table 3.12 Projected labour productivity growth (1995–2030)

	1995–2010	2011–2015	2016–2020	2021–2025	2026–2030
GDP annual growth(%)	9.9	8.6	7.0	5.9	5.0
Labour growth(%)	0.9	0.3	−0.2	−0.2	−0.4
Labour productivity growth(%)	8.9	8.3	7.1	6.2	5.5
Share of employment in agriculture(%)	38.1	30.0	23.7	18.2	12.5
Share of employment in service(%)	34.1	42.0	47.6	52.9	59.0

Source: The World Bank, DRC, 2012, 'China 2030: Building a Modern, Harmonious, and Creative High-Income Society'.

of people working in agriculture, while raising both services and industries in urbanized areas. Policies that facilitate the mobility of labour will thus play a crucial part in ensuring rising labour productivity.

7. Concluding observations and suggestions

The sustainability of the Chinese public pension system (in most cases, the system refers to the BOAI program) has been studied a lot in the literature. As China's public pension system is aiming (and approaching) one of universal coverage, with more people being covered by one of several types of available pension schemes, the foreseeable challenges during a process of rapid population ageing have come to the fore. An immediate outcome is simply that pension expenditure as a percentage of GDP will keep increasing. At the present moment, both central and local governments have continually subsidized pension funds, using around 2 percent of total fiscal expenditure over the past decade.

In this chapter, we estimate the public pension liabilities from several perspectives which are unique to the existing literature. First, in view of the specific urbanization process in China, we consider the effect of an expansion of coverage of the pension system on old-age dependency ratios and on financial balances of the public pension system. Second, we consider the possibility of reducing contribution rates as a mechanism to provide greater incentives for participation. A lower contribution rate will lead to higher rate of compliance, which will, in turn, generate more contributions to offset the effect of the reduction of the contribution rate. Third, we argue that an explicit subsidy from the government should be inputted into the BOAI system to finance the transitional cost caused by the reform during the middle of 1990s. Fourth, we simulate several reform scenarios to study the feasible improvement in the financial balances of the Chinese public pension system.

Our main observations are the following:

Current BOAI for urban employees in private sectors is unsustainable; the annual deficit of the system will be 5 percent of GDP in 2030, and the accumulative deficit in 2030 may be potentially as high as 32 percent.

Expanding coverage to rural migrant workers will improve the OADR and could improve the financial balance by a large margin.

Increasing retirement age by 5 years in a 20-year period of time starting in 2014 will significantly improve the financial situation of the BOAI system over the next 30 years.

Cutting contribution rates does not necessarily reduce the revenue in the pension fund. Instead, it provides an incentive for participation and could potentially increase collection rates. If the retirement age is increased together with a concurrent annual input of subsidies amounting to 1 percent of the GDP, the BOAI system will maintain a surplus till 2040.

The BOAI scheme is the core program of the Chinese public pension system. The reform objective of the system is to provide a uniform scheme with broad coverage to all employees in the industry and service sectors. It is unrealistic to provide a uniform system where the contribution rate is as high as 28 percent. Our core suggestion, therefore, is for a reduction in the contribution rate.

In our simulations, we treat the individual account as a notional account and the BOAI system as a DB program. This is in line with the current situation in China, where most individual accounts are empty and a target replacement ratio is employed in practice. It is also closely related to the current proposal from the World Bank and other scholars that adopting a notional defined contribution (NDC) in the Chinese public pension system is a possible policy option (e.g. Dorfman *et al.*, 2013).

The advantage of the NDC scheme is that it offers only the notional rate of return that keeps the system solvent, even during adverse economic times and under severe population aging. However, there are still a few conceptual and operational issues that have not yet been satisfactorily solved, such as the design of an effective balancing mechanism (Holzmann, 2012).

We argue that there should be additional fiscal expenditure to the pension system based on the requirement for financing the transition costs. There have been several estimates of the legacy costs (or transition costs) incurred from the pension reform in the middle of the 1990s in urban China (see Dorfman *et al.*, 2013).[23] The current high contribution rate is largely due to the fact that part of the contribution is used to cover part of the transition costs. We thus also suggest that fiscal funding should be used for this purpose in order to alleviate the pressure of the contributors. Our simulation shows that if the retirement age is raised to 65 and 60 for males and females respectively, the coverage is extended to as much as 80 percent of urban employees. Coupled with an annual fiscal subsidy at 1 percent of GDP, a contribution rate of only 20 percent could be sufficient to ensure the financial balance of the pension system.

China has some special tools to provide the necessary fiscal space to cope with the projected increase in pension expenditures. The National Social Security Fund has been established as a strategic reserve fund to cope with future pension needs. Dividends from state-owned enterprises and investment return from foreign exchange reserves are another two important instruments to supplement fiscal subsidies, but it should be noted that reforming the pension system relies on a comprehensive set of social and economic reforms.

The ability of an aging society to afford its elderly people is also dependent on productivity increases. Therefore, one of the fundamental solutions to solving the problem of financing an aging society lies with increasing human capital investment and changing economic growth patterns, e.g. transferring labour from low-productivity sectors to higher productivity sectors and increasing the effective pool of labour supply.

The policy implication of our paper is in line with some future reforms in the government's roadmap. The third plenary session of the 18th Communist Party of China (CPC) central committee in 2013 set out several important reforms related to the sustainability of public pension. China will loosen the one-child population policy, allowing couples to have two children if one of them is an only child. The new policy is expected to increase future fertility rates. The government will increase spending on medical services, social security, and environmental protection while at the same time considering reducing the contribution rate of social insurance. Another important policy currently in discussion is to increase the dividend rate submitted by SOEs to 30 percent by 2020. All of these are likely to help further enhance the preparedness of China's pension system to meet the challenges of an aging society.

Notes

1 Source of data: China statistics yearbook, 2013.
2 Source of data: China Pension Report (Zheng, 2012).
3 Please refer to the following government documents for current pension schemes: State Council, 1997, "The Decision on the Building of Unified Enterprises Employee's Basic Pension System", No. 26; State Council, 2005, "The Decision on Improvement of Unified Enterprises Employees' Basic Pension System", No. 38; State Council, 2009, "The Guidance on the Pilot of New Rural Resident Pension Scheme", No. 32; State Council, 2011, "The Guidance on the Pilot of Urban Resident Pension Scheme", No. 18.
4 Replacement ratio of 59.2 percent is of social average wage at retirement age.
5 Source of data: China statistics yearbook, 2012.
6 Ministry of Human Resources and Social Security: Annual Report on National Social Insurance System, 2012.
7 To simulate the rural/urban demographic change, we use the rural/urban definition of the Bureau of Statistics instead of the agricultural/non-agricultural *hukou* of the Ministry of Public Security in this chapter. According to the 2010 definition, urban areas should be located in or contiguous to the area where the local government is located. The only difference in the 2000 definition is that if a region is *not* located in or contiguous to the area where the local government is located, but located in a municipal district with population density above 1500 people per square km, it would be classified as urban, while it is rural by the 2010 definition. The difference is negligible since it is hard to find a discontinuous area in a high-density municipal district.
8 We assume no misreporting in mortality rates and sex ratios at birth. Few studies cast doubt on the reliability of mortality rates, while sex ratios at birth are believed to be over-reported; i.e. the births of females are under-reported (e.g. Goodkind, 2004). Nevertheless, none of the variables is quantitatively important for our main results.
9 This is a reasonable assumption for China, since the reported labor participation rate is lower than 10 percent after retirement age, and most people in enterprises working after retirement age are retirees and reemployed. In such cases, they get pension benefits and do not have to contribute.
10 We set new the labor participation rate (LPR) for each working age after the retirement age is increased following the method:

$$LPR_{new,\,age} = LPR_{old,\,age^*} \text{ in which } \frac{age - 16}{Retirement\;age(old) - 16} = \frac{age^* - 16}{Retirement\;age(new) - 16}$$

(The numerator population at age t minus 16 years. Similar for the denominator)
11 CHFS, the China Household Finance Survey, was conducted in 2011 and surveyed 8000 households around the 30 provinces in China.

12 Higher total fertility rate of 1.44 is a conservative assumption. TFR in China is believed to be 1.64 and the UN population projection is assumed to be 1.6 in middle variant.
13 Oksanen (2012) assumes that initially in 2010 part of the assets held by the pension system, equal to 2 percent of GDP, are assigned for the individual accounts.
14 Average replacement rate is the average pension benefit as a percentage of average wage in the same year. According to the policy laid out in the BOAI, the first year replacement rate for a person who entered the system after 1997 and earned average wage is about 55 percent. Those employees who started earlier have a higher entry replacement ratio. However, there is no clear growth rule afterwards, so the replacement ratio in terms of social average wage in later years is declining. Average replacement rate of 2010 is 45 percent.
15 Contingent liabilities are liabilities that may be incurred by an entity depending on the outcome of future events.
16 If growth slows down, then non-performing loans and other liabilities are likely to rise. When they increase to an extent that leads to a financial crisis, the government may have to inject capital into the financial sector.
17 This argument is not only related to revision of the sharing agreements between the central and local government, but also to facilitate the portability of the contribution when an employee moves from one city to another. Designing a plan to pool at the national level is under discussion by the Ministry of Human Resources and Social Security.
18 Sources of data: China statistics yearbook, 2012.
19 In recent years, while achieving relatively high investment returns, the NSSF's overhead is high. Its overhead is 3 times Norway's sovereign pension level and 1.5 times Ireland's sovereign pension fund level.
20 Sources of data: China fiscal yearbook, Ministry of Finance of China.
21 World Bank policy note "SOE Dividends: How Much and to Whom?" October 17, 2005, prepared by Louis Kuijs, William Mako, and Chunlin Zhang in the World Bank's Beijing Office.
22 Data from the 3rd, 5th, and 6th national population censuses.
23 Legacy costs can be broadly defined as the actuarial deficit of a reformed pension scheme. In China legacy costs come from the movement from higher benefits for old men and middle men (participants before the reform) to lower benefits for new entrants since 1997 and establishment of individual accounts. The legacy costs are aggregate liabilities accrued to date, which is equal to the present value of pensions in disbursement and the present value of any acquired rights to future benefits. (Dorfman *et al.*, 2013).

References

Barr, N. (2000). Reforming pensions: Myths, truths, and policy choices. IMF Working Paper 00/139. Washington, DC: International Monetary Fund.
Chen, Q. & Song, Z. (2013). Facing aging: Can urbanization help? *Financial Research* 396(6): 1–15. (In Chinese).
Dorfman, M. C., Holzmann, R., O'Keefe, P., Wang, D., Sin, Y. & Hinz, R. (2013). *China's pension system: A vision*. Washington, DC: World Bank.
Feldstein, M. & Liebman, J. (2008). Realizing the potential of China's social security pension system. In Jiwei Lou & Shuilin Wang (Eds.), *Public finance in China, reform and growth for a harmonious society* (pp. 309–315). Washington, DC: World Bank.

Feng, J. & He, L. (2012). Reforming China's public pension system: Coping effectively with aging, urbanization and globalization. In Wing Thye Woo (Ed.), *A new economic growth engine for China* (pp. 93–117). London, UK: World Scientific & Imperial College Press.

Goodkind, D. M. (2004). China's missing children: The 2000 census underreporting surprise. *Population Studies* **58(3)**: 281–295.

Hemming, R. (2012). Public debt sustainability and hidden liabilities in the people's Republic of China. In B. Ferrarini, R. Jha & A. Ramayandi (Eds.), *Public debt sustainability in developing Asia*. London, UK and New York, NY: Routledge.

Herd, Ri., Hu, Y., & Koen, V. (2010). Providing greater old-age security in China. OECD Working Paper.

Holzmann, R. (2012). Global pension systems and their reform. Social Protection & Labor, Discussion Paper, No. 1213, The World Bank.

ILO (International Labour Organization). (2010). *World social security report 2010/11: Providing coverage in times of crisis and beyond*. Geneva, Switzerland: ILO.

Johnson, D. G. (2003). Provincial migration in China in the 1990s. *China Economic Review* **14(1)**: 22–31.

Kawai, N. & Morgan, P. J. (2013). Long-term issues for fiscal sustainability in emerging Asia. ADBI Working Paper Series, No.432.

Morgan, S. P., Guo, Z., & Hayford, S. R. (2009). China's below-replacement fertility: Recent trends and future prospects. *Population and Development Review* **35(3)**: 605–629.

Oksanen, H. (2012). Pensions in China: Results from model simulations. Presentation at the International Academic Conference on Old-Age Security Center for Social Security Studies (CSSS) of Wuhan University, 21–22 October, 2012.

Sin, Y. (2005). Pension liabilities and reform of pensions for old-age insurance in China. World Bank Discussion Paper, No.2005–1.

Wang, Y., Xu, D., Wang, Z. & Zhai, F. (2004). Options and impact of China's pension reform: A computable general equilibrium analysis. *Journal of Comparative Economics* **32**: 105–127.

World Bank. (2012). *China 2030: Building a modern, harmonious, and creative high-income society*. Washington, DC: World Bank.

Zhang, G. & Zhao, Z. (2006). Re examining China's fertility puzzle: Data collection and quality over the last two decades. *Population and Development Review* **32(2)**: 293–321.

Zhang, W. & Cui, H. (2003). Estimation of accuracy of 2000 national population census data. *Chinese Journal of Population Research* **27(4)**: 25–35. (In Chinese)

Zhang, Y. & Barnett, S. (2014). Fiscal vulnerabilities and risks from local government finance in China. IMF Working Paper, WP/14/4.

Zheng, B. (2012). *China pension report 2012*. Beijing, China: Economic & Management Publishing House. (In Chinese)

4 Age related pension expenditure and fiscal space in India

Mukul G. Asher and Yutika Vora

1. Introduction

India is projected to exhibit rapid population ageing, increased urbanization, rising household incomes, and heightened societal expectations about income security over the next several decades. This strongly suggests that the initiatives to make explicit or implicit pension promises more credible deserve high priority in India's public policy agenda.

Two characteristics of pension arrangements are relevant in this context. The first is the long time period (around 75 years) for which pension arrangements must exhibit sustainability, affordability, and fairness, while providing adequate levels of benefits as a system throughout the retirement period, covering most of the population. The second is the tyranny of small numbers, as seemingly small changes in pension parameters (e.g. unanticipated increases or decreases in the life expectancy of a relevant cohort, the rate of return obtained on an investment of pension assets, and inflation rates) could have a disproportionate impact on the viability of pension arrangements.

Making pension promises credible involves policy, organizational, work-process, regulatory, data systems, and management reforms in many sectors and finding the requisite fiscal space for the funding of pensions, consistent with other public policy priorities (Asher and Bali, 2014). A systemic approach that links various sub-sectors (such as labour markets, public delivery systems, financial and capital markets, and fiscal systems) is therefore essential.

It is in this context that this chapter aims to project the age related pension expenditure in India, and discusses the initiatives for generating fiscal space for the expenditure share likely to be borne by the fiscal system. Both the projections of age related expenditure for various components of India's pension system and the linking of them with how to generate fiscal space are relatively unexplored areas in India's pension system literature. Exploring ways to generate fiscal space usually represents a flow-type analysis involving increases in tax rates, expanding the tax base, and changing existing license and other fees. It is, however, essential to link the flow with the stock analysis, involving using assets of the government more productively, and to also examine the characteristics of the stock of public debt and its dynamics in India. This chapter, therefore, is designed to fill this gap in the literature.

The chapter is organized as follows. This introduction is followed by a brief overview of India's demographic, labour market, and urbanization trends and characteristics. The overview illustrates not only that the need for credible pension arrangements will increase markedly, but also that this need will have to be met in the context of continuing significant informality in the labour markets and rapid but uneven urbanization in India. In Section 3, key characteristics and challenges of India's pension system are discussed. This sets the context in which the projection of age related pension expenditure is made in Section 4. As India's pension system is fragmented, such a projection is undertaken for each of the major components of the pension system separately, using a mix of quantitative and qualitative reasoning. The issue for generating fiscal space given the key features of India's fiscal system is discussed in Section 5. The final section concludes the chapter with some key observations and suggestions.

2. Demographic and labour market trends: an overview

This section provides an overview of demographic, labour market, and urbanization trends as population ageing impacts the size of the elderly population and the duration for which provision for each individual is needed. The labour market characteristics impact the extent to which pension systems can be based on formal and lessened roles of family-based support system relationships with wages and salaries as the basis for pension contributions, and the extent to which all workers are able to contribute throughout working life. Urbanization has traditionally increased the role of state-mediated pension arrangements. Regional variations in demographic trends and functioning of the labour markets leading to significant internal migration or mobility of labour[1] within India also need to be considered (Mahapatro, 2012). This suggests that portability of pension arrangements across occupations and geography should be an essential component of pension arrangements.

2.1. Demographic trends

India is currently in a demographically advantageous position, with a rising working age population to total population ratio (Government of India, 2013–2014). The population profile for 2011 exhibits a relatively low median age of 25 years and a correspondingly high old-age support ratio at 13 persons aged 15–64 for every person above the age of 65. However, the corresponding number for 2050 is expected to decline significantly to only 5, a decline of 61 percent.[2] This suggests that each elderly person will have to be supported by only 5 economically active persons. It is the moderately rapid pace at which the support-ratio will be declining that will pose challenges, as pension reform initiatives will need to be made effective in a relatively short time.

The changing population pyramid of India (Figure 4.1), based on the United Nations Population 2012 Projection, vividly exhibits India's moderately rapid population ageing and feminization of the elderly. Between 2010

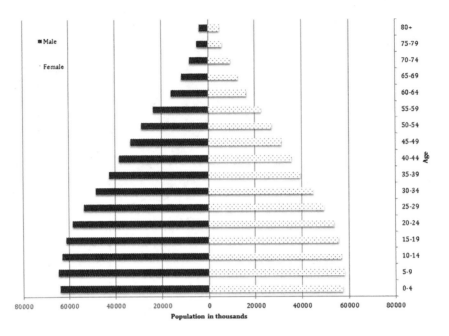

Figure 4.1a India's population pyramid, 2010

Source: UN. (2013). Accessed on 30 September 2014

Note: Population in thousands

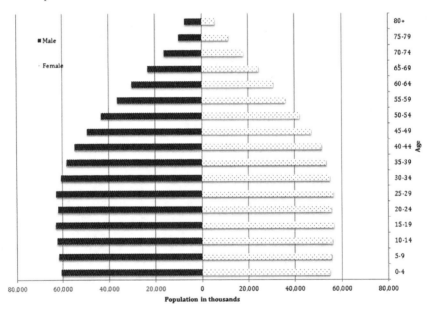

Figure 4.1b India's population pyramid, 2030

Source: UN. (2013). Accessed on 30 September 2014

Note: Population in thousands

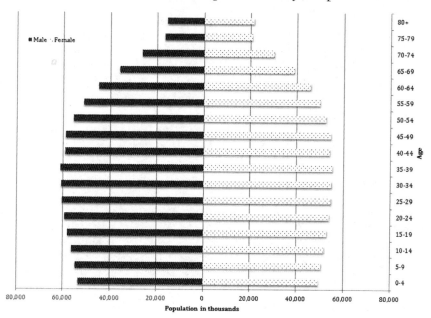

Figure 4.1c India's population pyramid, 2050

Source: UN. (2013). Accessed on 30 September 2014

Note: Population in thousands

and 2050, the number of those above 60 years of age will increase by more than three times, from 93 million in 2010 to 296 million in 2050 (United Nations, 2013). The number of those above 70 years of age will increase rapidly, so that by 2050 the single largest population cohort in India's population will be females above the age of 70, followed by males above the age of 70.

The feminization of the elderly is relevant for pension related expenditure, as females as a group have lower labour force participation rates, and as a group their average income is lower than that of men. But they live longer than men and require more resources of the society (family, community, and fiscal resources) to finance old age.

India will also experience the old-old phenomena as the share of those above 75 years will rise by over 5 times, from 0.9 percent of total population in 2010 to 4.6 percent in 2050 (United Nations, 2013). India's life expectancy at birth is projected to increase from 63.1 in 2000–05 to 72.9 by 2045–50 (United Nations, 2013). The life expectancy at 60, which is more relevant in analysing age related pension expenditure, has increased from 15 in 1990 to 17 in 2012, the latest year for which this figure is available (WHO, 2013). A significant contributory factor in increased longevity is reductions in mortality rates at older ages.

The difference between life expectancy at 60 between males and females has remained at 2 years since 1990. India's total fertility rate (TFR)[3] in 2012 is projected by the United Nations to reach replacement rate of 2.15 around 2030, and be at 1.92 in 2045–50. However, both these projections are likely to undergo revisions, portending even more rapid ageing if the policy initiatives of the Prime Minister Narendra Modi–led government on improving health sanitation and status of women translate into desired outcomes. In particular, planned improvements in public hygiene and sanitation, and better access to health care may reduce mortality rates at older ages, especially in those states where such rates are much above the national average.

More rapid reductions in the TFR than projected by the United Nations are indicated by a recent official report (Government of India, 2014a). The report estimates that in 2013 India's overall TFR was 2.3, (as compared to about 3.0 projected by the United Nation);[4] in rural areas it was 2.5, and in urban areas it was 1.8. Thus, India's urban population is already exhibiting below replacement TFR of 2015. Moreover, two thirds of the states (in 2013, India had 28 states) exhibited TFR below the replacement rate in 2013.

Faster than the projected decline in TFR leaves Indian policymakers with even less time for constructing modern pension system. Variations in the rate of TFR decline among states will further encourage internal labour migration and business location decisions, impacting economic growth and fiscal capacity.

In addition to the demographic trends portending rapid ageing and feminization of the aged, a change in family structures is also occurring. Traditionally, older persons were part of a joint family that led to economies of scale within the family. However, in the past few years there has been a transition to nuclear families, with more older persons choosing to live on their own. The estimates are that one in seven elderly persons in India live in all elderly households and that one in four household have at least one elderly person living with younger household members (Government of India, 2011). With an increasing number of older persons, this trend is only expected to increase the number of older persons living alone.

2.2. *Labour market trends and characteristics*

Trends and characteristics of the labour market in India have implications for pension coverage and age related expenditure in India. Three characteristics may be noted: livelihoods generation in relation to need; low overall – and especially – female labour force participation rates; and significant internal (and external) migration of workers, requiring robust arrangements for portability of pensions (and worker) benefits. The urban population is projected to rapidly increase from 340 million in 2008 to 590 million by 2030, an increase of 250 million people in just 22 years (Sankhe *et al.*, 2010). As a result, the regional variations will be significant, as some states will have a majority of urban and peri-urban populations by 2025.

2.2.1. *Livelihood creation*

India's current favourable demographic profile suggests that the country will need to generate significant number of livelihoods in the coming decades, while enhancing value added per worker. India's overall labour force was 484 million in 2011–12, about two fifths of the total population (Census of India, 2011). If this share increases to the level it was in 2004–05, of 43 percent, then by 2030 India will need to generate a minimum of 160 million net additional livelihoods[5] (1.476 population in 2030 multiplied by 0.43), or nearly 9 million livelihoods per year. This is a conservative estimate, and the needs are likely to be around 10 million per year.

In contrast, during the 2004–05 to 2009–10 period, net livelihoods generation, including self-employment, was less than 0.5 million per year, in spite of the real GDP increasing by an average of 8.6 percent per year in the same period (CRISIL, 2011). Thus, employment elasticity with respect to GDP needs to be enhanced through economic reforms. The potential of disruptive technologies affecting current livelihoods patterns will accentuate this crisis.

2.2.2. *Informality of the labour market*

India's labour force has a relatively low share of wage and salary workers, whose rising share has historically contributed to employment earnings–related pensions and other social security arrangements. Thus, in 2011–12 the share of wage and salary workers in India's total labour force was only 18 percent, while self-employed (52 percent), and casual labour (21 percent) accounted for the rest. The prospects for significantly increasing the share of wage and salary workers, especially in medium to large firms who have relatively better pension arrangements, are not bright. The reports suggest that the aggregate employee number for 185 of the BSE (Bombay Stock Exchange) 500 companies was only 27.9 million (less than 6 percent of the labour force), in 2013–14, a growth of only 2 percent over the previous year (Yoosef and Datta, 2014).

India is also unlikely to be immune to the global trend towarding increasing share of contractual work, with limited pension and healthcare benefits. This suggests that in extending the pension coverage, India cannot simply rely on expansion of formal employment, or on an 'unorganized sector' to which pension, provident funds, and many other labour regulations apply.

2.2.3. *Labour force participation rates*

Labour Force Participation Rates (LFPR) data for 2011–12 indicate that there exists an unusually large gap between men (56 percent) and women (23 percent) in India in their LFPR. For females in the same year, LFPR is much lower in urban (16 percent) than in rural areas (25 percent). The worker to population ratio in 2011–12 was 54 percent for males and 22 percent for females with societal changes and rising income; female worker to population is likely to rise significantly. This could help improve India's potential growth rate, as low participation rates of women in the labour force has been among the constraining factors in India's economic growth and social development.

India's pension arrangement initiative will need to take this trend into account. In particular, budget financed social pension programs will be of greater relevance to females, as they are more likely to be exhibiting informal work arrangements, and as their longevity is higher. This in turn would add to the fiscal space needed for pensions.

3. India's pension system: key characteristics and challenges

India is a federal state with a Union government, twenty-nine states, and seven Union territories. India's complex but fragmented pension system comprises several programs directed at different but sometimes overlapping groups.[6] Moreover, pension-like arrangements are included in several occupational welfare funds, such as for *beedi* (hand-rolled tobacco in Tendu leaves) workers (Rajan and Mathew, 2008). All of these programs have been introduced at different points of time with differing responsibilities of the Union government and individual states, and reflect lack of policy and organizational coherence (Asher, 2010). India does not have a unified national pension system, even when only urban or only rural populations are considered.

As a result of this lack of a unified system, data collection and reporting systems for pensions are undertaken by each organization, with varying degrees of transparency and professionalism. It is therefore difficult to put together nationwide indicators of the pension system – a gap that needs to be addressed. The data provided in Table 4.1 are approximate and not amenable to rigorous statistical or economic analysis even on an aggregative basis.

A summary of the main pension programs in India is provided in Table 4.1, on the basis of which the following observations may be made.

i   The two main groups covered by the mandatory pension programs are civil servants of the Union and the state governments and private sector employees in establishments with more than 20 employees and with a starting monthly wage below a stipulated amount.[7] For civil servants employed by the Union and state governments, the pension system has traditionally used the defined benefit (DB) method, with no requirement for any contribution by civil servants.

In principle, each state has the flexibility to formulate pension systems for its own civil servants. In practice, the states follow the Union government's design for their own civil servants, with some variations. The Union government reformed its pension system for those joining after January 2004. The method was changed from DB to defined contribution (DC), with mandatory annuitization of a portion of the accumulated balances, and robust pension architecture, including a pension regulator, was established (Shah, 2005). As of October 2014, only 2 of the 29 states (West Bengal and Tripura) have not adopted the Union government's basic 2004 design for their civil servants, though some are in the process of implementing it.

Table 4.1 Pension system in India: An overview

Program	Method	Responsible Ministry	Source of Funding	Membership (in million)	Criteria	Accumulated Balances in INR Bn (% of GDP)	Annual Expenditure in INR Bn. (% of GDP)
Mandatory Programs: Public Sector							
Union Civil Service Pension	Defined Benefit	Personnel, Public Grievance and Pension;	Consolidated Fund of India	3.5	Civil Servant Hired before January 2004	NA	428.39 (0.48)
State Civil Service	Non-contributory Scheme	Varies within State Governments'	Statutory Expenditure	18.5	Civil Servants Hired before a Cut-off Date (mostly 2004–2006)	NA	1463.45 (1.46)
National Pension Scheme (NPS)	DC Scheme; Mandatory Annuity Requirement for a Portion of Accumulated Balances	Finance; State Governments	Contribution by Employee and Government as Employer	Union Government: 1.4 / State Government: 2.5	Civil Service Employee Hired after January 2004	192.3 (0.19) / 133.3 (0.13)	NA / NA
Mandatory Programs: Private Sector							
Employees' Provident Fund Organization (EPFO)	EPF – DC / EPS – DC / 76741.5	Labour and Employment / NA	Employees & Employers from Formal Sector / Government Subsidies	4.69	Formal Sector Starting Wage/Salary below Rs. 15000 per month / (6.07) / (0.03)	4663.7	NA / NA

(Continued)

Table 4.1 (Continued)

Program	Method	Responsible Ministry	Source of Funding	Membership (in million)	Criteria	Accumulated Balances in INR Bn.(% of GDP)	Annual Expenditure in INR Bn. (% of GDP)
Voluntary Programs: Private Sector							
NPS – Corporate	DC	Finance	Employees & Employers	0.4	Private Sector as Per Scheme	17.67(0.02)	NA
Non-contributory and co-contributory schemes							
NSAP – Indira Gandhi Old Age Pension	Non Contributory Pension for Older Persons	Rural Development	Sharing of Finances by Union and State Government	16.5	Below Poverty Line and above 60 Years of Age	NA	106(0.08)
Swavalamban (under NPS) (Subsumed under Atal Pension Yojna)	Co-contributory DC Scheme	Finance	Contribution by Employee and Government	3.5	All Citizens	12.94	2.2

Source: Compiled by authors from various sources; PFRDA Annual Report 2013–14 and Monthly News Roundup Nov 2014; Budget Documents, Government of India

Notes: *8.5 million total contributors but only 4.69 active; ^ 1.16% of covered wages contributed by government for EPS

ii   Each of the pension programs or schemes, implemented by a different ministry or department, have dissimilar administrative structures and database maintenance responsibilities. There is very little cohesion or coordination between the schemes to provide a clear social security landscape for older persons. There are multiple schemes for the formal sector based on whether the employer operates in the private or public sector.

iii Actual membership numbers, as a result of limited publication of membership details, are difficult to get in each of these schemes, therefore making it challenging to provide the current membership of those contributing to and receiving pension benefits in the country. The absence of a unique identification makes it additionally challenging to estimate the number of beneficiaries. It is difficult to avoid double counting of beneficiaries within each scheme and also between schemes while trying to measure and project fiscal cost. For example, for civil service employee pensions there are currently at least two possibilities – those employees that were hired before 2004 are still on the old civil service pension program, and those hired after 2004 are on the National Pension Scheme (NPS) program with a defined contribution. The numbers for each of these needs to be estimated separately from separate databases. To complicate matters further, there is no uniformity in the state schemes for pensions for civil servants, even though they broadly follow the design of the Union government.

iv   For the Indian system, it is necessary to estimate the projections for each of the components separately using different assumptions. The fragmentation and absence of a complete pensions database make it difficult to project the age related expenditure as a whole.[8] In addition, the paucity of information in the public domain on funds utilization makes it additionally challenging to project the expenditure.

v   While the overall issue is aggregation of data, there are estimation issues. Within each scheme, dearth of analysis in the estimation of retirement income is exacerbated by a dearth of updated mortality tables. The few mortality tables available are constructed from non-representative insurance data. Low insurance coverage results in mortality tables cannot be considered representative of the population. In addition, there is no cohort-wise data available in order to make detailed projections of mortality rates (James and Sane, 2003).

vi   Undocumented income, expenditure, and savings behaviour data for the informal sector (a large section of the population) make it difficult to estimate their capacity to contribute and whether benefit levels are appropriate compared to the optimal income. Sometimes, even where data is clear, as in the case of salaried employees, calculation of payouts can be underestimated if they are not inflation indexed and based on the wrong wage-level criteria.

vii The estimation of administrative costs is especially complex. Disaggregated channels of delivery, even within a scheme like the National Pension Scheme, and the absence of consolidated data make it difficult to calculate administrative costs. These costs could be a key factor in increasing participation in India, where pension balances are expected to be among the smallest in the world.

An overview of India's pension system provided in Table 4.1 strongly suggests that an aggregative projection of India's age related pension expenditure based on a single macro-economic model is inappropriate. The projection will need to be made by each component, based on incomplete fragmented data, and uncertainty about the pace of population coverage and risks benefit levels will occur. The projections will also need to take in to account potential fiscal risks and contingent liabilities of individual components of India's pension system.

4. Age related pension expenditure analysis

4.1. Literature review of current projections

The age related expenditure projections by major multilateral organizations on the fiscal cost of pension and age related expenditure vary. These projections are part of studies that typically cover OECD countries as well as developing countries. In order to provide comparable results, the studies have a number of assumptions that inadequately reflect institutional and other aspects of India's pension system. These include India's fragmented social security system (rather than a national system found in most OECD countries), absence of relevant good quality data, and uncertainties surrounding pension and other policies impacting future pension costs.

Table 4.2 summarizes the available projections of India's social security expenditure by IMF and by Standard and Poor's (S&P). In view of the moderately rapid ageing projected for India and the probable expansion of non-contributing pension schemes, it is improbable that the public pension spending projected by the IMF will remain constant between 2010 and 2030 at only 1.0 percent of GDP, and decline thereafter to reach 0.7 percent of GDP in 2050. Similar trends are projected by the S&P (2010) study for public pension spending.

Table 4.2 India – Social security expenditure projections (percentage of GDP)

	2010	2020	2030	2040	2050
Public Pension (IMF 2011)	1	1	1	0.9	0.7
Pension Spending (S&P 2010a)	1.7	–	–	–	0.9
Total Age Related* (S& P 2010b)	2.6	3.2	3.4	3.2	2.7
Total Age Related* (S&P 2013)	2.2	2.7	3.3	3.9	4.4

Source: Compiled from Junichiro Takahata; total age related spending includes public pensions, health care, long-term care, and unemployment benefits.

In these projections both the IMF and S&P focus only on public spending. They also appear to focus only on public pension spending at the Union (or Central) government level. This is inappropriate for a country with a federal structure and in a country in which a significant proportion of pension expenditure is undertaken through non-public channels. This is one of the illustrations of how cross-country projections do not sufficiently take into account individual country contexts relevant for understanding the dynamics of age related pension expenditure, and for linking them with the fiscal institutions and practices.

The projection of total age related expenditure (including public pensions, healthcare, and unemployment benefits) by S&P 2010 and S&P 2013 studies exhibit anomalies. In the 2010 study, total age related expenditures are projected to increase from 2.6 percent of GDP to 3.4 percent in 2030, but thereafter decline significantly to 2.7 percent of GDP in 2010. The 2013 study, however, revises age related expenditure to exhibit steady increase from 2.2 percent of the GDP in 2010 to 4.4 percent in 2050. The different between the two projections is almost double for the 2050.

Within India, the Planning Commission (as of 2014, it has been replaced by the National Institution for Transforming India, NITI Aayog) and the Reserve Bank of India (RBI) have made projections on civil service pensions for the Union and state governments. In 2004, the former Planning Commission's Perspective Planning Division published a paper titled "Pension Liabilities of the Central Government: Projections and Implications". This paper attempted to project the payments to Central (Union) government employees up to 2009–10. According to these projections, the pension payment to Central (Union) government employees would be Rs. 367.06 billion (0.57 percent of GDP) in 2009–10 and Rs. 428.4 billion (0.56 percent of GDP) in 2010–11. The actual spending was one and a half times in nominal terms at Rs. 561.49 billion (0.87 percent of GDP) in 2009–10 and reduced to 1.3 times the projected in nominal terms at Rs. 574.05 billion (0.74 percent of GDP) in 2010–11.

There have been very few comprehensive projections of state-level civil service pensions expenditure. The "Report of the Group to Study the Pension Liabilities of the State Governments", published by the Reserve Bank of India, highlights that there is great variation at the state level for eligibility of pensioners or the payout for the pensioner. For example, some states cover employees of grant-in-aid organizations and urban local bodies, whereas others do not cover this cohort of employees.

In projecting the pension payout between 2002 and 2011, the RBI group requested the state governments to provide various details, including the age-wise and category-wise particulars of pensioners and employees. The information provided was deemed to be grossly inadequate to conduct an actuarial estimation of future pension liabilities. Therefore, the taskforce made projections based on the historical growth rate. They estimated that if the consolidated pension payments grow at the high levels of the 1980–81 to 1995–96 periods of 23.5 percent, the pension payout by 2011 would be approximately Rs. 1.89 trillion. The consolidated pension expenditure for the year 2011–12 was, however, much lower at Rs. 1.22 trillion (1.37 percent of GDP) (RBI, 2012).[9]

The Economic Survey of India 2001–02 reports that the pension liabilities would go up as a result of increased life expectancy, indexation of pensions to wage of employees, full neutralization of inflation linked to cost of living index; and many more reasons (Economic Survey of India, 2001–02). However, there has been little recent research in projecting pension liabilities of the Union and state governments, and of the country as a whole.

4.2. Analysis of age related pension expenditure by components

This section approaches the age related pension expenditure projections in India by focusing on the key components contributing to the pension expenditure. These components include civil service pensions for the Central (Union) government, state governments, and National Pension System (NPS), Employee's Provident Fund Organization (EPFO), and the old age pensions of the National Social Assistance Program (NSAP).

4.2.1. Civil service pensions: Union and state governments

The payment of civil service pensions, consistent with the international practice, is a statutory requirement that has to be met before any other expenditure. In 2014–15, the actual expenditure on civil service pensions for the Union government as well as the states combined was 2.14 percent of the GDP, with the states incurring about 70 percent of the total (Table 4.3).

Two types of civil service pension schemes exist in India – the older defined benefit scheme and the newer defined contribution scheme. Public sector employees that joined the government organization before April 1, 2004, are members of the traditional defined benefit civil service pension scheme. Those employees that joined the civil services after April 1, 2004, are on a defined contribution scheme, the National Pension Scheme (NPS).

Furthermore, the rules for civil service pensions may for the Union government employees and the various state government employees differ. Individual states employ a larger proportion of government employees accruing pensions. In order to project an estimate of pension expenditure, state expenditure needs to be examined as well. However, each of the states administers its pension programs differently, making it difficult to get aggregate data. For example, over the last decade some states have made the transition to NPS, with only two states continuing to use the traditional civil service pension.

Even when examining just the central government, there is an added complexity, as the central government employees include five types – civil, defence, postal, railways, and telecommunications.[10] The payouts for each of these departments differ in terms of amount, duration, and eligibility of the employee (Swain and Sen, 2004). Since the railways and telecommunications departments have been corporatized, they are required to establish their own dedicated pension funds to meet their respective liabilities (Sane and Shah, 2011).

However, in general one can expect that in the transition to the DC scheme, civil service pension liabilities could decline in the long run. The rate of decline

Table 4.3 Trends in aggregate civil service pensions expenditure, in percentage of GDP. (Figures in parentheses are percentage of total)

Year	Union	State	Total
2004–05	0.56	1.2	1.76
	(32)	(68)	(100)
2005–06	0.61	1.1	1.71
	(36)	(64)	(100)
2006–07	0.56	1.1	1.66
	(34)	(66)	(100)
2007–08	0.49	1.1	1.59
	(31)	(69)	(100)
2008–09	0.59	1.2	1.79
	(33)	(67)	(100)
2009–10	0.87	1.3	2.17
	(40)	(60)	(100)
2010–11	0.74	1.4	2.14
	(35)	(65)	(100)
2011–12	0.68	1.4	2.08
	(33)	(67)	(100)
2012–13	0.69	1.4	2.09
	(33)	(67)	(100)
2013–14	0.65	1.4	2.05
	(32)	(68)	(100)
2014–15	0.64	1.5	2.14
	(30)	(70)	(100)

Source: Government of India. Fourteenth Finance Commission Report, http://fincomindia. nic.in/ShowContentOne.aspx?id=9&Section=1. Accessed on 3 June 2015

may not be rapid, and under certain condition, expenditure to GDP ratio may increase because of the following reasons.

First, the Central Pay Commission (CPC) appointed every 10 years revises pensions as well as salaries of civil servants, affecting the pension expenditure of civil servants on the DB scheme. For example, the latest available pay commission, the sixth pay commission (released in March 2008) announced that the pensions were to be paid at 50 percent of the average emoluments/last pay without linking it to 33 years of qualifying service for grant of full pension. In addition, higher rates of pension for retirees and family pensioners on attaining 80, 85, 90, 95, and 100 years of age was announced. The Seventh CPC is expected to provide its recommendations in the second half of 2015.

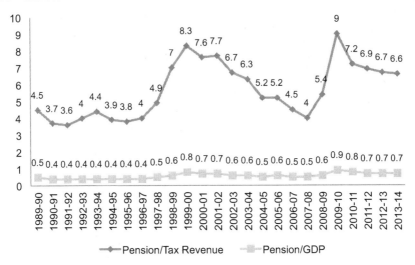

Figure 4.2 Pension expenditure as percent of GDP and tax revenue
Source: PFRDA 2013–14

Some estimates suggest that pension expenditure may increase by about 30 percent with the seventh CPC report (Economic Survey of India 2014–15). Along with the direct impact on the Union government, the recommendations of the CPC have in the past created major fiscal dislocations in the states, adversely impacting fiscal consolidation and fiscal flexibility. This has been particularly the case with the states under fiscal stress.

Linking of pensions with revisions in salaries of existing government employees is a very unusual and unhealthy practice, especially given frequent salary revisions and indexation for cost of living. Indexing to both cost of living and to wage increases is not found in the vast majority of middle- and high-income countries. Nevertheless, this policy is politically entrenched and will require strong leadership and consensus across political parties to modify. This will at best be a medium-term process in India; setting an overall ceiling on civil service pensions to GDP ratio is an option that is worth exploring by Central and state governments in India.

Second, the size of government increased rapidly in the 1970s and 80s and then contracted drastically in the 1990s post the IMF austerity measures – as a result, the NPS was launched in 2004 (Sane and Shah, 2011). As a result there would be spike in the pensions when these cohorts retire. Given that this group of pensioners will not increase any further, there is a possibility to project relatively accurately. With projections, it is possible to plan for these changes, especially since the benefit structure of these schemes were extremely liberal, providing gracious benefits not only to the civil servants but also to the families of the civil servants for years after retirement or death of the civil servant.

Third, the armed forces continue to be part of the traditional civil service pension with a DB scheme. With the low retirement age, the eligibility to claim pensions at 20 years of service, and higher benefit levels, the net present value of lifetime benefits is relatively large (Sane and Shah, 2011). In 2010–11 the total expenditure on military pensions accounted for approximately 0.3 percent of GDP (Sane and Shah, 2011). Currently there has been no discussion of absorbing the armed forces into the NPS, especially since it has such a unique demographic, and one of the features that attracts citizens to join any of the forces is the liberal benefit structure during service and post retirement. In principle, the proposal for One Rank One Pension (OROP) has been accepted by the Cabinet. Under this system, the armed forces personnel will receive the same pension if they hold the same rank, regardless of the years of service; last pay drawn of the years served in a particular rank. This is expected to have some fiscal impact on the pensions expenditure.

Fourth, two states continue to follow the traditional civil service pension defined benefit scheme – West Bengal and Tripura. The liabilities of these states will continue to accrue until they decide to switch to a defined contribution scheme.

PROJECTION OF CIVIL SERVICE PENSION EXPENDITURE

The pension expenditure projections for civil servants estimated by the fourteenth Finance Commission are presented in Table 4.4. It is unclear whether the model takes into consideration the possible impact of the Seventh Central Pay

Table 4.4 Summary of projections for civil service pension

	Expenditure Union and State Government (% of GDP)		
Year	*Union*	*State*	*Combined*
2015–16	0.61	1.4	2.01
	(30.35)	(69.65)	(100)
2016–17	0.59	1.5	2.09
	(28.23)	(71.77)	(100)
2017–18	0.57	1.5	2.07
	(27.54)	(72.46)	(100)
2018–19	0.55	1.5	2.05
	(26.83)	(73.17)	(100)
2019–20	0.53	1.5	2.03
	(26.11)	(73.89)	(100)

Source: Government of India. "Fourteenth Finance Commission Report", Table 7.2 and Annex 6.2, http://fincomindia.nic.in/ShowContentOne.aspx?id=9&Section=1 Accessed on 28 March 2015.

Commission (CPC), which is expected to submit its report in the last quarter of 2015. In the 2015–16 Union budget speech, the Finance Minister estimated that in addition to the increasing rate of growth in pension expenditure as a result of higher retirements and increased life expectancy, the impact of the seventh CPC is likely to be approximately 0.7 percent of GDP in 2016–17 and 2017–18 (Union Budget Speech 2015–16, Paragraph 42). This will then have a cascading effect on the state expenditure on pensions as the state governments start implementing the recommendations of the pay commission. As a result, these estimates are likely to be the lower bound of the projections.

4.2.2. National Pension Scheme

The National Pension Scheme is a defined contribution scheme undertaken in 2004 in response to the high pension liabilities for civil servants under the DB scheme. The scheme has been opened up to the private sector as well as the informal sector. Therefore, under the NPS there are currently a number of schemes: Civil Service Pensions is mandatory, whereas the NPS-corporate and the *Swavalambhan* Scheme (in 2015, Swavalambhan was incorporated into the Atal Pension Yojna) are voluntary schemes meant for the private and informal sectors (Government of India, 2014b). This is a significant achievement in the civil service pension landscape in India, to make the transition from a DB scheme to a DC scheme, which can be challenging in the developing country context. All state governments (except two) have implemented the scheme on a rolling basis since 2004, with the last state starting implementation in 2012.

MANDATORY SCHEME

Civil servants hired on and after April 1, 2004, for the central government have been mandatorily enrolled in this scheme. The total contribution rate under this scheme is 20 percent of monthly earnings split between the employee and the employer (the government). Members have some choice in the investment instrument; however, most civil servant employees continue to use the default option of investing. Under the default scheme employees contribute 85 percent in fixed income government instruments and 15 percent in equity and equity related instruments.

Respective state governments can select their scheme preference; however, all state governments as of now have selected the default scheme as prescribe by the government, as already mentioned. In the default scheme, the contribution is allocated to three provident fund managers, namely SBI Pension Funds Private Limited, UTI Retirement Solutions Limited, and LIC Pension Fund Limited, in a predefined proportion that is decided by the NPS Trust after looking at previous years returns generated by the respective fund manager.

As of November 2014, 1.4 million central government employees were enrolled in the NPS Scheme and 2.3 million state government employees were enrolled. Implementation has already been well established in 22 of states, with

5 states still in the initial stages of implementation. As the scheme gets implemented fully in the states, the number of members in the states will increase. The states have the option of choosing different investment packages as well; however, so far most states continue to use the default investment package. The accumulated balances under the central government civil service pensions were approximately 0.25 percent of GDP and 0.23 percent of GDP for the state government civil service pensions.

In principle, the government has met its pension obligations for those employees who are mandatorily under the NPS scheme by meeting its share of the monthly contribution. This imposes fiscal discipline in meeting pension obligations, as these cannot be deferred to a future date. Fiscal risks, however, could arise from a variety of sources, impacting age related pension expenditure.

Some sources of concern include the following: (i) annuity markets in India are not well developed. The mandatory requirement for annuity in the NPS scheme could thus potentially require some government support, directly or indirectly through public sector annuity providers bearing the costs; (ii) it is probable that taxes on withdrawals at retirement may be rescinded, as no such tax is levied on pension products of EPFO. This would imply foregone revenue, reducing tax revenue; (iii) moral liability of NPS fund managers is also ultimately on the government.

VOLUNTARY SCHEMES

In addition to the civil service pensions, the NPS has the unique opportunity to expand its coverage and provide pension coverage for a large proportion of India's workforce. Of India's 425 million–strong labour force, approximately 372 million (87.5 percent) could potentially enrol for the NPS. Currently, only approximately 4.4 million are covered (1.2 percent) through the NPS. Of these, most are public sector workers. The NPS was envisioned to cover the labour force that is not covered by the formal sector programs. To this end, the NPS has been expanded to the private sector as well as to the informal sector on May 1, 2009. One scheme to encourage workers from the private sector to join is NPS-lite that has been subsumed under Atal Pension Yojna as of 2015. The fees for the NPS-lite or Atal Pension Yojna accounts were much lower for those in the unorganized sector (Rs. 70 for opening an account vs. Rs. 350 for civil servants). It is too early to know the impact of this program and other strategies undertaken by the government to expand coverage.

By November 2014, the private sector voluntary NPS scheme had 403,000 members, and the NPS-lite scheme already had 3.5 million members. These numbers continue to be relatively small; however their membership is expected to increase with the introduction of the Atal Pension Yojna that has been launched as a part of the Prime Minister's Jan Dhan Yojna.

To further encourage the unorganized sector workers, the Union government introduced a scheme with co-contributions in 2010–11, called the Swavalambhan scheme, to help lower-income individuals voluntarily become members of the

NPS. Like NPS-lite, this has also been subsumed under Atal Pension Yojna since 2015. Swavalambhan's co-contributory arrangements have been in place for only a limited number of years, but they could become permanent with the Atal Pension Yojna. The participation under the Swavalambhan scheme had been extremely low (only 3.5 million members). However, if the number of enrolees in this scheme increases, then there could be some cost in the form of co-contributions. In the 2014–15 budget, Rs. 1.95 billion (0.002 percent of GDP) was earmarked for this scheme. The Union government urged state governments to undertake similar schemes as well.

If the informal sector starts enrolling in the Swavalambhan with the Rs. 1000 matching contribution, there is a possibility that the cost would rise significantly. If all informal sector workers take up the program, the annual cost just for NPS-lite would reach 0.3–0.4 percent of GDP (Palacios and Sane, 2012). However, more realistically, if approximately a quarter of the workers enrolled in the program, the cost would be about 0.07–0.1 percent of GDP (Palacios and Sane, 2012).

The cost of the mandatory component will increase in the next decade based on the number of people being hired in the civil services. Compared to the traditional civil service pension, NPS increases expenditure in the initial phases but reduces the pension liabilities in the long run. With NPS, the government has to pay out 10 percent of the civil servant's monthly pay into the NPS account. This will increase the cost in the initial stages. However, in the Indian context this increase is advantageous, even though these funds would have an opportunity cost. First, this improves fiscal discipline, as the payments have to be made every month to the individual accounts. Second, as pension contributions are made monthly by the government (as the employer), and as these can be withdrawn anytime before the employee leaves the government, there is greater security and confidence in the pension scheme. Finally, it makes the cost of hiring an additional civil servant more transparent, as the current cash accounting system does not include accrued liabilities.

There will be contingent liabilities and fiscal risks if the NPS is not well managed and does not provide adequate returns in the range of 10 percent for the three main fund managers. So far the returns have been encouraging (see Table 4.5), but if the returns become less than adequate, there could be political pressures on the fiscal system to assist in providing a reasonable replacement rate.

In October 2013, India passed the Provident Fund Regulatory and Development Authority (PFRDA) Bill, which made India one of the few countries with a dedicated pension regulator. The PFRDA is an autonomous body set up by the Government of India in 2003 to regulate and develop the pension market in India. The passage of this bill is a big achievement for the pensions market in India. As a result of the bill there have been some changes to the NPS. First, members will now be allowed to make partial withdrawals. However, there is a limit on the amount and number of withdrawals. Only 25 percent of the total contribution can be withdrawn for specific purposes. Second, the

Table 4.5 NPS rates of return

Name of Scheme	Compound Annual Growth Rate (since inception) in %	Rate of Doubling	Real Rate of Return	Real Rate of doubling
Public Sector				
Central Government (CG) (w.e.f. April 1, 2008)	9.1	7.9	1.5	48.0
State Government (SG) (w.e.f. June 25, 2009)	8.59	8.4	0.99	72.7
Private Sector				
E	9.2	7.8	1.6	45.0
C	10.53	6.8	2.93	24.6
G	7.93	9.1	0.33	218.2

Source and Notes: Source: Adapted from Government of India, Pension Fund Regulatory Development Authority. (2014). *Annual Report*, http://pfrda.org.in//MyAuth/Admin/showimg.cshtml?ID=459 Accessed on 3 October, 2014

Note: Doubling rate calculated using 72 rule.; E F and G (w.e.f. May 1, 2009); E – Index funds/ exchange traded funds that replicate the portfolio of either BSE Sensex index or NSE Nifty 50 index; C – Fixed deposits of scheduled commercial banks, credit rated debt security with residual maturity of not less than three years, credit rated public financial institution, rated asset backed securities, debt mutual funds regulated by SEBI; G – Government of India bonds and state government bonds; inflation rate average 2008–12 – 7.6 percent

fund managers are now allowed to provide minimum assured returns on contributions. The details of the implementation of these two arrangements are not clear; however, there are likely to be some implications on costs. The biggest challenge faced by the NPS has been to get more enrolees. However, with the passage of the PFRDA bill NPS is better placed to get more enrolees. Most recently, in the 2015 budget the government announced its plans to allow members to transition from the EPFO to the NPS schemes. This could have further cost implications.

4.2.3. Employee's Provident Fund Organization

EPFO, the formal sector pension scheme, is unusual in that there are two separate schemes operating under it: first, a defined contribution scheme (Employees' Provident Fund, or EPF) and second, a defined benefit scheme (Employees' Pension Scheme, or EPS). The parameters for both these schemes are different, therefore necessitating different calculations in trying to project the fiscal implications of these schemes. EPFO schemes are concentrated in upper income formal sector workers.

Some estimates suggest that the government subsidies for EPFO amount to approximately 0.04 percent of GDP (Palacios and Sane, 2012). The actuarial deficit for EPS, the DB scheme, is estimated to be approximately Rs. 540 billion (0.6 percent of GDP) in 2013. In January 2014, the government increased the minimum pension payments under EPS to Rs. 1000 per worker. This is expected to directly benefit at least 2.7 million pensioners. For this, the government will provide an additional subsidy of Rs. 12.17 billion in the next fiscal year 2014–15.

To get a complete picture of the EPFO landscape, it is important to look at the number of members and their balances in the schemes. The first challenge is that these essential numbers are not always available in the public domain. From the scanty published reports, in 2011 the EPF scheme covered 0.66 million establishments and had 61 million members. It was estimated in 2009–10 that 30 million accounts were not operational. In 2009, for example, of the 44 million members only 22 million were active contributors. As of March 31, 2012, the EPS scheme had 85.5 million members from 691,000 business establishments. However, monthly pension payout was being made to 4.1 million members. A total of 708.89 billion were received as contributions, of which Rs. 555.55 billion were received as contribution to the employees provident fund, Rs. 147.67 billion for the employees pension fund, and the rest for the linked insurance fund. A total of Rs. 269.14 billion was paid as benefits to members.

There is currently a limited contribution from the government to the EPFO. However, if not managed well there are contingent liabilities and fiscal risks

Table 4.6 India EPFO investments: 2008–09 to 2012–13 (in Rs. billion)

	Investments	Employees' Provident Fund	Employees' Pension Fund	Total*	% of GDP	Growth
2008–09	Yearly	290.1	144.76	443.64	0.79	
	Cumulative	2331.05	1085.78	1488.39	2.64	
2009–10	Yearly	354.59	152.12	516.88	0.80	16.51
	Cumulative	2685.65	1237.9	4005.27	6.20	14.82
2010–11	Yearly	464.16	182.6	658.43	0.86	27.39
	Cumulative	3149.81	1420.5	4663.7	6.08	16.44
2011–12	Yearly	586.62	197.29	797.11	0.88	21.06
	Cumulative	3736.44	1617.8	5460.82	6.08	17.09
2012–13	Yearly	630.18	216.25	860.77	0.85	7.99
	Cumulative	4366.6	1834.05	6321.59	6.30	15.76

Source: Employees' Provident Fund Organization (EPFO). Annual report, various years, http://search.epfoservices.org:81/OperationStatistics/operational_stats_en.php Accessed on 23 September 2014;

Note: Total includes employees' deposit linked insurance fund that will finally be on the government. It is under these circumstances that it is possible that the EPFO might need some fiscal space in the future.

4.2.4. National Social Assistance Program

The National Social Assistance Program is a centrally assisted program that provides the finance for social pensions programs that is implemented by the state government. The Indira Gandhi National Old Age Pension Scheme (IGNOAPS) is one component of the NSAP that provides a minimum pension payment of INR 3600 annual (4.72 percent of per capita income in 2012–13), at INR 300 every month to persons above the age of 60 that are considered to be below the poverty line. In addition, persons above the age of 80 years are entitled to INR 6000 per year (7.87 percent of per capita income in 2012–13), at INR 500 every month. The central government provides state governments with funding based on the estimates of persons above 60 years of age and considered to be below the poverty line. States are then free to top up the benefit with their own funding or provide the same benefit level but to increase coverage based on a lower poverty line estimate. Therefore, funding for this program is accrued both by the Central (Union) government as well as by state governments.

There might be some changes in the future that could result in increased expenditure on the program. First, there has been a call to universalize the old age pension scheme from the current means tested scheme. If this scheme is universalized, there could be a dramatic increase in the expenditure on social pensions given that a majority of India's population currently has no access to employment related social security. Second, the benefit level is currently very low as a percentage of the per capita income of the country. Third, there has been some pressure on the states to provide matching benefits as provided by the central government. This could be a burden to fiscally weak states. This could result in indirect fiscal costs through contingent liabilities if the requisite budgetary resources are not set aside for future liabilities.

In regards to the current social pension scheme, the coverage levels are relatively low, as are the benefit levels. If the benefit levels were to be increased and indexed to the per capita income of the country, this would result in some increases in spending on social pensions.

Asher and Bali (2014) undertake an analysis of the possible costs with an increased benefit level. The benefit level is tied to the per capita GNI, with Variant A having benefit at 15 percent of per capita GNI and Variant B with benefit at 20 percent of per capita GNI. Under this model it is assumed that the aim of the social pension is to mitigate relative poverty and that it is not based on the notion of absolute poverty. The GNI is assumed to grow at 11 percent per annum in nominal terms, allowing for real growth of 5–6 percent and inflation of 5–6 percent per annum. Finally, this model does not have any behavioural foundations, does not incorporate any administrative costs, does not impose any means test, and does not differentiate between individuals living in rural and urban areas.

Table 4.7 Projections of expenditure for national old age scheme component of NSAP (percentage of GDP)

Scenario		2010	2020	2030
A.	If all persons above 60 years covered at:			
A1.	10% of per capita GDP benefit level	0.77	0.99	1.23
A2.	15% of per capita GDP benefit level	1.16	1.48	1.84
B.	If 70 % of all persons above 60 years covered at:			
B1.	10% of per capita GDP benefit level	0.54	0.69	0.86
B2.	15% of per capita GDP benefit level	0.81	1.04	1.29

Note and Source: Calculations by authors. Calculated GDP assuming nominal growth rate of 12 percent p.a.; Population figures from UN 2013

In March 2013, the Task Force constituted by the Ministry of Rural Development provided a report that among other things recommended the universalization of the NSAP to all older persons above the age of 60. If this is done, the fiscal implications as provided by the task force would increase expenditure from the current of Rs. 45.99 billion with coverage of 16.5 million members to Rs. 278.61 billion in year five for 42.6 million members.

As indicated earlier, the NSAP is a shared program. The fiscal capacity of the Union government and of the individual states to deliver social pensions without type one and type two errors at an appropriate transaction cost should be important. Therefore, in delivering this social pension program the capacity at the sub-national level will be extremely important. For example, the NSAP scheme itself relies on state-specific lists for eligibility, but again because of a lack of accurate income-expense data on households this is still error prone and may increase the number of beneficiaries.

4.2.5. Pension expenditure for the military personnel

In 2013–14, the pension expenditure for the defence expenditure was INR 545 billion (equivalent to 0.47 percent of the 2013–14 GDP at market prices). Two broad factors are expected to increase this ratio, requiring additional fiscal space.

The first is the submission of the report of the Seventh CPC (see section 4.2.1) in the second half of 2015. In the past, such reports have made recommendations for military personnel as well as for civilian employees. This practice is expected to continue.

The second factor is the acceptance by the government of the long-standing demand of the armed forces for One-Rank-One-Pension (OROP) in May 2015. This would require payment of uniform pension to military personnel retiring with the same rank with the same length of service, irrespective of their date of retirement About 80 percent of the armed forces personnel retire between ages of 34 and 37.

As of end May 2015, the final details on the terms of OROP have not been made available, but the one-time fiscal costs if OROP is backdated and the recurring fiscal costs are likely to be substantial, particularly when combined with the Seventh CPC recommendations.

The future fiscal space needed to implement OROP will depend on several factors. The first concerns the design. The number of those eligible for armed forces pensions is relatively large: there are about 1.3 million armed forces personnel currently serving in the armed forces and 2.4 million ex-service persons (Business Standard, 2015). The potential pension beneficiaries to current personnel of OROP will be nearly two to one. Moreover, with about four fifths of the armed forces personnel retiring in their thirties, as noted, pension retirement age is very low. The length of time an armed forces pensioner will receive pensions is also quite long. With longevity expected to increase, this implies a long-term recurring burden.

Another design issue of relevance for fiscal space is the formula adopted for OROP. This will involve a decision concerning references date for determining the OROP pension payments. The more recent the date of retirement that is taken as a reference point, the higher the potential of fiscal costs are likely to be. Each rank in the armed forces has a salary range, so another detail impacting the fiscal costs concerns the particular point in the range aimed. The decision on the level of pension benefits provided to the survivors will also impact fiscal costs.

The second broad factor concerns the effectiveness in delivering promised pensions with low transaction costs. The strategic use of appropriate technology, combined with complementary instruments such as the use of Aadhar card[11] (unique identification) and bank accounts, as well as robust pension beneficiary profile, including reliable death registration arrangements, will be needed.

The third broad factor concerns the political economy of pensions: would OROP for armed forces personnel create an environment leading to demands for more generous pensions for other uniformed government security personnel and civilian employees? How these expectations can be managed will affect the fiscal cost of the employee. The additional fiscal costs would thus also depend on uncertain political economy factors.

This discussion suggests that the fiscal costs of the OROP are likely to be significant, but are difficult to quantify. Our assessment is that the OROP will require additional fiscal expenditure of between 0.8 and 1.2 percent of GDP. This is quite disproportionate to the relatively small number of labour forces involved in the security forces, mainly in the armed forces.

4.2.6. *Other fiscal costs*

In addition to the four pension programs mentioned above, there are a number of smaller pension programs with smaller coverage levels that will also accrue costs. For example, a state such as Rajasthan has co-contributory schemes that would have additional fiscal costs. In addition, some state-owned enterprises run their own pension programs. The contingent liabilities of these programs will be on the government.

4.3. Summary

The total expenditure on age-related social security would be an addition of all the fragmented schemes given above.

The above analysis of the various components of India's pension system suggests that by 2030 somewhere between 2 to 4 percent of GDP will account for pension expenditure alone. The higher estimate in the above range is more likely if military personnel are eventually provided with OROP. There are also contingent liabilities implicit in many co-contributory schemes, such as APY targeted at low-income groups. Their value has not been fully accounted for in the above estimates. Some of the pension schemes by the states, particularly those financed from the budget as social pensions, may also contain future contingent liabilities. If age related expenditure in healthcare were added, the fiscal space needed would be even higher.

India thus faces a major challenge in generating fiscal space. Before considering how this challenge can be met, a brief overview of India's fiscal system may be instructive.

5. Key characteristics of India's fiscal system

India's federal system necessitates an analysis of the Union and state governments' public finances. The combined government expenditure in 2013–14 was equivalent to 28.2 percent of GDP (Government of India, 2014c). The fiscal deficit, using the cash accounting system, has averaged 6.6 percent annually during the 2005–06 to 2013–14 period; while the corresponding primary deficit (which excludes debt-related expenditure), averaged at 2 percent of GDP. The corresponding tax-to-GDP ratio was, however, only 17.9 percent, implying that only 63.4 percent of total combined expenditure was financed out of tax revenue. The rest was from non-tax revenue, capital receipts, and borrowing. This suggests a need for tax revenue to increase at a faster rate than government expenditure until a more appropriate level is obtained.

India's public debt is largely internal, with only approximately 8 percent being external debt as of December 2014–15 (Government of India, 2015b). The weighted average maturity of India's stock of public debt in 2014–15 was 10.25 years, and the corresponding figure was 14.7 years for government debt issued in 2014–15 (Government of India, 2015b). A large proportion of the debt was owned by domestic public sector financial institutions, and much of the rest was owned as part of statutory requirements.

The IMF's 2015 Article IV consultation reports on India has indicated that India's fiscal consolidation has continued on a trajectory broadly consistent with the Union government's deficit reduction path (IMF, 2015). The report indicates that the primary deficit (overall deficit less public debt–related expenditure) has narrowed by 2 percentage points of the GDP since 2010–11. The report concluded that "India's public debt is projected to decline over the medium term and remains on a sustainable path". The reasons for the projected decline suggested by the report include India's relatively high nominal GDP growth rate, favourable majority structure and currency composition, and captive domestic investment base.[12] The report, however, notes that large negative growth shocks represents one of the major risks to the declining growth trajectory.

The Union government 2015–16 budget speech reported that the overall deficit target of 3.9 percent of GDP has been met (Government of India, 2015a). Reforms of some of the subsidies, such as the LPG subsidies and lower and subdued oil prices, have helped India's fiscal consolidation. However, this has been achieved through compression of capital expenditure and other priority areas. The quality of fiscal consolidation therefore needs to be improved, and revenue enhancement measures need to be pursued more vigorously.

The Union government has indicated its willingness to improve the quality of fiscal consolidation and to find ways to improve fiscal flexibility that would permit higher public investment and growth-enhancing public expenditure. The Union government has exhibited competence in generating additional resources through the use of balance sheet items as well. This has been illustrated by successful auctioning of coalmines, of spectrum for telecommunications, and of FM radio licenses between October 2014 and July 2015. These have reportedly generated fiscal revenue equivalent to 2.5 percent of the GDP, albeit to be realized over a period of time. As the Union and state governments become more competent in using auctions and other methods for more productive use of state assets, the revenue enhancement component of fiscal consolidation can be expected to improve.

Since the new government was formed in May 2014, its policy measures have improved India's growth prospects.[13] India, however, needs to continue to focus on policy initiatives, such as emphasis on greater physical and digital connectivity, application of technology to a wide variety of activities including agriculture, and the generation of skills relevant for productive livelihoods, which are broad based and sustain high growth, particularly as India's demographic advantage is likely to diminish significantly around 2035. Sustaining such growth trajectory and characteristics will be a major challenge, and there is little room for complacency.

5.1. Changing dynamics of union – state fiscal relations

The 'Co-operative Federalism' approach of the Prime Minister Narendra Modi–led government envisages much greater flows of resources and commensurate responsibilities to the states and to Urban and Local Bodies (ULBs), requiring substantially greater competence and professionalism in managing their public finances (Asher, 2015).

Two of the most important initiatives in this context are the following. First, acceptance of the recommendations of the 14th Finance Commission (FC) to increase the statutory share of divisible tax revenues of the Union government from 32 percent to 42 percent (Government of India, 2015c).

Second, larger statutory transfers to states are to be accompanied by significant reduction in ad-hoc Union government schemes, reportedly from about 70 such schemes to 20. The remaining schemes are also to be rationalized to give greater flexibility and control, and therefore accountability, to the states. The above alters the dynamics of Union-state fiscal relations from a scheme- and grant-based support to a devolution-based support.

The intention of the Fourteenth Finance Commission appears to be to delink the classification of government expenditure into planned and non-planned expenditure and to foster the cultivation of development outcomes orientation in the budgeting process.

The above two initiatives, along with the replacement of the previous unlamented Planning Commission with National Institution for Transforming India (NITI) Aayog on January 1, 2015, with a mandate to render expert advice to government organizations at all levels, without any role in financial transfers between the Union and the state governments, are expected to fundamentally alter India's fiscal system.

6. Avenues for generating fiscal space

As noted previously, moving India's fragmented pension system towards a more robust system, covering a significantly increased proportion of the population and improving benefits, implied by the recent measures, is likely to require between 2 and 4 percent of fiscal space by the year 2030.

The policy dilemma is that enhanced expenditure on the social sector would have significant opportunity costs, particularly in providing infrastructure and productivity improving expenditure. To minimize the adverse impact of such trade-offs, pension arrangements will also need to be directed towards resource savings through better design and reducing transaction costs, while minimizing leakages from the pension benefit delivery mechanisms.

Measures to effectively utilize avenues for generating fiscal space in India need to be multidimensional, and need to use a systemic rather than a ad-hoc approach. The three broad avenues under which measures could be undertaken by the Union and state governments may be characterized as enhancing rate of economic growth and broadening its base, improving revenue performance from conventional and non-conventional sources, and better managing expenditure to obtain greater value for money from budgetary outlays. As an illustration, improving procurement practices of governments in India (around 12 to 15 percent of India's total government expenditure-to-GDP ratio of 28.2 percent in 2013–14 was on procurement of goods and services), which generate savings of 5 percent, could generate fiscal space equivalent to 0.60 and 0.75 percent of GDP.[14]

Generating fiscal space in India involves not only flows of receipts and expenditure, but also the balance sheet items. Thus, preparing asset registry of the government organizations and accounting reforms enabling better understanding of accrued and contingent liabilities are essential prerequisites for generating fiscal space. The above suggests that generating fiscal space in India in a systemic and integrated manner will be a complex exercise, requiring greater competence and professionalism and focusing on citizen centric outcomes.

As noted before, the Union government has exhibited competence in generating fiscal resources from government assets and creation of property rights. The state governments will also need to increasingly exhibit similar competence and willingness to generate resources from their assets and property rights. The Mines and Minerals (Development and Regulation) Amendment Bill, 2015, does enable the states to potentially generate higher fiscal resources from mining activities and to retain the revenue for the state's fiscal activities.

The Constitutional Amendment Bill (122nd Amendment) for the nationwide Union and state government goods and services tax (GST) has been tabled in parliament. The official implementation date for GST is April 2016. This, however, may be somewhat optimistic. Even then, the probability of the adoption of GST by the country is quite high. The GST has the potential to generate 0.5 percent additional revenue to GDP.

The Union government also aims to expand the income tax base in the country. Thus the government has asked the income tax department to increase the number of individual taxpayers by around 10 million within the next 12 to 16 months. According to official estimates, the current number of individual taxpayers is approximately 35 million. Similar efforts are needed for expanding the tax base of other taxes, such as the companies' tax. The states also need to exhibit similar willingness to expand the tax base of the taxes and charges levied by them.

In addition to this, there are other measures that could indirectly generate fiscal space by improving the design, administration, and effectiveness of delivery of pension and other public services. These include:

i   Greater professionalism among provident and pension fund organizations in performing core functions. This will include more extensively using transaction costs–reducing technologies, developing more appropriate skill sets among the staff, and implementing more modern investment policies.

ii Actuarial aspects that permit better matching of long-term assets and liabilities will also need to be addressed.

iii Better organizational and policy coherence: given the number of organizations already involved in age related pension expenditure, it is pivotal that these organizations work in a cooperative manner as well as work with policies that are coherent and sound.

iv Reducing expenditure needs in old age while creating policy environment conducive to prolonging economic activity in old age.

v   Indexing benefits in payment to prices rather than civil-service earnings (Palacios and Whitehouse, 2006).

To meet the anticipated future fiscal costs of the pensions for military personnel, including the costs arising from the OROP, an important option would be to use the assets of the defence forces more productively. This task can be approached through several initiatives. The first is to create a registry of physical assets, particularly land holdings and public amenities. This would assist the government in prioritizing non-essential physical assets to be monetized. A component of the resulting funds could be put into a separate fund, income from which could help contribute towards meeting future pension liabilities of the armed forces.

The second initiative meriting consideration is to explore ways to monetize intangible assets, such as airspace and other rights of the defence facilities. The cantonment areas managed by the defence organizations may provide several such opportunities. Again a portion of the funds could be used to meet pension liabilities. The tangible and intangible assets of the public sector defence organizations, such as ordnance and other factories, could also provide opportunities for revenue generation. These non-conventional revenue sources and the creation of sinking funds to meet in an orderly manner future pension liabilities would also increase the credibility of pension promises. Similar arrangements could be considered for other large government organizations, such as the Indian Railways and India Post.

7. Concluding remarks

India's demographic trends, with a faster than expected decline in fertility rate, suggest that it has only about two decades to construct a modern pension system. Population ageing and the concomitant issue of how to generate fiscal space to fund age related expenditure while sustaining broad-based high growth and fairness in pension arrangements have therefore become pressing.

The analysis in this chapter suggests that it would be prudent for Indian policymakers to generate an additional 2 to 4 percent of fiscal space by the year 2030 to progress towards pension arrangements suitable for a middle-income country. Generation of the additional fiscal space in India will be a complex exercise, involving a systemic and integrated approach. This will involve measures to enhance the economic growth rate and to widen its reach among regions and sectors: reforms of conventional taxes, rationalization of fees and charges for public amenities and services, resource generation from non-conventional sources such as auctioning of state assets, and better government expenditure management.

In addition, enhancing the professionalism with which India's social security organizations are governed and managed will also be essential. This will involve organizational restructuring and great reliance on technology-enabled processes. The responsibilities and accountability for generating fiscal space will need to be shared by the Union government and States and Urban and Local Bodies (ULBs) in the spirit of 'Co-operative Federalism'. Those governmental organizations that are not adapting to changing dynamics of Union-state fiscal relations are less likely to be able to fulfil the responsibilities entrusted to them, which could bear adverse electoral and other consequences.

Generating additional fiscal space in India will be aided by construction and policy-relevant usage of relevant age-related databases. This could also improve the quality of public policy debates on pension arrangements and enable the achievement of more sustained focus over a longer term on pension policy issues.

Notes

1 India's 2001 census data suggest internal migration of about 300 million, nearly 30 percent of the total population (Census of India 2001).
2 Old-age support ratio is the number of persons aged 15–64 per person aged 65 and over.
3 Total fertility rate is the average number of children a hypothetical cohort of women would have at the end of their reproductive period if they were subject during their whole lives to the fertility rate of a given period and if they were not subject to mortality. It is expressed in children per woman.
4 This wide difference in the TFR between the United Nations projections and the national data suggests using trends in TFR and resulting population figures in a nuanced manner. Using range of population, estimates depending on future TFR trends could assist in better planning of ageing policies.
5 Net of persons retiring or losing jobs, or withdrawing from self-employment.
6 For a detailed discussion of the evolution of India's pension system and its challenges, see H. Sadhak (2013); Asher and Bali (2009); Dave (2000).
7 In October 2014, this amount was INR 15,000 per month.
8 There is strong case for modernizing the communication practices of India's social security organization, including publishing analytically relevant and informative reports, both in print and on the websites of the respective organization.
9 This number also includes some Miscellaneous General Services expenditure, which would be a small percentage of the total amount.
10 Employees of the armed forces in India are all on a defined benefit program.
11 Aadhar card is a unique biometric identification provided to residents by the Government of India.
12 For a detailed analysis of India's debt sustainability, see Asher (2012).
13 Thus the World Bank (2015) projects India's real GDP growth for 2015, 2016, and 2017 at 7.5 percent, 7.9 percent, and 8 percent respectively. The projections by the IMF are similar, but OECD projects 2015 and 2016 real GDP growth rates at 6.9 percent and 7.6 percent respectively.
14 India is considering introducing a procurement bill. For an analysis of how this bill could be improved, see Asher *et al.* (2015).

References

Asher, Mukul. (2010). Pension plans, provident fund schemes and retirement policies: India's social security reform imperative. *ASCI Journal of Management* **39**(1): 1–18.

Asher, Mukul. (2012). Public debt sustainability and fiscal management in India. In ADB (Ed.), *Public debt sustainability in development Asia*, https://openaccess.adb.org/bitstream/handle/11540/1356/public-debt-sustainability.pdf?sequence=1

Asher, Mukul. (2015). The road to cooperative federalism. *Swarajya Link*, http://swarajyamag.com/economy/the-road-to-co-operative-federalism/ Accessed on April 7.

Asher, Mukul & Bali, Azad Singh. (2010). India's social security system: An overview. In Mukul Asher, Sothea Oum, & Friska Parulian (Eds.), *Social protection in East Asia – Current state and challenges*. ERIA Research Project Report 2009, No. 9, http://www.eria.org/publications/research_project_reports/images/pdf/y2009/no9/SP_Compiling_corrected_2010–09–15_FINAL.pdf Accessed on February 2014.

Asher, Mukul & Bali, Azad Singh. (2014). An assessment of India's recent pension reforms. In Thom Reilly (Ed.), *Pensions: Policies, new reforms and current challenges*. New York, NY: Nova Science Publishers.

Asher, Mukul G., Sharma, Tarun, & Sheikh, Shahana. (2015). Public procurement legislation essential for improving public financial management in India, 17 April 2015. Takshashila Institution, Policy Brief, 2015–01, Lee Kuan Yew School of Public Policy Research Paper No. 15–20

Business Standard. (June 2015). A fiscal nightmare, **XXII(35)**, 5 June 2015.

CRISIL Research. (August 2011). *Employment in India: Uneven and weak*, http://www.crisil.com/pdf/corporate/EmploymentInsight_CRISILResearch_Aug2011.pdf Accessed on 6 October 2014.

Dave, S. A. (2000). Project OASIS report. *Committee report*, Ministry of Social Justice, Government of India.

Employees Provident Fund Organization. (EPFO). *Annual report various years*, http://www.epfindia.com/annual_reports.html Accessed on February 2014.

Government of India. (October 2011). Ministry of statistics and programme implementation, *Selected socio-economic statistics: India, 2011*.

Government of India. (2013–2014). Seizing the demographic dividend. *Economic survey of India*. http://indiabudget.nic.in/es2012-13/echap-02.pdf

Government of India. (2014a). Office of registrar general and census commissioner 2014. *Sample Registration System Statistical Report 2013*, New Delhi, Report No. 1 http://www.censusindia.gov.in/vital_statistics/SRS_Reports_2013.html

Government of India. (2014b). Pension fund regulatory development authority 2014. *Annual Report*, http://pfrda.org.in//MyAuth/Admin/showimg.cshtml?ID=459 Accessed on 03 October 2014.

Government of India. (2014c). Indian public finance statistics 2013–14. *Ministry of Finance 2014*, http://finmin.nic.in/reports/IPFStat201314.pdf Accessed on 02 August 2015

Government of India. (2015a). *Budget at a glance 2015–16*, http://indiabudget.nic.in/ub2015–16/bs/bs.pdf

Government of India. (2015b). *Public debt management – Quarterly report*, January–March 2015. May 2015, http://www.finmin.nic.in/reports/PDM4th201415.pdf Accessed on 02 August 2015.

Government of India. (2015c). *Report of the fourteenth finance commission*, 24 February 2015, http://fincomindia.nic.in/ShowContentOne.aspx?id=9&Section=1 Accessed on 02 August 2015.

International Monetary Fund. (2011). *The challenge of public pension reform in advanced and emerging economies*. http://www.imf.org/external/np/pp/eng/2011/122811.pdf Accessed on 15 October 2015.

International Monetary Fund. (2015). *India: Staff report for the 2015 Article IV consultation*. 26 January 2015, https://www.imf.org/external/pubs/ft/scr/2015/cr1561.pdf Accessed on 02 August 2015

James, E. & Sane, R. (2003). The annuity market in India: Do consumers get their money's worth? What are the key public policy issues? Rethinking pension provision in India. *Economic and Political Weekly* **38(8)**: 729–734, 736–740.

Mahapatro, S. R. (2012). *The changing pattern of internal migration in India*. Paper presented at the European Population Conference, 2012, http://epc2012.princeton.edu/papers/121017 Accessed on 05 October 2014.

OECD. (2015). Economic outlook annex tables. *Annex Table 1. Real GDP*. June 2015, http://www.oecd.org/eco/outlook/economicoutlookannextables.htm Accessed on 02 August 2015.

Palacios, R. & Sane, R. (2012). Learning from the early experience of India's matching defined contribution scheme. Matching Contributions for Pensions: A Review of International Experience, 243–260, World Bank Group, Washington DC, USA.

Palacios, Robert & Whitehouse, Edward. (2006). *Civil servants pension schemes around the World. Pension reform primer*. Washington, DC: World Bank.

Reserve Bank of India. (2012). *Handbook of statistics on Indian economy, Table 112: Expenditure patter of the state governments*, http://www.rbi.org.in/scripts/PublicationsView.aspx?id=14468

Rajan, S. I. & Mathew, E. T. (2008). India. In S. I. Rajan (Ed.), *Social security for the elderly*. New Delhi, India: Routledge.

Sadhak, H. (2013). *Pension reform in India: The unfinished agenda*. New Delhi, India: Sage Publications.

Sane, R. & Shah, A. (2011). Civil service and military pensions in India. In N. Takayama (Ed.), *Reforming pensions for civil and military servants*. Tokyo, Japan: Marusen Publishing.

Sankhe, S., Vittal I., Dobbs R., Mohan A. & Gulati A. (2010). *India's urban awakening: Building inclusive cities, sustaining economic growth*. McKinsey Global Institute.

Shah, A. (2005), A sustainable and scalable approach in Indian pension reform, Working Papers id:237, eSocialSciences. http://www.esocialsciences.org/Download/repecDownload.aspx?fname=Document18112005170.2944605.pdf&fcategory=Articles&AId=237&fref=repec Accessed on 21 November 2015.

Standard and Poor's (2010a). *Global aging 2010: An irreversible truth*, http://www2.standardandpoors.com/spf/pdf/media/global_aging_100710.pdf

Standard and Poor's (2010b). *Global aging 2010: An irreversible truth: Methodological and data supplement*, http://www.standardandpoors.com/en_EU/web/guest/article/-/view/sourceId/6245230

Standard and Poor's (2013). *Global aging 2013: Rising to the challenge*, https://www.nact.org/resources/2013_NACT_Global_Aging.pdf

Swain, Sibani & Pronab, Sen. (2004). Pension liabilities of the central government: Projections and implications, perspective planning department, planning commission, Government of India. Working Paper Series Paper No. 1/2004-PC.

United Nations, Department of Economic & Social Affairs, Population Division. (2013). *World population prospects: The 2012 revision*, DVD Edition, http://esa.un.org/wpp/ Accessed on February 2014.

World Bank. (2015). Global economic prospects. *Table 1.1. Global Outlook Summary*, http://www.worldbank.org/content/dam/Worldbank/GEP/GEP2015b/Global-Economic-Prospects-June-2015-Table1.pdf Accessed on 02 August 2015.

World Health Organization. (2013). *Life expectancy data by WHO region*, http://apps.who.int/gho/data/node.main.688 Accessed on 04 October 2014.

Yoosef, K. P. & Data, Aveeka. (2014). Strain's showing: India Inc hiring slowest in 3 years, up by Mere 2% in FY14. *Financial Express*, 04 October 2014, http://www.financialexpress.com/news/strains-showing-india-inc-hiring-slowest-in-3-years-up-by-mere-2-in-fy14/1295377 Accessed on 05 October 2014.

5 Pension system and its fiscal implications in Indonesia

Hefrizal Handra and Astrid Dita

1. Introduction

1.1. Background

Indonesia is currently reforming its social security system to implement Law 40/2004, the Law of *Sistem Jaminan Sosial Nasional* (SJSN). The future system under the SJSN framework will cover five areas: healthcare, work accident, old-age savings, pension, and death. The pre-SJSN scheme has proven inadequate in providing social security benefits to the population because of a low coverage ratio, limited benefits, and low investment returns, together with issues of poor governance and management (Arifianto, 2004).

The overarching institution undertaking the reform is the National Agency for Social Security, or *Badan Pengelola Jaminan Sosial* (BPJS), with subordinate agencies bearing the responsibility for specific areas of coverage as mandated by the new legislation (Law 24/2011 on National Agency for Social Security). The new and reformed healthcare insurance system comes under the purview of BPJS Health (dubbed BPJS I),[1] while labour security, old-age savings pension system, and death benefit falls under the scope of BPJS Labour (dubbed BPJS II).[2] Although BPJS Labour will start its operation in early 2015, full implementation of the new system – where institutional transformation will have been completed – will not take place until 2029. By that time, Indonesia's population demography will have begun ageing.

From a macro perspective, Indonesia's governance system and political economy have been evolving since the decentralization initiative began in 2001. Local Governments now hold more power and responsibilities relative to before. Agencies within the Central Government, which used to receive instructions and directives from a considerably central deliberative and decision body, are now liberated, with considerable freedom to operate on their individual agendas. Unsurprisingly, this decentralization has also led to conflicts, due in no small part to what is termed as 'sectoral ego' between agencies, where each attempts to exert and extend its influence over the passing of laws, regulations, and budgetary/resource allocation. Such conflicts however, will clearly have a significant impact on the ability of the government to undertake any reforms and financing of the pension system.

Abstracting from the inter-agency political economy concerns, the key concerns which affect the government's long-term ability to fund the pension system are the dynamics of the population demography and the governance policies. With the government committed to reforming and maintaining the state pension system (as legislated by the SJSN), an estimation of the possible future burdens this may incur will benefit the Indonesian government in anticipating future unfunded state liabilities.

1.2. Challenges

The SJSN reform for Indonesia's social security system faces several challenges:

- *Fragmented Stakeholders.* SJSN Law was supposed to have been in effect since 2009, but the numerous stakeholders took an additional three years just to agree on the form of the operator for the SJSN. Current social security operators will be grouped into two *Badan Penyelenggaraan Jaminan Sosial* (BPJS),[3] governing healthcare (BPJS I) and labour (BPJS II). Agreements were hard to reach, especially for the BPJS II, where extra effort from the governing authority of the social security reform – *Dewan Jaminan Sosial Nasional* (DJSN) – was needed to persuade non-governmental stakeholders, particularly the labour unions, to agree to the new operating structure and institution.
- *Transparency.* The reform demanded better transparency than today's management of the social security funds – particularly in the public sector.
- *Myopic Vision.* Despite the global trends to the contrary, SJSN has purportedly chosen the path of opting for the defined-benefit regime. This may indicate that the policymakers are more concerned about the political economy of the social security promises rather than the sustainability of benefit deliverance.
- *Low Awareness.* Low awareness on the importance of labour social security is reflected in the low compliance rate in the mandatory Jamsostek scheme. In case of the pension programs, only a fraction of national labour force is covered; more than half of the force has neither the certainty for retirement allowance nor pension.
- *Heterogeneity Disparity.* As mentioned in Guerard *et al.* (2012), there is disparity present on the social security coverage among different sectors, with the informal sector being the worst.
- *Limited Fiscal Space.* Even without the burden of the new national social security system, the government has to deal with various annual budget constraints; total deficits of central and subnational annual budgets must not exceed 3 percent of GDP, while there are several earmarks for spending as required by sectoral laws (e.g. education spending should be 20 percent of the total budget, health spending must be 5 percent of total budget), and the energy subsidy is ever growing (usually at 20 percent).

1.3. Main research questions

Given the issues and challenges to reform mentioned, any analysis is suggestive at best. Thus, this chapter takes an exploratory study of the fiscal implications, in particular to that of demographic changes, which Indonesia may face in adopting any one of a number of potential pension schemes. Some of the related policy considerations, with suggestions for a strategy to meet the government's fiscal needs, will also be discussed.

This study will not try to address and propose potential solutions to all challenges mentioned. Instead, the focus here will only on those pertaining to the policy options for the government – particularly in improving the fiscal space. Specifically, the study in this chapter aims to provide some insights/answers to the following questions:

1   What is the estimated future age-related expenditure of Indonesia?
2   How much fiscal space/resource will be required to address the expenditure need?
3   What are the policy initiatives/options for financing, to provide the needed fiscal space?

The rest of the chapter is organized as follows. The next section will give an overview of the demographic and labour trends of Indonesia from the literature. Section 3 covers the key characteristics of the current pension system in Indonesia and also the future pension system under the SJSN Law. Section 4 examines the key characteristics of the fiscal policy in Indonesia. Section 5 covers the projection of the population (and demography) and the age-related pension expenditure under different scenarios. The projection methodology, assumptions and analysis is also covered in this section. Section 6 will discuss the policy options available to improve and find the necessary fiscal space for financing pensions in Indonesia. Finally, the last section concludes the chapter, along with some recommendations for future works.

2. Demographics and ageing trends

2.1. Labour market trend

In 2010, population of the Indonesian archipelago stood at around 237.6 million, with a particularly unequal spread of inhabitation. Approximately 78.8 percent of the population resides on the main islands of Java and Sumatra, generating 81.2 percent of total output in the Indonesian economy.[4] Higher per capita incomes and a better quantity and quality of physical and social infrastructure relative to the rest of the archipelago are reasons accounting for the significant population concentration in Java and Sumatra. This has also had the effect of promoting even more migration to the main islands. In 2000, population density in Java and Sumatra was at 270 people per square km, as compared to just 32 people per square km in the other islands.

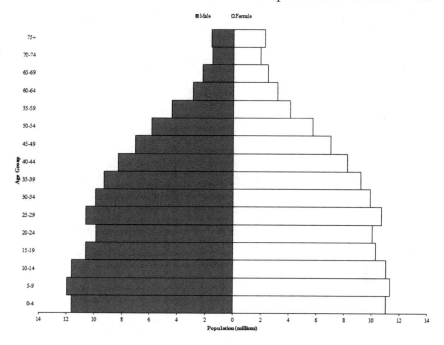

Figure 5.1 Indonesia population pyramid 2010

Source: Indonesia Census Bureau (2010). 2010 Population Census. Jakarta: BPS

Indonesia's 2010 population pyramid (see Figure 5.1) illustrates that the country has a large youth population. The population of under-15-year-olds accounts for 28.9 percent of the total population, and above-65-year-olds is 5 percent of the population. The age group of 15–65 years is the majority, as it forms 66.1 percent of the population. Currently, Indonesia's old-age dependency ratio stands at 8 percent, the young-age dependency ratio at 43 percent, and the overall dependency ratio is 51.3 percent. The overall gender ratio of males to females is approximately equal at 101 males to every 100 females. In the higher demographic age group of over-65-year-olds however, this ratio decreases significantly to 81 males for every 100 females.

Post-2010 Indonesia is projected to enjoy and reap a demographic dividend for the period of 2020–2030. A demographic dividend results when the OADR is at its lowest, thereby supplying the country with its highest numbers of abundant productive-age labour. Combined with lower OADRs, will result in a rapid growth of per capita income (Adioetomo, 2005). The latest official projection based on 2005 inter-census population data (Bappenas, 2005) estimates that Indonesia's population will reach 273.65 millions in 2025, with an 8.5 percent senile population of over 65. Life expectancy is projected to be 73.7 years on average, the total fertility rate is projected at 2.07, and the infant mortality rate at 15 per 1000 in the population. Generally, most provinces will reap the benefits of the demographic dividend from 2020, albeit different starting points and few outliers. For instance, in 2020 Prov. Jakarta will start entering the demographic dividend phase, while Prov. Yogyakarta will have already started to age.

For longer-term demographic trends, different studies suggest a wide variation in the possible total future population of Indonesia. ADB's (2012) projection suggests that Indonesia's population will reach 296.9 million in 2050, with 24.8 percent in the senior age group. World Bank (2010) estimated that total population will reach 289.5 million in 2050, with the estimated inflection point of ageing projected to be in 2030 (see Figure 5.2), the prior years being the demographic dividend window. UN (2012) suggested four different fertility scenarios, where total population will be somewhere between 277.1 million (for a low-fertility scenario) to 369.9 million (for a high-fertility scenario). The common consensus among these studies, however, is that Indonesia would have already started to age by 2050.

The structure of Indonesia's projected population structure for 2050, as projected by the World Bank, is presented in Figure 5.3. The figure clearly reflects an ageing society, a stark contrast to the present condition. In 2050, the population younger than 15 years of age will decline to 16.5 percent of the total population. At the same time, the population older than 65 years of age will gain more dominance in the society, forming 18.7 percent of the total population. The overall sex ratio of male to female will also fall to 98 males for every 100 females.

As Indonesia's economy is projected to continually develop, increasing longevity risk and decreasing fertility rate are expected as side effects. The changes in these trends must be followed closely, suggesting that the usefulness of long-term projections is no more than for pointing the directions, and periodical reviews are needed to adjust the projections.

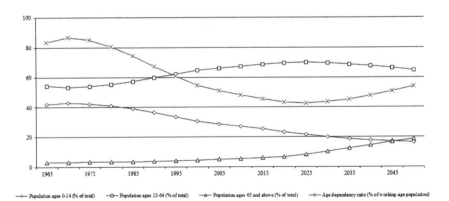

Figure 5.2 Indonesia's demographic trend 1965–2050

Source: World Bank (2010)

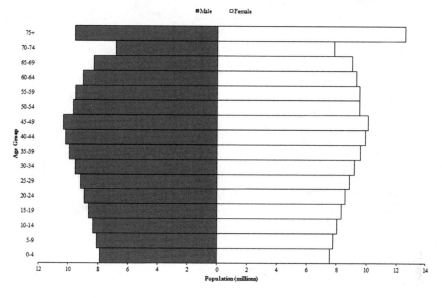

Figure 5.3 Indonesia's population pyramid 2050
Source: World Bank (2010)

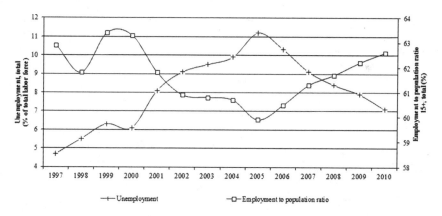

Figure 5.4 Indonesia's employment trend, 1997–2010
Source: World Bank (2012)

2.2. Labour market trend

Indonesia has experienced a steady decline of unemployment that once peaked in 2005 with the rally of positive economic growths after the Asian financial crisis. In 2010, 63 percent of the adult population was employed (see Figure 5.4. below). This is not without caveat; Indonesia's employment is mainly informal.

In the formal sector, labour unions have been gaining more influence, resulting in more rigid labour regulations and hikes in the minimum wage.[5] However, the hikes in wages have not been followed by an increase in productivity. Indonesia's labour productivity is below the neighbouring countries of Malaysia, Thailand, and the Philippines (CSIS, 2014).

The prevalence of informal employment in Indonesia is reflected in the numbers. Based on the official labour force survey conducted by the Indonesia Census Bureau (2012), of those employed, approximately two-thirds or 66.6 millions work in the informal sector, mainly in the non-agriculture field (61.26 million workers). The formal private sector follows with 39.7 million active workers, while there are only 4.5 million active civil servants (sum of Central and Local Government employees) in the public sector. Although the informal sector has always been historically larger than the formal sector in Indonesia, Matsumoto and Verick (2011) have predicted the trend that the economy will continue to be more casual in employment. If the indication is coupled with rigid labour laws, a decline in Indonesia's informal sector, particularly in the number of informal sector workers, is less likely.

As with other Southeast Asian countries, Indonesia's labour market is also biased toward men (Figure 5.5). Whereas more than 80 percent of adult males participate in the labour force, the rate slumps to around 50 percent for adult females. Nevertheless, the role of females in the labour force has been improving, and this is likely to be the trend, especially taking into account the rapid urbanizations occurring in the secondary cities in Java and Sumatra (ILO, 2012).

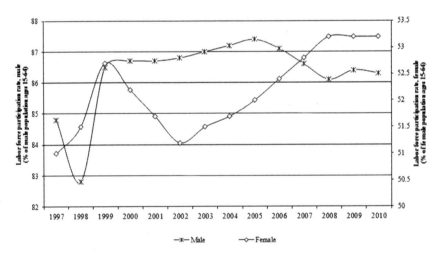

Figure 5.5 Male vs. female labour force participation rate, 1997–2010

Source: World Bank (2012)

2.3. Key characteristics of Indonesia's pension (old-age security) system

The nature of Indonesia's old-age public sector security programs differs from the private sector's, but these programs can generally be classified into mandatory and voluntary ones (Figure 5.6).

Before SJSN, the mandatory old-age security program for the public sector covers the civil servants (currently managed by PT. Taspen) and armed forces (currently managed by PT. Asabri). It is delivered through a pay-as-you-go (PAYG) scheme with a defined benefit (DB). The private sector – both State-Owned Enterprises (SOEs) and non-SOEs – is obliged to participate in the mandatory retirement scheme of PT. Jamsostek.

Additionally, formal private sector workers may use other voluntary programs as top-ups for their mandatory old-age security programs. The voluntary (private) pension funds can be managed by the employer through *Dana Pensiun Pemberi Kerja* (DPPK), or handled by other financial institutions through the *Dana Pensiun Lembaga Keuangan* (DPLK). The pension programs under the DPPK scheme can be either DB or defined contribution (DC); the ones in DPLK are DC, as the payouts are subject to returns on investments funded by the contributions.

While the formal workers in public and private sectors are guaranteed by law to be at least covered in a mandatory old-age security program – with contributions coming from both the workers and their employers – this is not the case for the informal sector. Their only option for obtaining some type of pension is to participate in the private voluntary system. Table 5.1 reports the typical contribution rates for each sector for the types of benefit schemes currently available.

Despite its considerably smaller number of workers, the mandatory old-age security coverage in the public sector far exceeds the (formal) private sector (Table 5.2). This is primarily because of the low compliance rate in the (formal)

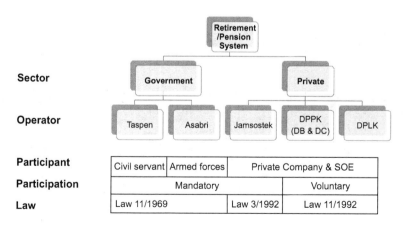

Figure 5.6 Structure of old-age security system in Indonesia, pre-SJSN

Table 5.1 Contributions of public and private sectors employer and worker, pre-SJSN[1]

Contribution*)	Public Sector		Private Sector**)		Informal***)
	Gov't****)	Civil Servant	Employer	Worker	Worker
Endowment fund	–	3.25	3.7	2.00	2.00
Pension fund	–	4.75			
Employment accident			Varies	–	1.00
Death benefit			0.30	–	0.30
Health insurance	–	2.00	3.00	–	3.00
			6.00		6.00
Housing	–	1.00			

[1] 2012 data
*) As a percentage to the base salary
**) Mandatory Jamsostek's scheme for contracted workers
***) Voluntary Jamsostek's scheme for non-contract (self-employed/informal) workers
****) The government is supposed to pay some contribution, but never do so because they opt for the PAYGO payment.

Table 5.2 Sectoral comparison, pre-SJSN[1]

	Public Sector	Formal Private Sector
Mandatory Pension/ Retirement Coverage	4,700,000	18,000,000 (non-active) 11,200,000 (active)
Participants	Central and Local Government employees	Employees of private companies (SOE & non-SOE)
Funding	Pay-as-you-go	Fully funded
Type	Defined benefit	Defined contribution
Replacement Rate	75%	Vary
Normal Retirement Age	56 (male & female) 50 (military)	55–60 (male & female)

[1] 2012 data

private sector. Less than half of formal workers are active participants in the mandatory Jamsostek scheme, while the rest are non-contributing registrants.

2.4. Mandatory public sector system

Civil servants and armed forces in the public sector are provided with non-portable, for-life, defined benefit (DB), pay-as-you-go (PAYGO) pension funds, which covers survivors as well. They are also provided with the lump-sum endowment fund known as *Tabungan Hari Tua* (THT), as well as with survivors' and disability benefits. At retirement, a lump sum is paid to the employee, and the amount of the lump sum is calculated using a formula.[6] Following the lump sum payout, the employee will receive a regular monthly pension which varies according to the rank/position at retirement. Currently, in addition to the twelve monthly pension payments, pensioners also receive a thirteenth payment in July every year. This follows the government's practice of providing a thirteenth-month salary for all active civil servants.

The Ministry of Finance supervises the pension program and endowment plan for civil servants. However, the pension program and endowment plans for members of armed forces are under direct supervision of the Ministry of Defence. Both the pension and endowment funds are managed separately, and in both cases the employee's contributions are a small share to government financing, the latter of which is funded through the state budget.

PT. Taspen has been tasked to collect contributions from the employer (government) and the employee (Central and Local Governments' civil servants) and manage the public sector pension fund; however, it has not been making any pension payouts. It has cited the small size of the fund as the cause, and the same time, the government is non-contributing to the fund. Government has deemed it trivial to make contribution which will not even be sufficient to cover the payout, opting for paying it as it goes.

PT. Taspen had only made token payouts in 2005–2010, since the fund managed is smaller than the annual public pension payout. The case is similar for PT. Asabri, where its total assets were 9 trillion IDR, but the expected payout was 8.5 trillion IDR. The government has essentially borne the entire civil service pension costs in its annual budget since 2011.[7] As a result, the roles of PT. Taspen and PT. Asabri have become cashiers to retirees – the government transfers the sum of the payment to them, and they then pay out the benefits to the pensioners (see Figure 5.7 below).

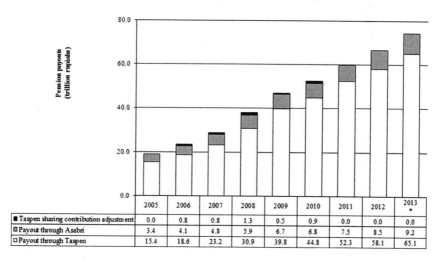

	2005	2006	2007	2008	2009	2010	2011	2012	2013 *
■ Taspen sharing contribution adjustment	0.0	0.8	0.8	1.3	0.5	0.9	0.0	0.0	0.0
▨ Payout through Asabri	3.4	4.1	4.8	5.9	6.7	6.8	7.5	8.5	9.2
▢ Payout through Taspen	15.4	18.6	23.2	30.9	39.8	44.8	52.3	58.1	65.1

Figure 5.7 Pre-SJSN public pension payouts, 2005–2013

(*) Proposed Budget Plan

Source: State Budget, Ministry of Finance, 2005–2013

Overtime, the government is burdened with increasing public pension payouts. The budget has doubled from 38.1 trillion IDR in 2008 to 74.3 trillion IDR in 2013, to pay for nearly 2 million civil servants and armed forces pensioners. Given that there will also be an increasing number of retiring civil servants, it is likely that the fiscal burden on the government's budget will be untenable. To try to mitigate/delay this outcome, the government has attempted to extend the retirement age, extending it to 65 years of age for several official ranks, as a form of temporary relief (Government of Republic of Indonesia, 2013: Government Regulation 19/2013).[8]

2.5. *Mandatory private sector system*

The mandatory private sector programs are operated by PT. Jamsostek and supervised by the Ministry of Labour. Since 2007, it is compulsory for all private companies with 10 or more employees or a monthly payroll of at least 1 million IDR to participate. The programs are on a fully funded defined contribution (DC) basis, providing members with a retirement fund, healthcare, employment accident insurance, and death insurance. PT. Jamsostek collects contributions, administers benefits, and manages the investment of the funds.

At the end of 2012, there were about 11.25 millions active individual members of PT. Jamsostek, supported by about 167,893 employers. The contribution rate to the provident fund is set at 5.7 percent of the base salary, where employees contribute 2 percent and employers contribute an additional 3.7 percent. Contributions to the fund are tax-deductible; investment income of the fund from certain types of investment is exempt from taxation; but pension benefits are taxed as regular income. Lump-sum benefits are taxed at personal income tax rates, ranging from 5 to 35 percent.

Participants are allowed to withdraw accumulated contributions before retirement if they have contributed for five years or have been unemployed for at least six months. Lump-sum retirement benefits are granted when a member reaches age 55 or over, in the case of death prior to age 55, or in the case of total and partial disability. The amount is equal to total employee and employer provident fund contributions plus accrued interest (about 14 percent). The nominal interest rate is set by the government and does not reflect actual investment earnings. Members with more than 50 million IDR in their retirement fund account may also opt for a periodic pension payment.

Although the number of Jamsostek participants is far larger than both Taspen and Asabri combined, payouts have been relatively small due to the DC nature of the programs. Jamsostek has been handing 6–7 trillion IDR payouts in recent years (Table 5.3), which was covered by investment returns alone. In 2012, PT. Jamsostek gave 10.82 percent yield of investment of its 133 trillion IDR asset.

2.6. *Voluntary system*

The voluntary private old-age security system was introduced in 1992 as a part of a major reform of the national retirement income policy to extend the coverage of old-age security plan holder. The programs in the voluntary system are

Table 5.3 Pre-SJSN number of participants of Indonesia's voluntary private pension funds

	Cases	Payouts (trillion IDR)
2008	693,199	3.73
2009	884,930	5.79
2010	867,723	5.88
2011	904,927	6.83
2012	943,324	7.97

Source: Jamsostek (2012)

Table 5.4 Pre-SJSN number of participants of Indonesia's voluntary private pension funds

Year	DPPK	DPLK
2007	1,350,967	1,081,474
2008	1,380,115	1,178,999
2009	1,378,981	1,302,245
2010	1,382,741	1,435,256
2011	1,412,827	1,669,881

Source: Bapepam (2012)

Table 5.5 Pre-SJSN number of operators of Indonesia's private pension funds

Year	DPPK (DB)	DPPK (DC)	DPLK
1995	147	20	18
1997	245	36	22
1999	268	40	23
2001	275	42	27
2003	271	36	29
2005	250	36	26
2007	226	36	26
2009	210	41	25
2011	204	41	25

Source: Bapepam (2012)

managed by the employer (DPPK) and/or financial institution (DPLK), and can be either a DB or a DC plan (Law 11/1992).

The participants in the voluntary system can be employee of a company that provides DPPK or DPLK as additional benefit, or individuals who already possess a mandatory social security plan and wish to have more benefits, or workers who are not covered in mandatory plan, e.g. formal workers in company whose employment is less than 10, or self-employed/informal workers. The following table shows the steadily increasing number of voluntary system participants.

A small amount of DPLK operators manages relatively equal number of participants with that of the DPPK. Operators of DPPK are largely offering a defined benefit (DB) program rather than a defined contribution (DC) program at present, although the numbers appear to be decreasing. The possibility of switching to the DC plan can be seen from the table below.

2.7. Corporate participation in voluntary system

An employer can either establish a pension fund (DPPK) directly providing DB or DC benefits, or sign a contract with a financial institution that will set up and manage pension fund (DPLK) operating on a DC basis. The law gives employers discretion on their pension policy and also permits employers to arrange different schemes for different groups of employees, but in practice many employers affiliate their employees to a single scheme. Currently, about 2.8 million workers of SOE and private sector companies participate in corporate voluntary pension schemes (comprising about 2 percent of the employed labour force).

Pension funds can be financed either solely by the employer or via joint contributions by both the employer's and employees' contributions. In the latter case, it is unambiguous that there is a consensus between the employer and employee on the scheme to be enrolled. If only the employer contributes to any scheme, however, the employee can be enrolled by default into the same, but they ultimately retain the right to decide if they want to join a particular program.

Participants are allowed to receive pension benefits after three years of participation in the pension fund and may transfer their rights and accumulated funds to another pension fund upon termination of employment or just prior to retirement. In the case of employment termination before reaching the mandatory retirement age, employees can decide (i) to transfer present value of accrued benefits to the financial institution, (ii) to transfer present value of accrued benefits to the new employer, or (iii) to transfer the accrued benefits to a deferred pension to be paid by the former employer. Payment of the benefits can be claimed when a member reaches the retirement age, at age 55.

2.8. Personal participation in voluntary system

Financial institutions may also establish private pension funds (DPLK) which are open to all individuals (regardless of employment status) willing to make a contributions towards retirement savings. However, this scheme only operates as a DC scheme. Ideally, every individual is statutorily allowed to establish a voluntary private pension plan managed by private financial institutions. However, the providers of the voluntary system often prefer to only target the middle-to high-income groups (Bloomberg Businessweek Indonesia, 2013). Subsequently, this significantly reduces options which the unprotected poor workers in informal sector have available to them.

Members are generally entitled to receive benefits upon reaching the legal retirement age, in a range of 45 to 65 years. Members may also opt for early retirement from the pension scheme, where the accrued benefits may be received as lump sum or annuity depending on the accumulated amount. The contribution rate is usually defined in the contract established between the individual and the financial institution. For example, Jamsostek's voluntary program requires that the self-employed contribute at least 2 percent of gross monthly income, and another 1 percent for employment accident insurance to the provident fund.

2.9. Shortcomings of current pension system

The current social security system, particularly the pension system, is unfair, discriminatory, and limited. It lacks intergenerational equity in the case of the PAYG public sector pension, where the government uses the present income tax to finance the gap between the limited contributions made by the retirees in the past and pensions they receive in the present. It discriminates in that only the civil servants are entitled to guaranteed pension and retirement funds, while private sector employees' retirement welfare and needs depend on the policy and contingency of their employer. It is limited that only the workers in the formal sectors (approximately a quarter of the workers in formal sector) are insured in Taspen, Asabri, and Jamsostek schemes, with informal workers mostly omitted.

Performance of the public sector in managing its fund assets is lagging far behind the private sector. Table A5.1 in the Appendix shows the shift of the composition of DPPK and DPLK investments over time. Their performance is in contrast to the public sector's performance.[9]

2.10. Future pension system under SJSN Law

The reform legislated by the SJSN Law (Law 40/2004 on National Social Security System) proposed a framework consisting of the following:

- Five mandatory programs, namely work-accident protection, life insurance, provident fund, pension, and health maintenance programs.
- All-worker coverage, including informal workers, with gradual inclusion.
- Pre-funding for all programs.
- A tripartite board to assist the President in formulating policies on a national social security system.
- Several state companies to run the program

However, the details on how the programs are managed and financed and how to collect contribution are still unclear (Rachmatawarta, 2004).

The government is yet to complete the tasks of (i) designing the system (the contribution, the benefit, managing the contribution of informal sector, the role of state, etc.), (ii) increasing the coverage (especially for informal sector), and (iii) determining the financing-mix (contribution collections, state's share of contribution for the poor, etc.).

2.11. Institutions

The future social security system will consist of two building blocks, *Badan Penyelenggara Jaminan Sosial* (BPJS) I of the Healthcare, and BPJS II of the Labour. The pension system falls into the latter, which will merge the current major operators of PT. Taspen, PT. Asabri (operators of mandatory social security for civil servants and armed forces – the public sector), and PT. Jamsostek (operator of private mandatory social security), into one BPJS II of Labour within the following timeline:

1   PT. Jamsostek (formal private sector) will become BPJS Labour from 1 January 2014 and start to operate from 1 January 2015, including the accommodation of new members. Jamsostek aims at having 4 million new members in 2013 and 31 million active members by the end of 2017.[10]
2   PT. Taspen and PT. Asabri (public sector) will become part of BPJS Labour on 2029 at the latest and gradually shift their insurance programs and pension payment to BPJS Labour.

2.12. Pension program

Essentially, the new program under the SJSN framework is a DB pension program with universal coverage. This means that citizens, including the informal workers, the disabled, and the poor are also covered in the program, possibly with aided contribution. The details of the benefits and the minimum benefits ceiling are yet to be formulated by the government; although numerous studies like Wiener (2009)[11] and Park and Estrada (2012)[12] try to look into the issue, the bottleneck seems to be more on the political than the technical side.

Employers and employees are required to pay equal contributions to the provident fund. Contribution rate is yet to be determined by a set of government regulations. It is not clear how the rate will be adjusted to respond to the potential emergence of surpluses and deficits.

Jamsostek is the first to join the BPJS Labour, and the new program will first apply to its participants. For the private sector, the pension program under the SJSN will solve the problem of portability and mobility, whereas companies can still opt for additional DPPK or DPLK. The challenge will be to enforce the private sector participation and contribution, since the current contribution for the majority of the formal sector is considerably low.

The current mandatory retirement fund for the private sector managed by Jamsostek is on a DC basis. Since the first 15 years of SJSN Law will be carried out by Jamsostek, the program will still be in DC form during that time, with only those with more than 15 years of contribution eligible for full pension benefits instead of mere accumulated contributions. Participants may also borrow from the provident fund by pledging their benefits after a minimum period of participation. If the new pension program begins in 2014, only those reaching age 55 in 2029 or later would be eligible to receive pension benefits.

PT. Taspen and PT. Asabri will not join the system until 2029 at the latest, buying the government the time to figure out the new form of pension for civil servants. The fully funded DB scheme has been proposed as a plausible reform option, but the government has yet to decide, since transition from a PAYG to a fully funded scheme will require a large amount of funding upfront. This should be addressed soon since the uncertainty of new civil servant pension programs and the government's say to contribute for the payment of pension of the poor may potentially create unfunded benefits in the next decades.

3. Indicators of Indonesia's fiscal system

3.1. Current fiscal condition 2001–2012

Indonesia's fiscal condition after the financial crisis in 1998 has been more stable. During the period of 2001–2012, the Central Government budget deficit was relatively stable in the range of 0.7 percent to 2.5 percent of GDP (Table 5.6). In line with controlled deficit, the government debt gradually decreased from about 100 percent of GDP in 1999–2000 to about 24 percent of GDP in 2012.

3.2. State revenues

In the last decade, Central Government revenue was dominated by tax revenue, while non-tax revenue tended to gradually decrease. Nevertheless, a small increase in tax ratio has not fully substituted the reduction in non-tax revenue. As a result, the ratio of domestic revenue to GDP has slightly decreased during the period 2001–2012.

There are two main taxes levied by the Central Government in Indonesia: income tax (corporate and personal) and value-added tax. Corporation income tax is calculated on the basis of income – less certain deductions, tax rate varies from 10 percent to 30 percent. In similar fashion, different tax brackets are applied for individual income taxes.[13] Value-Added Tax (VAT) is levied on delivery of taxable goods, on imports of goods, and on services (including services furnished by foreign taxpayers outside Indonesia if the services have a benefit in Indonesia). Unless specifically exempt, the VAT is 10 percent. There

Table 5.6 Indonesia fiscal condition 2001–2012 (in percentage of GDP)

Year	State Internal Revenue			State Expenditure			Surplus/ Deficit	Debt Ratio
	Taxes	Non Taxes	Total	Central Government	Transfers to Regions	Total		
2001	11.3	7.0	18.3	15.8	4.9	20.7	−2.5	77.3
2002	11.5	4.9	16.4	12.3	5.4	17.7	−1.3	67.2
2003	12.0	4.9	16.9	12.7	6.0	18.7	−1.7	61.2
2004	12.2	5.3	17.6	13.0	5.7	18.6	−1.0	56.6
2005	12.5	5.3	17.8	13.0	5.4	18.4	−0.5	47.3
2006	12.3	6.8	19.1	13.2	6.8	20.0	−0.9	39.0
2007	12.4	5.4	17.8	12.7	6.4	19.1	−1.3	35.1
2008	13.3	6.5	19.8	14.0	5.9	19.9	−0.1	33.1
2009	11.0	4.0	15.1	11.2	5.5	16.7	−1.6	28.3
2010	11.2	4.2	15.4	12.1	5.3	17.5	−0.7	26.1
2011	11.8	4.5	16.2	11.9	5.5	17.4	−2.1	24.4
2012	12.3	4.1	16.5	13.0	5.8	18.8	−1.5	24.0

Source: Writer's calculation from the data at the MOF

Note: Data from 2001–2011 are the realization, while data from 2012 is the revised budget

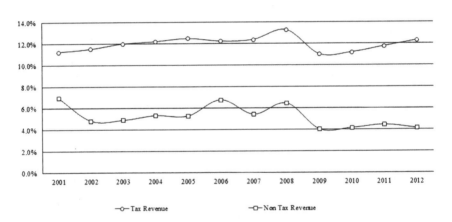

Figure 5.8 Central government tax and non-tax revenue (percentage of GDP)

Source: Writer's calculation from the data at the MOF

is also sales tax – rates vary – on luxury goods, imposed in addition to the VAT on the delivery of luxury goods manufactured in or imported into Indonesia.

Although the rates of corporate and personal income taxes are relatively low compared to developed countries, there is a low compliance problem faced by Indonesia's tax administration, as reflected in the low tax ratio (see Figure 5.8).

Taxpayers are concentrated on the formal sector and on the urban area. At the end of 2012, there are only about 20 million registered taxpayers from about 120 million workers, and there are only about 8.5 millions taxpayers which conduct the tax self-reporting. The government should take the growing middle-income class and urbanization as opportunity to improve the tax ratio in next decades, and to reduce the reliance on natural resource-based revenues.

3.3. State expenditures

State expenditure in Indonesia comprises Central Government expenditure and transfers to Local Governments (provinces, districts, and cities). Since the implementation of Decentralization Law in 2001, about one third of state expenditure is in form of transfers to Local Governments. Meanwhile, the Central Government expenditure in 2012 is dominated by personnel expenditures (20 percent), energy subsidy (19 percent), capital expenditure (16.5 percent) and operation and maintenances (15 percent) (see Table 5.7). Subsidy for energy tends to increase since Indonesia adopts the price control policy for fuels and electricity.

3.4. Central government expenditure for pension of civil servants

In Indonesia's system, civil servant salaries are paid by each level of government. The salaries for civil servants at the Central Government and for military personnel is the responsibility of the Central Government. Meanwhile, the civil servants at the Provincial, District, and Municipal Government are paid by the level of government in which such personnel are employed. In 2012, the number

Table 5.7 Composition of central government expenditures (percentage of total budget)

Item	2005	2006	2007	2008	2009	2010	2011	2012
Personnel	15.0	16.7	17.9	16.3	20.3	19.0	19.9	19.8
Operation and Main.	8.1	10.7	10.8	8.1	12.8	12.5	14.1	15.1
Capital Expenditure	9.1	12.5	12.7	10.5	12.1	10.3	13.3	16.5
Interest Payment	18.1	18.0	15.8	12.7	14.9	11.3	10.6	10.6
Subsidies	33.4	24.4	29.8	39.7	22.0	24.7	33.4	23.4
Energy Subsidies	28.9	21.5	23.2	32.2	15.0	17.9	28.9	18.9
Non-Energy Subsidies	4.5	2.9	6.6	7.5	6.9	6.7	4.5	4.5
Social Grant	6.9	9.3	9.9	8.3	11.7	8.8	8.0	8.0
Other Expenditures	9.4	8.5	3.1	4.4	6.2	2.8	0.6	6.6
Total	100.0	100.0	100.0	100.0	100.0	100.0	100.0	100.0

Source: Writer's calculation from the data at the MOF

Note: Data from 2001–2011 are the realization, while data from 2012 is the revised budget

Table 5.8 Central government expenditure to cover the payment of state's pensioners

Expenditure	2005	2006	2007	2008	2009	2010	2011	2012
Percent of GDP	0.7	0.7	0.7	0.8	0.9	0.8	0.8	0.8
Personnel Expenditure	31	31	31	33	38	35	33	31
% Central Government Expenditure	5.3	5.2	5.6	5.4	7.6	7.4	6.6	6.9

Source: Author's calculation from the data at the MOF

of civil servants attached to Central Government and Local Government was about 916,500 and 3.8 million personnel respectively.

Importantly, while salaries are paid by the relevant government, the pension payments are mainly the responsibility of Central Government. The Central Government has to make up the amount of pension that should be paid by PT. Taspen and PT. Asabri to the pensioners (see Table 5.8). In case of PT. Taspen, the accumulation of employee contributions for the pension program into a fund was initially to cover 25 percent of the pension cost. The Central Government should cover the rest of the 75 percent from general revenue. ADB (2007) noted that the contributions collected and the accumulated interest earned are not sufficient to pay the planned share. Therefore the government share has been increasing. In 2007, PT. Taspen only covered 15 percent, whereas the government added 85 percent (ADB, 2007).

In practice, the pension payment for civil servants and military is on a PAYG basis, not from the accumulated pension fund. The total amount of expenditure for pensions from Central Government was approximately 0.8 percent of GDP in 2012 or about 7 percent of the Central Government expenditure. This PAYG basis is unlikely to change for the next 20 years. Currently the contribution of active civil servants to pension fund is only 4.75 percent of basic salary. In order to fund 25 percent of benefits, the contribution should be about 17 percent of basic salary (ADB, 2007). Therefore, the government should make some changes in the design of the pension program in the future to maintain its fiscal viability.

3.5. Age-related pension expenditure: Projection and analysis

In this section, we estimate and project the state pension expenditure, in accordance with the SJSN Law, for a mandatory pension fund with defined benefit system (Article 36 verse 3). A majority of the state's future pension liabilities are likely coming from two components. The first is the state expenditure for civil servants and military (civil servants). This has been practiced for the last two decades in the DB plan. The government is now spending about 0.8 percent of GDP to be able to fund the payment of this pension benefit, while the contribution of employee is only about 0.1 percent of GDP. This is likely to be continued for the next decades since there is no request for changing the system in the SJSN Law.

The second part of state future liabilities will be the basic pension benefit, which is explicitly mentioned in the SJSN Law. In Article 39 it is mentioned that the pension system is conducted nationally on the basis of the social insurance principle. The pension system should be able to secure the basic living standard for those who are already at pension age. Although the pensioners should be those who are registered in BPJS, the SJSN Law requests the government to register those who will receive the pension contribution to be paid to BPJS (Article 14).

The SJSN Law prescribes that the pension program will continue to be a DC plan for the next first 15 years (Article 41) since the law mentioned that only those who have contributed for 15 years are eligible for a pension benefit. That means that if the pension program began in 2014, only those reaching age 55 in 2029 or later would be eligible to receive pension benefits. Moreover, those who retire prior to the time the system begins will receive no pension benefit at all. Under the SJSN Law, all existing pensioners plus another generation of retiring workers will not receive a pension (ADB, 2007).

The new pension system under the SJSN Law as well as the BPJS Law is not yet clear in term of the contribution, the benefit, the role of state, etc. At the moment, the pension system for civil servants is PAYG. If the state contributes for the payment of pension of the poor, the disabled population, and the informal sector, there is a potential of unfunded benefits in the next decades. Regarding the pension benefit for the next 15 years, the initial solution could be a basic benefit, which is different from the benefit received by civil servants and private voluntary schemes. The basic benefit may only cover the basic need for living, such as for foods and other basic living costs.

There are three possible scenarios of projection for the basic pension benefits. The first is that the state will be liable to pay the basic pension benefit for the poor pensioners. This is the most probable scenario. According to the SJSN Law the government should pay the pension contribution of the poor and the disabled population (Article 14). Nevertheless, the state's future liability is likely to be extended to the pensioners who are not working in the formal sector, since they could fall into poor categories at age 60 due to their inability to work normally.

The second scenario is that the state will be responsible to pay the basic pension benefit for those who have never worked in the formal sector. This scenario implicitly assumes that those who have been working in formal sector have covered themselves with a pension insurance based on contribution. The last scenario is that the state will pay the basic pension benefit for all populations at pension age (other than civil servants).

Figure 5.9 summarizes the results of public pension expenditure for the three scenarios. The error bar of each point shows the deviation of decreasing/increasing the pension age by 5 year from the basis of 60 years.

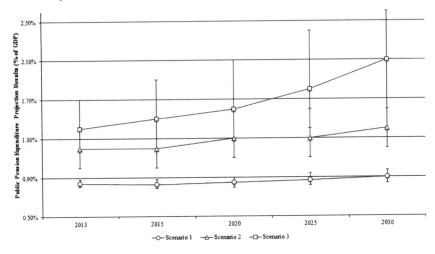

Figure 5.9 Public pension expenditure projection results (percentage of GDP)

Table 5.9 Projection of public pension expenditure in 2030 (in percentage of GDP), Scenario 1

	Pension Age	2013	2015	2020	2025	2030
Basic Pension for Poor	55	0.12%	0.14%	0.16%	0.19%	0.23%
	60	0.08%	0.09%	0.11%	0.13%	0.16%
	65	0.05%	0.05%	0.06%	0.08%	0.10%
Pension Benefit for Civil Servants	55–65	0.76%	0.74%	0.74%	0.74%	0.74%
Total	55	0.88%	0.88%	0.90%	0.94%	0.97%
	60	0.84%	0.83%	0.85%	0.87%	0.90%
	65	0.81%	0.79%	0.80%	0.82%	0.84%

Source: Authors' calculation based on the data of WB population projections (2012)

3.6. First scenario

The projection of the first scenario can be seen in Table 5.9. The additional future state liability for this scenario is only about 0.23 percent of GDP in 2030 if the pension age is 60 and about 0.16 percent of GDP if the pension age is 55. Including the pension benefit for civil servants, the total state pension expenditure in 2030 is projected to be about 0.97 percent of GDP for pension age at 60 and about 0.90 percent of GDP for pension age at 55. The

Table 5.10 Assumptions for Scenario 1 projection

	2013–2030	Note
Annual Growth of Nominal GDP	11%	
Monthly Benefit per Pensioner in 2013 (Rp)	300,000	The income line of poor individual
Annual Growth of Basic Pension Benefit	10%	Equal to annual growth of GDP per capita
Annual Growth of Benefit for Civil Servants	10%	
Annual Growth of State Pensioners	0.7%	Average annual growth of population (2013–2030)
% Poor pensioners	12%	Percentages of the total population

projection for total basic pension benefit is based on several assumptions (see Table 5.10): (i) the nominal GDP will grow by 11 percent annually, (ii) monthly basic benefit is at 300,000 IDR[14] in 2013 and will grow annually by about 10 percent (which is equal to the annual growth of GDP per capita), and (iii) the poor pensioners in 2013 are 12 percent of the total number of pensioners' population. Meanwhile, the projection for civil servants' pension payment assumes that the benefit will also grow about 10 percent[15] annually and that pensioners will grow by 0.7 percent[16] annually.

The above projections show that the basic pension payment for the poor in 2030 is lower than in 2013 due to the reduction in the proportion of poor pensioners and because the growth of nominal GDP is much higher than the increased benefit. Moreover, the difference between the social pensions at age 55 is a little bit higher than it is at age 60. This suggests that the government should consider increasing the pension age to 60.

3.7. Second scenario

The projection of the second scenario can be seen in Table 5.11. If the pension age is at 55, the state expenditure for basic pension benefit and for civil servants is expected to be about 1.7 percent of GDP in 2030. Meanwhile, if the pension age is at 60, the expenditure for social pension will be about 1.4 percent of GDP in 2030. The projection of social pension benefit for all pensioners of informal sectors (included poor pensioners) uses this similar assumption as the first scenario. Nevertheless, this scenario assumes that the proportion of informal sector workers will gradually decrease from 66 percent in 2013 to about 50 percent in 2030 (see Table 5.12).

The above projections also show that the social pension payment for the pensioners in the informal sector (including the poor) in 2030 is lower than it

Table 5.11 Projection of public pension expenditure in 2030 (in percentage of GDP)

	Pension Age	2013	2015	2020	2025	2030
Basic Pension for Non-formal	55	0.6%	0.7%	0.8%	0.9%	0.9%
	60	0.4%	0.5%	0.5%	0.6%	0.7%
	65	0.3%	0.3%	0.3%	0.4%	0.4%
Pension Benefit for Civil Servants	55–65	0.8%	0.7%	0.7%	0.7%	0.7%
Total	55	1.4%	1.5%	1.6%	1.6%	1.7%
	60	1.2%	1.2%	1.3%	1.3%	1.4%
	65	1.0%	1.0%	1.1%	1.1%	1.2%

Source: Authors' calculation based on the data of WB population projections (2012)

Table 5.12 Assumptions for the percentage of informal sector in the economy

	2013	2015	2020	2025	2030
% Informal Sector	66%	65%	60%	55%	50%

in 2013 due to the expected reduction in the proportion of informal sector – and also the growth of nominal GDP is much higher than the increased benefit. Moreover, the difference between the social pensions at age 55 is much higher than at age 60. Similar to the first scenario, it suggests that the government should increase the pension age to 60.

3.8. Third scenario

This scenario will result in the highest burden to the state since the government should provide the basic pension benefits to all pensioners (other than civil servants) regardless of their pension contributions. This is unlikely to happen, since the rich and the worker at the formal sector will follow the defined contribution pension scheme. Nevertheless, considering the coverage and contribution of the current formal sector employee, there is a possibility for the government to receive a part of this burden if the BPJS is not able to collect the contribution from the formal sector.

The projection of the third scenario can be seen in Table 5.13. If the pension age is at 55, the state expenditure for basic pension benefits is expected to be about 1.9 percent of GDP in 2030. Meanwhile, if the pension age is at 60, the expenditure for basic pension benefits will be about 1.3 percent of GDP in 2030. Combined with the future pension liabilities for civil servants, the total

Table 5.13 Projection of public pension expenditure in 2030 (in percentage of GDP)

	Pension Age	2013	2015	2020	2025	2030
Basic Pension for all Pensioners	55	1.0%	1.2%	1.4%	1.6%	1.9%
	60	0.6%	0.7%	0.9%	1.1%	1.3%
	65	0.4%	0.4%	0.5%	0.7%	0.9%
Pension Benefit for Civil Servants	55–65	0.8%	0.7%	0.7%	0.7%	0.7%
Total	55	1.7%	1.9%	2.1%	2.4%	2.6%
	60	1.4%	1.5%	1.6%	1.8%	2.1%
	65	1.2%	1.2%	1.3%	1.4%	1.6%

Source: Authors' calculation based on the data of WB population projections (2012)

state liabilities will be about 2.6 percent if the pension age is 55 and 2.1 percent if the pension age is 60.

Comparing these projections with the projection of public pension expenditure done by others such as ADB (2007), IMF (2011), Standard and Poor's (2010), the difference is due to assumptions and scenarios. The projection of the first scenario (about 0.94 percent of GDP) is lower than the IMF projection (1.1 percent in 2030) and also much lower than the ADB projection (1.84 percent in 2030). Meanwhile, the projection of the third scenario is much higher than both ADB (2007) and IMF (2011), although the pension age is assumed to be at 60.

This projection also suggests that the government should change the age of retirement from 55 to 60, as also suggested by ADB (2007), to recognize higher life expectancies and to control the cost of the pension program in the future.

3.9. Fiscal space-improving options for future pension liabilities

The gap between the future pension liabilities in the one hand, and the accumulation contribution and its potential future return on the other hand, can be filled in various ways: (i) increasing tax revenue, (ii) regularly increasing contribution from civil servants, as well as from the private sectors, including the informal one, (iii) maximizing the return of investment of the accumulated pension fund, and (iv) burden-sharing between the Central and Local Governments for the local civil servants – aside of improving awareness and thus participants' compliance with the social security programs.

3.10. Tax revenues

Indonesia's tax revenue was still much lower in terms of tax-to-GDP ratio in comparison to other countries, as explained in the previous section. There is a possibility that the tax ratio will increase in the future due to an increasing number of formal sectors and middle-income population for the next 20 years. Increasing the tax ratio by 2 to 3 percent for about 20 years a head is a highly possible for Indonesia, given that current economic stability is maintained. Other countries, such as Turkey and Korea, were able to increase approximately 9–10 percent of their tax ratio within 20 years. In Korea, for example, the tax ratio increased from approximately 16 percent in 1988 to 25.6 percent in 2009. Turkey's tax ratio jumped up from 13 percent in 1986 to 24.6 percent in 2009 (data from OECD). Turkey's experience is relevant to Indonesia since in 1988 this country was still a middle-income country.

Nevertheless, there are also many examples of countries where the tax ratio gradually decreased or stayed at the same level. The tax ratio of Chile during the period of 1990–2009, for example, stayed at 18 percent of GDP, while the tax ratio of New Zealand decreased gradually from about 37 percent in 1990 to about 31 percent in 2009. In the case of Indonesia, the tax ratio during the last 20 years only increased about 1 percent, since there was almost no change in Indonesia's tax rate (except for the income tax administration system, it has changed from the official assessment to a self-assessment system). Moreover, considering the current fiscal condition in Indonesia, the increased tax ratio is likely to be used for purposes other than the pension fund.

Therefore, there should be a specific earmarked tax or a new tax rate earmarked for the pension fund. An alternative to an increase in Indonesia's tax ratio, especially to cover the need of future public pension expenditure, is to introduce a payroll tax earmarked for pension expenditure for all sectors of the economy, including the Central and Local Government. Currently, the individual income tax in Indonesia contributes about 2.5 percent of GDP at an average tax rate of 15 percent. Adding payroll tax at the rate of 4 percent of total salaries, the tax ratio will increase to about 0.6 percent of GDP. The amount could be sufficient to cover the needs for the second scenario, but would be much lower than that needed for the third scenario.

3.11. *Potential contributions from civil servants*

While the burden for civil servants pension payment is increasing, the contribution of civil servants to the fund remains the same. It is highly possible to increase the contribution, since civil servants' salaries already gone up in nominal term as well as in real term. Current contributions from civil servants is only about 15 percent of the total state pension payment, while the other 85 percent (0.8 percent of GDP) is coming from the state budget. Table 5.14 shows that raising employee's contribution to 35 percent (0.2 percent of GDP) will improve the balance between the state and the employee contributions.

An alternative to reducing the state burden to pay the pension of civil servants is by gradually increasing the contribution of civil servants. The projection in Table 5.15 shows that if the contribution of civil servants is set at 2.5 percent of the total state personnel expenditure (Central and Local Governments'

Table 5.14 Projections of increased civil servants' contribution to pension fund

		2013	2015	2020	2025	2030
State Expenditure	% Total	85%	80%	75%	70%	65%
	% of GDP	0.7%	0.6%	0.5%	0.5%	0.5%
Employee Contribution	% Total	15%	20%	25%	30%	35%
	% of GDP	0.1%	0.1%	0.2%	0.2%	0.2%

Source: Authors' calculations.

Table 5.15 Projection of civil servants' contribution to pension fund

		2013	2015	2020	2025	2030
Total State Expenditure for Personnel (Including Sub-National Government)	Trillion IDR	398	526	1,059	2,130	4,283
	% GDP	4.3%	4.5%	5.4%	6.4%	7.6%
2.5% of Personnel Expenditure	Trillion IDR	10.0	13.2	26.5	53.2	107.1
	% GDP	0.11%	0.11%	0.13%	0.16%	0.19%

Source: Authors' calculations.

Table 5.16 Projection of informal sector contribution to pension fund

	2015	2020	2025	2030
% contribution of informal sector	10%	14%	18%	22%
% of GDP	0.11%	0.16%	0.18%	0.21%

Source: Authors' calculations.

employees), the contribution will be about 0.19 percent of GDP in 2030. It could be about 0.38 percent of GDP if the contribution from civil servants is 5 percent of salaries.

3.12. Potential contributions from the informal sector worker

Another possible way to reduce the burden of social pensions is to increase coverage and contributions in the informal sector. If some workers in the informal sector are joining the BJPS scheme or other private schemes voluntarily, they will be a part of the defined contribution pension system. The projection in Table 5.16 shows that, if the contributions of informal sector can achieve the level of 10 percent in 2015 and gradually increase 1 percent per year, that will reduce the state burden to about 0.2% of GDP by 2030.

3.13. Projection of state fiscal condition 2013–2030

Given these projections, it is also important to make a projection of the state's fiscal condition to 2030 in order to see if the state fiscal capacity can meet the future burden of social pensions. Assuming that the state will run as usual, with some adjustment in the revenue side and in the expenditure side (other than for social pensions), the assumptions are that:

- Indonesia's tax ratio will be gradually increased from 12.4 percent of GDP in 2013 to 15.4 percent in 2030 (tax ratio will increase to 3 percent of GDP within 17 years)
- Non-tax revenues will be gradually decreased from 8 percent of GDP in 2013 to 6 percent in 2030
- The growth of personnel expenditure will fluctuate at the rate of 15 percent to 16 percent
- The growth of capital expenditure will be at the rate of 15 percent to 16 percent
- The growth of transfers to Regional Governments will be at the rate of 14 percent to 15 percent.

Moreover, it is also assumed that the government will reduce the subsidy gradually, especially the energy subsidy, during this period. The price of fuels and electricity should be adjusted for every three years. Such assumptions are based on the experiences (data history) during the period of 2001–2012 (Bappenas, 2007). The projection can be seen in Table 5.17.

Fiscal projection show that the state's fiscal condition will be stable during the period of 2013–2030 as long as the Central Government can maintain the growth of revenue and expenditure along with the assumption. Moreover, the deficit level is quite low to anticipate the needs for social security spending. There will be a space from about 1.2 percent to 1.7 percent of GDP if the maximum deficit is set from 2 percent to 2.5 percent of GDP in 2030.

The future fiscal burden from the pension system has been estimated in the previous section. State liabilities for public pension will depend very much on the design of the pension system. Assuming that the pension age will be at 60 years in 2030, additional burden for social pensions will range from 0.16 percent of GDP (Scenario 1 with 60 years as the pension age) to 1.3 percent of GDP (Scenario 3 with 60 years as pension age), other than state liabilities for civil servants. Such liabilities will be partly funded by the contribution, as discussed before. Therefore, the maximum additional liabilities to the state will be about 1.1 percent of GDP. Comparing with the above projection of fiscal space, such a number will be able to be funded by the state in 2030.

Table 5.17 Projection of state fiscal condition 2013–2030

Year	State Revenue	Central Expenditure	Transfer to Local Government	Surplus/ Deficit
	% of GDP			
2013	16.2%	12.4%	5.8%	−2.0%
2014	16.2%	11.6%	5.9%	−1.3%
2015	16.2%	11.7%	5.9%	−1.4%
2016	16.2%	11.8%	5.9%	−1.5%
2017	16.2%	11.3%	6.0%	−1.0%
2018	16.3%	11.4%	6.1%	−1.2%
2019	16.3%	11.4%	6.2%	−1.2%
2020	16.3%	11.1%	6.3%	−1.0%
2021	16.4%	11.1%	6.4%	−1.1%
2022	16.4%	11.2%	6.5%	−1.2%
2023	16.5%	11.0%	6.5%	−1.0%
2024	16.6%	11.0%	6.6%	−1.0%
2025	16.7%	11.1%	6.6%	−1.0%
2026	16.8%	11.0%	6.6%	−0.9%
2027	16.8%	11.1%	6.7%	−0.9%
2028	16.9%	11.0%	6.8%	−0.9%
2029	17.0%	10.9%	6.9%	−0.8%
2030	17.1%	10.9%	7.0%	−0.8%

Sources: Authors' calculations.

3.14. Sharing of responsibility with Local Government

Civil servants are currently recruited by both Central and Local Governments. The Local Government's decision to recruit new employee is independent from the Central Government's, as the salary is paid wholly by Local Governments from local budgets. However, for most regions the largest part of their local budget revenue is the intergovernmental grants from the Central Government, particularly the *Dana Alokasi Umum* or DAU (a block grant). There is a false notion amongst the Local Government that the grant is to be used for paying Local Government salaries.

Although the Local Government is responsible for paying their civil servants' salaries, the case does not apply for their pensions. The DB pensions of Central and Local Government employees are fully born by the Central Government and transferred to the recipients through Taspen. Currently, the ratio of Central to Local Government civil servants is around 1 to 3.8. An increase in the number of civil servants is mostly due to new recruits in the regions.

Whatever reform options the Central Government is considering for the future civil service pension, it should not disregard the issue of unfairness, where the Central Government would bear the entire future pension burden for the recruitment decision made by the Local Governments. This creates a moral hazard for the Local Government to be less prudent in recruiting new employees, as well as endangering the fiscal robustness of the Central Government. There needs to be burden-sharing between the Central and Local Government for the local civil servants, whichever form the future system may adopt (e.g. burden-sharing in terms of percentage of total payments in the PAYGO system, or contribution-sharing in the funded system). It is very likely that the final incidence will still be on the Central Government's side (since one third of the state budget is transferred to the regions as their revenue). Nevertheless, explicitly stating Local Government responsibility for its recruitment decisions will be likely to improve future public sector employment.

3.15. *Other contingent liabilities*

Other than the above three scenarios of future state liabilities for social pension and pension schemes for civil servants, there are also some possible future burdens due to a mismatch between contributions and benefits in each of other mandatory programs, namely work-accident protection, life insurance, and provident funds. The shortfalls in each scheme will require state intervention as the ultimate guarantor of fund solvency. However, these three schemes of labour and old-age protections are purportedly not discussed in detail.

3.16. *Concluding observations and suggestions*

Although the SJSN Law has been legislated for almost a decade now, Indonesia's future pension system is still unclear in term of the design, particularly in the aspect of contributions, benefits, and the role of the state. Thus any attempt to analyse the future sustainability of the pension system in tandem to the government's fiscal position is, at best, exploratory.

What one may perhaps be able to draw with some confidence is that the defined benefit PAYG system for the civil servants is likely to continue. As part of the legislated requirement to provide some form of social security nationwide, the state will likely, or inevitably, have to contribute towards paying for the pension benefits of the poor, the disabled, and the informal sector workers who have no access to formal employment-linked pension schemes. The existing PAYG system by which (some of) the informal sector is covered under is likely to add on to the government's fiscal burden, owing to constraints in contribution collections from this sector.

Nonetheless, we have attempted some projections of the possible scenarios of a reform of the pension system following the framework and regulations spelt out in the SJSN legislation. The projection shows that the future public pension liabilities will depend very much on the design of a future pension system. If the government chooses to contribute only for the poor and the disabled population, the future liabilities will be much smaller than to contribute to all informal workers and to all pensioners. Nevertheless, the future burden for the informal sector pensioners may still be a part of the system, since this population is very large in Indonesia.

There are several ways in which the future liabilities can be met. The first is by increasing the tax effort. However, this choice will result in uncertainty for pension funds, since such resources could be used for other state expenditures. Second, the government could introduce a new tax whose revenue is earmarked for pension fund. An alternative would be the payroll taxes. Another alternative is by enforcing more contribution from civil servants and the workers from the informal sector in line with the increased salaries. The last alternative, especially for local civil servants, is burden-sharing between the Central and Local Governments. Moreover, this research suggests that the government should change the age of retirement from 55 to 60, which was also suggested by ADB (2007).

Notes

1 This will start in 2014 with the mergers of the existing health insurance systems under the current operators PT. ASKES, Jamkesmas (*Jaminan Kesehatan Masyarakat*, a social health insurance for poor people funded by the state budget), and the healthcare programs of PT. Jamsostek.
2 This will involve merging the existing state-owned operators of old-age savings and pension funds, i.e. PT. Jamsostek (the mandatory programs for private employers), PT. Taspen (for civil servants), and PT. Asabri (for the armed forces).
3 It is mandated by SJSN Law (Section 1 and Section 49) to have several BPJS to avoid cross-subsidy and to minimize adverse incentives when handling both contributions from the state and private sources.
4 This is calculated as the sum of nominal Gross Regional Domestic Product (GRDP) of the provinces in Java and Sumatra compared to the sum of nominal GRDP of 33 provinces in 2010. If national Gross Domestic Product is used, this ratio is 66.7 percent if oil and gas products are included, or 72.3% percent (excluding oil and gas product).
5 A recent win in their favor was the significant hike in Jakarta's monthly minimum wage in early 2013 – a 40 percent increase from 1.3 million IDR to 2.2 million IDR. It triggers companies to move out from Jakarta, increases the competition for formal sector jobs, and influences minimum wage hikes in other regions since the capital city Jakarta is regarded as a benchmark (Viva News Online, 2013).
6 According to IOPS (2011), the formula is determined by the Ministry of Finance of Indonesia, and equals between 1.875 percent and 2.5 percent of the final salary multiplied by the years of service.
7 Post decentralization, civil servants are grouped into Central and Local Government employees; pensions for both groups are still paid by the state via the state budget.
8 ADB (2007) suggested that the retirement age should be at least 60 today, to recognize higher life expectancies and to control the cost of the pension program in the future.

9 For example, PT. Taspen's total asset in 2008 was 19.65 trillion IDR (0.04 per-cent of GDP, 0.56 percent of annual benefits), but its return on invested assets in 2008 was only 9.12 percent – lower than the inflation rate of 11.1 percent, and about the same as yield on Central Bank Certificates (9.2 percent) (Guerard, 2010).

10 http://ekbis.rmol.co/read/2013/01/31/96525/Jadi-BPJS-Ketenagakerjaan,-Asset-Jamsostek-Rp-277,6-Triliun-di-Tahun-2017- accessed 11 March 2013.

11 Wiener (2009) suggests a DB pension equal to 0.5 percent of final pay per year of contribution, providing a replacement ratio of 20 percent for a 40-year career. The retirement age was to increase to 60, and then gradually to 65 by the year 2047.

12 Park and Estrada (2012) proposed that the normal retirement age should be gradually and dynamically adjusted to reflect increases in longevity, and lump-sum payments should be gradually converted to a life annuity to increase financial security in retirement.

13 Income range and its tax rate: <25 million IDR (5 percent), 25–50 million IDR (10 percent), 50–100 million IDR (15 percent), 100–200 million IDR (25 per-cent), >200 million IDR (35 percent).

14 This assumption is a possible alternative to implement the SJSN Law since this is based on the income line between the poor and non-poor in Indonesia. This assumption is much lower than the minimum basic needs defined by the World Bank, which is at US$2 per person per day or equal to about 20,000 IDR in 2013. The benefit is assumed to increase about 10 percent per year, which is equal to the projection of GDP per capita growth during the period of 2013–2030. This assumption is much lower than suggested by Arifianto (2004) as a percentage of an individual's average income from the previous year (between a minimum of 60 percent and maximum of 80 percent of the local minimum wage (UMR), and each worker will receive a guaranteed minimum pension of at least 70 percent of the UMR).

15 This assumption is lower that the growth of state pension expenditure for the last 12 years, which was about 14 percent annually.

16 The number of state pensioners rose as the result of population growth for the last 10 years. The annual growth of population during the period of 2010–2030 is projected to be about 0.7 percent.

References

ADB (Asian Development Bank). (2007). *Preparatory studies on national social security system in Indonesia*. Report of TA 4024-INO, Financial Governance and Social Security Reform.

ADB (Asian Development Bank). (2012). Social pensions for the elderly in Asia: Fiscal costs and financing methods. In Mukul G. Asher (Ed.), *Social protection for older persons: Social pensions in Asia* (pp. 60–83). Manila, PH: ADB.

Adioetomo, M. (2005). *Bonus demografi: Menjelaskan hubungan antara pertumbu-han penduduk dengan pertumbuhan ekonomi* (Demographic bonus: Explaining the relationship between population growth and economic growth), Professorship Inaugural Speech, Faculty of Economics, University of Indonesia, Depok, Indonesia.

Arifianto, A. (2004). Social security reform in Indonesia: An analysis of the national social security bill (RUU SJSN). SMERU, Working Paper.

Bappenas. (2005). *Proyeksi Penduduk Indonesia 2005–2025* (Indonesia population projection 2005–2025). Jakarta, Indonesia: Bappenas.

Bappenas. (2007). *Prospek sustainabilitas APBN dalam jangka menengah 2002–2007* (Medium-term sustainability prospect of state budget 2002–2007). Jakarta, Indonesia: Bappenas.

Bappepam. (2012). *Laporan tahunan dana pensiun indonesia 2011* (2011 Indonesia pension fund annual report). Jakarta, Indonesia: Bappepam.

Bloomberg Businessweek Indonesia. (2013). *Menanti kontribusi dana pensiun* (Waiting for the contribution of pension fund). Written by P. Iswara, D. Dewi Kusuma, and S. Fitra in Bloomberg Businessweek Indonesia No. 8, 28 February–6 March 2013 edition.

BPS (Indonesia Census Bureau). (2010). *Sensus Penduduk 2010* (Population census 2010). Jakarta, Indonesia: BPS.

BPS (Indonesia Census Bureau). (2012). *Survei Angkatan Kerja Nasional Agustus 2012* (National labour force survey August 2012). Jakarta, Indonesia: BPS.

CSIS (Centre for Strategic and International Studies). (2014). Chapter by Haryo Aswicahyono. In Yose Risal Damuri (Ed.), *Untuk Indonesia 2014–2019: Agenda ekonomi*. Jakarta, Indonesia: CSIS.

Government of Republic of Indonesia. (1992). Law 11/1992 on Pension Fund.

Government of Republic of Indonesia. (2004). Law 40/2004 on National Social Security System.

Government of Republic of Indonesia. (2011). Law 24/2011 on National Agency for Social Security.

Government of Republic of Indonesia. (2013). Government Regulation 19/2013 on Fourth Amendment on GR 32/1979 on Civil Servant Termination.

Guerard, Y. (2010). *Developing Asia's pension systems: A case study of Indonesia.* Manila, PH: Asian Development Bank.

Guerard, Y., Asher, M. G., Park, D. & Estrada, G. B. (2012). Reducing disparities and enhancing sustainability in Asian pension systems. Asian Development Bank Working Papers No. 313, October 2012.

ILO (International Labour Organisation). (2012). *Labour and social trends in Indonesia 2011: Promoting job-rich growth in provinces.* Jakarta, Indonesia: ILO.

IMF (International Monetary Fund). (2011). *The challenge of public pension reform in advanced and emerging economies.* IMF Fiscal Affairs Department, 28 December 2011.

International Organisation of Pension Supervisors (IOPS). 2011. IOPS member country or territory pension system profile: Indonesia. November 2011. Available at http://www.iopsweb.org/researchandworkingpapers/49240302.pdf

Jamsostek. (2012). *Annual report 2012: Membangun kekuatan menuju BPJS ketenagakerjaan (Building on strengths toward a employment BPJS).* Jakarta, Indonesia: Jamsostek.

Matsumoto, M. & Verick, S. (2011). Employment trends in Indonesia over 1996–2009: Casualization of the labour market during an era of crises, reforms and recovery. ILO Employment Working Paper No. 99/2011, Employment Analysis and Research Unit, Economic and Labour Market Analysis Department.

Park, D. & Estrada, G. B. (2012). Developing Asia's pension systems and old-age income support. Asian Development Bank Institute Working Papers No. 358, April 2012.

Rachmatawarta, I. (2004). *Indonesia pension system: Where to go? Pension in Asia: Incentives, compliance, and their role in retirement.* Tokyo, Japan: Hitotsubashi University.

Standard and Poor's. (2010). *Global aging 2010: An irreversible truth.* New York, NY: Standard and Poor's Financial Services LLC.

UN (United Nations). (2012). *World population prospects: 2012 Revision.* Geneva, Switzerland: UN.

Viva News Online. (2013). *90 Perusahaan akan relokasi pabriknya ke luar jakarta,* http://us.bisnis.news.viva.co.id/news/read/398283–90-perusahaan-akan-relokasi-pabriknya-ke-luar-jakarta Accessed on March 2013.

Wiener, M. (2009). Old age saving program, pension program, and death benefit program, national social security system. White Paper Draft. Jakarta, Indonesia: The Ministry of Finance, Republic of Indonesia.

World Bank. (2010). *Population estimates and projections 1960–2050,* http://data.worldbank.org/data-catalog/population-projection-tables Accessed on March 2012.

World Bank. (2012). *World development indicator,* http://data.worldbank.org/data-catalog/world-development-indicators/wdi-2012 Accessed on January 2013.

6 Policy challenges in Indonesian social security

Bambang P. S. Brodjonegoro,
Suahasil Nazara, and
Fauziah Zen

1. Introduction

Indonesia enacted the Law no 40/2004 on National Social Security System (*Sistem Jaminan Sosial Nasional* or SJSN hereafter) as a manifestation of Constitutional vision to protect all Indonesians. The law has the origin form the aftermath of from the Asian Economic Crisis that severely impacted Indonesia at the end of 1990s. In response, Indonesia launched several social safety net programs to protect the poor and vulnerable groups. Subsequently, policymakers realized that Indonesia needs a more comprehensive social security system, and the 2004 law was a major step towards addressing this need.

A social security system is very important for a country. One faces different risks over his/her lifetime, and one of the major risks is health. The rich may be able to afford the health costs without societal support, but the most of the population may not be able to. Risk-sharing and pooling arrangements are better options when compared to reliance on the government's medical coverage on a reimbursement basis, for especially the poor. The latter may be an appealing option in the short run, but for an economy with a growing population, income, and aspirations for improved living standards, it is not attractive in the long term. Different other kinds of risks may also be foreseeable among those at work. For Indonesia, implications of these risks must be carefully examined and calculated because of the demographic structure (Handra and Dita, 2016).

In 2015, Indonesia is in the middle of a population historical path. In terms of the dependency ratio[1] (DR), Indonesia has exhibited a declining DR since the early 1970s, when the government first launched the *Keluarga Berencana* (Family Planning) program. That led to a significant decline in population growth rates, and the projection shows that up to the year 2030 Indonesia will continue to have this declining DR (see Figure 6.1). The period when the DR is declining is considered to be a golden period for an economy to accumulate wealth. This is the period when the economy can increase its national savings, allowing for increasing investments and capital accumulation for development.

Along with the declining fertility, the population projections also suggest that in the next decade Indonesia will have an enormous working-age population (see Figure 6.2). As of 2014, Indonesia has about 118 million people in the

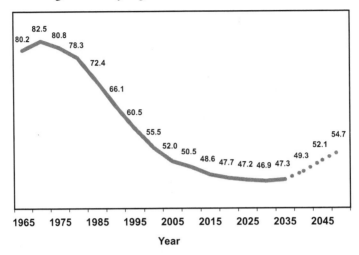

Figure 6.1 Old-age dependency ratio

Source: BPS Publication (2013), 2010–2035 from Bappenas-BPS Population Projection, 2035–2050 Author's estimation

labour force, and that would continue to increase to above 200 million in 2035. This is, again, a golden period. However, a careful macroeconomic policy and management are needed to ensure the availability of jobs as well as protection to the ever-increasing labour force.

The DR, however, will not decline forever. Estimates suggest that the DR will start to increase again around 2030. This is not spurred by fertility behaviour. Instead, the DR will increase because of the aging population (see Figure 6.2). Improvement in nutrition, medicine, and development as a whole will increase the life expectancy. In 2030 Indonesians will have life expectancies at birth of around 74 years, a significant bump from the current 69 years. Earlier literature suggested that the aging population may pose a potential burden to the economy. Recent discussions, however, suggest otherwise. Aging populations may become a source of potential improvement of societal welfare, provided that the elderly are healthy and productive. A key to that message is the understanding that the groundwork for healthy and productive elderly persons should be prepared as early as possible, and not when a person approaching the retirement age.

This situation is coupled with the fact that Indonesians are aspiring for higher economic status. Between 2003 and 2010, there were about 55 million people joining the Indonesian middle-income class (World Bank, 2011). This group has a defining role in Indonesia's long-term development features. The middle class in essence is the labour in the production process and the same time is the significant source of demand for goods, services, and assets. Members of this class have great expectations about a better life for their own generation,

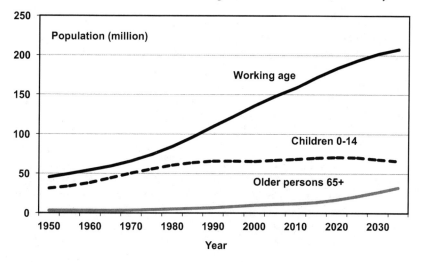

Figure 6.2 Population by age group

Source: BPS Publication (2013), 2010–2035 from Bappenas-BPS Population Projection, 2035–2050 Author's estimation

and more importantly for the coming generations. They would like to have better education, better health, and proper protections from different risks that life may pose to them. To facilitate attainment of these aspirations, the middle class needs government leadership and support in provision of public amenities and in social protection.

In addition to the middle class, Indonesia is also placing a great priority on poverty alleviation. Again, an important lesson from the end-1990s economic crisis is the need of proper social security (or more appropriately, a social safety net) for the poor. Although social security is not necessarily only for the poor, it is also very important to include the poor in Indonesian social security programs, especially for the programs covering health risks.

The Law no. 40/2004 on the National Social Security System mandates five different programs, namely (i) health insurance, (ii) public pension, (iii) old-age pension, (iv) working accident insurance, and (v) death benefit program (Republic of Indonesia, 2004). For the implementation, two social security agencies implementing agencies (*Badan Penyelenggara Jaminan Sosial*, or BPJS hereafter) were established. First is the BPJS Healthcare, which will be responsible to implement the National Health Insurance (*Jaminan Kesehatan Nasional*, or JKN hereafter), and the second is the BPJS Labour, which will be responsible for implementing the other four programs for all Indonesian workers.

An important feature for the implementation of Indonesian SJSN Law involves a transformation of existing programs to the two new BPJS agencies. Indeed, some of these programs have already been in place in Indonesia, but unfortunately they were rather scattered (in terms of the coverage) and were not in a structured fashion. The fact that these programs were actually in place also posed implementation challenges to the program. One of these implementation challenges is the fiscal policy strategy.

Despite the five-year preparation period granted by the SJSN Law, Indonesia only managed to establish the SJSN implementing agencies in 2011, by way of Law no. 24/2011 on BPJS (Republic of Indonesia, 2011). There are two implementing agencies, namely BPJS Healthcare and BPJS Labour. BPJS Healthcare – a transformation from PT Askes, a state-owned enterprise (SOE) that has been providing civil servant health insurance, including for retired civil servants – is responsible for organizing the national health insurance program, The BPJS Labour has been entrusted to organize the other four social security programs: public pension, old-age pension, work accident insurance, and death benefit program. BPJS Labour will be administered PT Jamsostek, another state-owned enterprise that has been administering income security and other programs for private sector workers. The transformation from SOEs to public entities on January 1st, 2014, was meant to comply with the SJSN administration principles, such as establishment of a trust fund and operating as a not-for-profit organization. In addition, two other SOEs, PT Taspen and PT Asabri, that managed the pension for government employees and army personnel respectively, will be integrated into BPJS no later than the year 2029.

Since the enactment of the law on BPJS, the government and related stakeholders have worked hard to formulate implementing regulations. The government and parliament agreed that BPJS Healthcare begin the implementation of JKN as of January 1, 2014. By the end of 2013, the government issued 10 Government Regulations and 5 Presidential Regulations to support the implementation. There is more to be done, but the success of SJSN implementation would have a significant impact on several aspects, impacting on the quality of life and well-being of the population of Indonesia.

Following this introduction, challenges of implementing agencies designated to implement the 2004 SJSN Law are discussed in the following section (BPJS healthcare), and in the section titled "BPJS labour". The final section provides concluding observations.

2. BPJS Healthcare

BPJS Healthcare is responsible for implementing the *Jaminan Kesehatan Nasional* (JKN). The law mandates that JKN must be implemented as a social insurance program under which risk is shared by the society, and membership is mandatory with universal coverage. This is not an easy task, since the most important task for the JKN is the integration of different existing systems.

To progress towards the objective of achieving universal coverage, WHO (2008) conceptualizes three dimensions (Figure 6.3). The three dimensions are (i) membership target, (ii) benefits covered, and (iii) proportion of cost covered. These dimensions are well understood by Indonesian policymakers, but taking

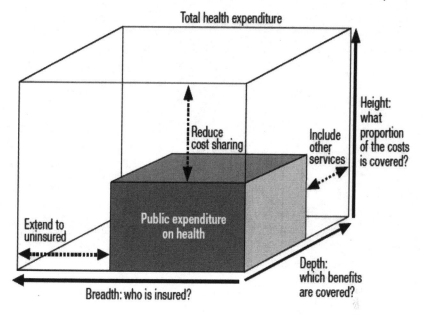

Figure 6.3 Three ways of moving towards universal coverage
Source: WHO (2008)

and implementing appropriate decisions regarding these dimensions is a complex taste with several challenges.

The first challenge is the membership target. The law mandates universal coverage. The challenge is to extend the coverage to all the uninsured so that universal coverage of the JKN is achieved. The BPJS Healthcare Roadmap sets the target of universal coverage in 2019. In June 2014, BPJS had a membership equivalent 50 percent of the population (BPJS Healthcare, 2014).

The roadmap of BPJS Healthcare suggested that the target for 2014 enrolment is 121.6 million people and that it should gradually reach the universal coverage in 2019, covering 257.5 million people. On January 1, 2014, all beneficiaries from the old system migrated to the new system (Table 6.1). Memberships of the old system comprised the Jamkesmas participants (known as Recipient of Contribution Subsidy (*Penerima Bantuan Iuran* or PBI hereafter) under the SJSN scheme), armed forces/polices, participants of PT Askes (civil servants), and participants of healthcare program for formal workers provided by PT Jamsostek (JPK Jamsostek). This is a challenging migration process. In addition, the Jamkesda, financed by local governments, is expected to join BPJS Healthcare by the end of 2016.

Employers who have not enrolled their employees in JPK Jamsostek have to register their employees to BPJS Healthcare during period of 2014 to 2019, according to a specified schedule. The employees of SOEs and private companies (from small size to large size) have to be enrolled in BPJS Healthcare by

Table 6.1 Indonesia JKN Membership in January 2014 (million people)

No.	Programs	Membership		
		Participating member	*Family members*	*Total*
1	Askes Sosial	7.26 (6.3)	8.88 (7.6)	16.14 (13.9)
2	Jamkesmas	86.40 (74.4)	nil	86.40 (74.4)
3	Army Personnel	0.43 (0.4)	0.43 (0.4)	0.86 (0.7)
4	Police Personnel	0.36 (0.3)	0.39 (0.3)	0.74 (0.6)
5	Jamsostek	3.40 (2.9)	5.05 (4.3)	8.45 (7.3)
6	Jamkesda (JKA and KSJ)	3.53 (3.0)	nil	3.53 (3.0)
	Total membership			**116.11 (100.00)**

Source: BPJS Healthcare (2014)

Note: Figures in brackets are percentage of the total membership

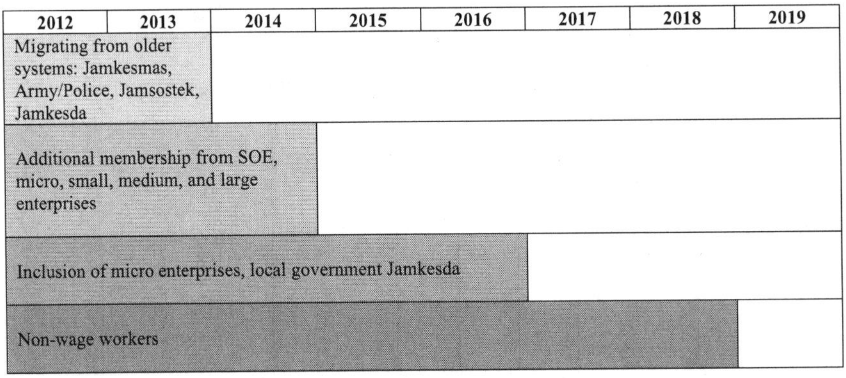

2012	2013	2014	2015	2016	2017	2018	2019
Migrating from older systems: Jamkesmas, Army/Police, Jamsostek, Jamkesda							
Additional membership from SOE, micro, small, medium, and large enterprises							
Inclusion of micro enterprises, local government Jamkesda							
Non-wage workers							

Figure 6.4 Membership road map towards universal coverage

January 1, 2015, at the latest, while for the micro size companies the deadline is January 1, 2016. Finally, the informal sector must enrol in BPJS Healthcare by January 1, 2019. A detailed schedule is provided in Figure 6.4.

Achieving the universal coverage in 2019 is ambitious. The government is fully aware that it would be a great challenge to accomplish it. In the Roadmap for Healthcare, there are three main strategies to meet this target, namely participant grouping strategy, regional-based strategy, and collaboration among all related parties. Although this is a mandatory program, some parties are sceptical that the target of universal coverage in 2019 can be achieved. It should be noted that one of the criteria of a successful healthcare program is the number of people enrolled in BPJS Healthcare.

The second challenge is the coverage of benefits provided to all participants. Of course, it is important to keep in mind that a sustainable insurance system must always link the benefits closely with the premiums paid. A higher premium would naturally entail greater benefits. The migration to the new system had to face a transformation challenge: different existing systems had various levels of premiums and benefits.

The most important challenge is posed by the previous program of Jaminan Kesehatan Masyarakat (Jamkesmas), which is the health insurance for the poor and vulnerable. Jamkesmas was previously part of the poverty alleviation program, providing health insurance covering individuals belonging to households in the lowest 30 percent of the income distribution. Despite its public appearance as an insurance, in practice Jamkesmas is just another program of the Ministry of Health (MoH). The participating health facilities can ask MoH for reimbursement of (Jamkesmas beneficiaries') health expenses in a fiscal year while not enabling MoH to take into account the over-time accumulation of the unspent funds.

The Jamkesmas benefits had been very generous since the beginning, while the premium allocations were very small, at around IDR 6,000 per person per month. There is a big question of system sustainability if the premium remains at this level, given the unlimited benefit coverage. In the previous system, some local governments also implemented the Jamkesda, a Jamkesmas-like program paid for by the local government budgets. This also added to the complexity of transformation, as Jamkesda has different premiums and benefits as well, and on some occasions may overlap with Jamkesmas.

The other health insurance systems, e.g. ones for government employee or army personnel, or private insurance, are more reasonable in terms of premium-benefit links. In general, the benefit packages of the old systems already covered primary and secondary outpatient services. Different classes of treatment were also evident. For example, civil servants in grade I and grade II are entitled to inpatient care in class 2, while civil servants who are in grade III and grade IV can get inpatient care in class 1. The participant of JPK Jamsostek gets inpatient services in class 2, while Jamskesmas participant members and most Jamkesda are entitled to services in class 3.

The rate for medical practitioners and health amenities also varies depending on the class of treatment. This affects the quality of service given to the lower class because this system discourages the health providers. Some institutions, such as PT Askes, implement managed care, while others use indemnity/fee-for-service plans where the participant has no restriction as to which healthcare facility he/she can attend. Despite Jamkesmas, there are several health services that are excluded, particularly those whose costs are high, e.g. hemodialysis, organ transplantation, and cancer treatment.

As mandated in the SJSN Law, benefits provided by the Healthcare Program is individual health care including promotive, preventive, curative, and rehabilitative care. It also provides prescription drugs and consumable health amenities. As long there is a medical case, there is no limit to the health care coverage, and there is no cost sharing.

For the inpatient care, due to inadequacy of existing infrastructures there are still some differences in treatment classes. However, this condition is expected to change by 2019. Another challenge is to incorporate more and more providers to have contract or agreement with BPJS Health, arrangements for healthcare outside the country, infertility treatment, treatment for *cosmetic* or *aesthetic* reasons, and alternative treatments.

The third challenge is to generate requisite financial resources. In a welfare state, all health expenses are financed through either designated or from general tax. With a 12 percent tax-to-GDP ratio, the Indonesian revenue budget is not able to finance the whole health expenses. Thus it is important to have an actuarial study of the financing needs and their dynamics for the next few decades. The government budget would fully cover the PBI, and those with a socioeconomic status above the PBI level would pay for the premiums either in a co-sharing basis (for workers) or full payment (for other individuals). This poses issues of targeting those who are eligible to receive subsidies and those who are not eligible.

The law also mandated that the insurance premiums for poor and vulnerable groups in the population are paid for by the government. At this moment there are about 86.4 million people registered as the premium beneficiaries (PBI). That covers people from the 35 percent of households with low incomes. Regarding this PBI, it is important to stress that BPJS Healthcare should not be aiming at greater government contribution by increasing the number of PBI. With the economic growth, the ability of some of the current PBI to pay or co-share the health insurance premium should also be increasing. Thus, the BPJS Healthcare should aim at higher government contribution by increasing the premium rate, and at the same time anticipating the reduction in the PBI beneficiaries. This may sound unpopular, but the system will be more sustainable and fair if this course is followed. It is also important to note that the PBI covering 35 percent of the lowest-income households in income distribution involves around three times the number of people below the poverty line, which in 2014 was only about 28 million or 11.3 percent of the population.

3. BPJS Labour

BPJS Labour is established to implement the other four social security programs, namely the old-age savings, pensions, working accidents, and death benefit programs. The main targets for these employment social securities are all workers in Indonesia, covering both those in formal and informal sectors. It is set to become effective on July 1, 2015, and it is expected that all formal sector workers should have enrolled in BPJS Labour by 2019, while the informal sector membership will be accelerated after that. By 2019, the plans are to cover about 46 percent of the labour force numbering 126 million (Table 6.3).

With the establishment of BPJS Labour, the most immediate challenge is to migrate the existing system. But more important than that is to prepare road-maps to expand the coverage of current social security programs. The existing social security programs for formal workers are operated by several SOEs, namely PT Jamsostek, PT Taspen, and PT Asabri. Details of the number of participants in 2012 by each of these organizations are presented in Table 6.2. It may

Table 6.2 Membership in Indonesia's social security organizations, 2012 (million people)

Participant	2008	2009	2010	2011	2012
Jamsostek	**11.85 (61%)**	**13.67 (64%)**	**13.67 (63%)**	**15.08 (65%)**	**15.37 (66%)**
Active Participants – JKK, JHT, JKm	8.22 (43%)	8.50 (40%)	9.34 (43%)	10.26 (44%)	11.25 (48%)
Participants from Construction Sector	3.63 (19%)	5.17 (24%)	4.33 (20%)	4.83 (21%)	4.13 (18%)
Taspen (for government employee)	**6.32 (33%)**	**6.50 (30%)**	**6.72 (31%)**	**6.98 (30%)**	**6.91 (29%)**
Active Participants	4.22 (22%)	4.33 (20%)	4.49 (21%)	4.69 (20%)	4.56 (19%)
Retiree (beneficiary)	2.10 (11%)	2.17 (10%)	2.24 (10%)	2.29 (10%)	2.36 (10%)
Asabri (for army personnel)	**1.14 (6%)**	**1.15 (5%)**	**1.16 (5%)**	**1.16 (5%)**	**1.16 (5%)**
Active Participants	0.86 (4%)	0.86 (4%)	0.84 (4%)	0.85 (4%)	0.84 (4%)
Retiree (beneficiary)	0.28 (1%)	0.29 (1%)	0.32 (1%)	0.31 (1%)	0.32 (1%)
Total	**19.31 (100%)**	**21.32 (100%)**	**21.55 (100%)**	**23.22 (100%)**	**23.44 (100%)**

Source: Adapted from BPJS Labour Roadmap, 2013

Note: Figures in bracket are percentage of the respective total.
JKK: *Jaminan Kecelakaan Kerja* (Work Accident Insurance)
JHT: *Jaminan Hari Tua* (Old Age Insurance)
JKm: *Jaminan Kematian* (Death Insurance)

Table 6.3 BPJS Employment membership targets (million people)

	2013	2014	2015	2016	2017	2018	2019
Indonesian Labour Market	**114.0**	**118.4**	**120.0**	**121.5**	**122.9**	**124.4**	**126.9**
Formal workers	45.6	47.3	48.0	48.6	49.1	49.7	50.3
Informal workers	68.4	71.1	72.0	72.9	73.8	74.7	75.6
Membership in BPJS Employment	**11.2**	**12.2**	**15.2**	**23.0**	**32.7**	**44.3**	**57.9**
Formal sector (cumulative)	11.2	12.2	14.5	21.2	29.4	39.1	50.3
Informal sector (cumulative)	–	–	0.7	1.8	3.3	5.2	7.6

Source: BPJS Healthcare (2013)

Note: – negligible

be observed that there are 15.4 million members of PT Jamsostek, of which 11.25 million people are active participants for JKK (Workers Accident Program), JKm (Death Benefit Program) and JHT (Old Age Saving Program). Under the PT Taspen, the total number of participants is 6.9 million, and 66 percent of them are active, the rest being retirees. On the other hand, there are 1.2 million participants in PT Asabri, with 73 percent active participants, the rest being retirees.

The membership trends in Table 6.2 suggest that the share of Jamsostek in total membership has increased from 61 percent in 2008 to 66 percent in 2012, and correspondingly the share of Taspen membership has decreased from 33 percent to 29 percent. The above coverage of social security employment program is far from the labour market conditions. The National Labour Force Survey (Sakernas) conducted by BPS in February 2014 suggested that the number of labour force in Indonesia is 113.2 million people, with about 43.3 million as workers. However, the number of participants in PT Jamsostek, PT Taspen, and PT Asabri is only 23.4 million people (approximately 20.7 percent of the total labour force, and about 54 percent of workers). The challenge for Indonesian BPJS Labour is the fact that about 60 percent of the Indonesian labour force is actually in the informal sectors. To get them to enrol in different social security programs that BPJS Labour will launch is a major challenge.

The BPJS Labour roadmap was then established, setting annual targets of membership (Table 6.3). The roadmap is based on two important assumptions for the 2014–2019 period: (i) working ratio of 65.1 percent of all Indonesian people age 15 or above, and (ii) a constant 40 percent ratio of the formal sector in the total labour force. Using these assumptions, the government projected the number of participant of BPJS Labour (Table 6.3). It suggests that the penetration rate for formal workers is gradually increasing from 6 percent (12.2 million workers) in 2014 to 100 percent (50.3 million workers) in 2019. This progress is lower for informal sector workers, with penetration rate of 1.5 percent in 2014, and increasing to only 10 percent (7.6 million workers) in 2019.

BPJS Labour's target to cover all workers in the formal sector in 2019 would not be an easy one. The roadmap sets out several strategies, namely:

- Focus on the province/municipality with highest participation coverage. Targets can be set for several BPJS Labour regional branches, and resources can be focused respectively. Naturally this will mean that BPJS Labour would start expansions in Java and Sumatra regions, where about 80 percent of Indonesia's population resides.
- Set the main priority to be sectors of businesses that already have associations or labour unions. Links to business associations as well as to labour unions may speed up membership expansion. However, approaching these organizations should not end up as a group bargaining process with underlying political transactions. BPJS Labour should not end up charging different premium nor benefit levels to different business associations or labour unions.
- Develop a solid database of BPJS Labour participants synchronized with the database of participants for the healthcare program in BPJS Healthcare and population registration data. In 2015, Indonesia does not have an effective single citizen identity number for the country as a whole. Hence, different agencies may operate on the basis of different datasets. It is expected that BPJS Labour would put priorities in the IT and data management. By early 2015, Indonesia already has a functioning single registry which is used for targeting social protection and poverty alleviation programs. BPJS Healthcare obtains the beneficiaries of premium subsidies from that single registry. BPJS Labour should synchronize the data with an existing single registry and the population registration data under the Ministry of Home Affairs.
- Implement public education, promotion, and advocacy. The majority of Indonesia's population, labour force, and workers need to know more about the both BPJS Healthcare and Employment. Indonesians also need to be made aware of the benefits of insurance available throughout their lifetimes. With a rapidly growing middle class, Indonesians can benefit considerably from insurance and shared risks.
- Use law enforcement as a strategy. Nevertheless, the transition period should not rely on the law enforcement in a rigid way. As Indonesia enters the transition period toward the full implementation of both BPJS programs, Indonesia needs to exhaust all other strategies first.

There are four programs that BPJS Labour is responsible for. The Workers Accident Program is to ensure that participants receive healthcare benefits and cash compensation if they get injured at work or suffer occupational diseases. The benefits includes health services according to the medical needs and cash benefits in case of total permanent disability or death. Healthcare benefit includes curative, promotive, preventive, and rehabilitative services. In addition, the Workers Accident Program provides benefits in the form of disability compensation. As for the Death Benefit Program, the benefits would be paid to the heirs in term of cash benefits, where the amount is based on a particular formula. In designing this program, the benefits provided by the Workers Accident Program and the Death Benefit Program should be at least equal to the current benefits provided by PT Jamsostek.

For retiree, there are two programs, namely the Old Age Saving Program and the Pension Program. Both programs basically have the same purpose of providing income protection during the retirement period. The Old Age Saving Program uses a defined contribution scheme with a lump sum benefit payable when the participant retires. The Old age Saving Program under the SJSN should continue the current system currently administered by PT Jamsostek.

All workers in formal sectors, excluding civil servants, are required to join this program. The amount of contribution is 5.7 percent of salary/wages, where 3.7 percent is the employer's portion and the other 2 percent is the employee's portion. Informal sector workers could join this program by contributing a fixed amount of money. The government as an employer provides similar benefits to civil servants and armed forces/polices, but using the defined benefit (DB) method. As of February 2015, policymakers have not finalized the details of the pension and savings programs.

The aim of the Pension Program of SJSN is to maintain a decent life when participants receive reduced income or even lose income due to retirement or permanent total disability. Currently only a few employers provide pension benefits to their employers. However, some medium- and large-scale companies already provide attractive retirement benefit packages, using either defined contribution (DC) or defined benefit (DB) methods. The government as an employer has provided pension benefits with DB methods for civil servants, armed forces, police, veterans, and people who fought for the independence.

The SJSN Pension Program uses the DB method. Every participant or his/her heir is entitled to retirement benefits after fulfilling a minimum period of 15 years of contributing. If the participant dies before reaching the retirement age or has not met the contributing period of 15 years, his/her heirs are still entitled to pension benefits with some benefit adjustment.

In term of benefits, the government's initial target for the Pension Program of SJSN is at least for retirement security to provide the minimum of a 40 percent replacement rate required by the ILO Convention. To meet the target of a 40 percent replacement rate, the government also has to consider similar programs that have same purpose of income protection after retirement, such as the Old Age Saving Program. Moreover, the employer's responsibility to give severance pay to its employee as a reward of loyalty and hard work also should be taken into account. The SJSN Pension Program should at least provide benefits to cover the gap between the current replacement rate provided by other mandatory programs with the minimum replacement rate of 40 percent required by ILO.

The Pension Program of SJSN would be financed by both the employer and the employee. The government must be sensitive in calculating the amount of contributions that are affordable for both the employer and employee to ensure that the resulting arrangements bring a positive impact on the economy and the sustainability of the program. If the amount of the contribution is too small, the benefit can be expected to be small and inadequate. Yet it is also not necessarily desirable to set a high contribution rate. The extra cost for paying a contribution that exceeds the employer's ability may negatively impact the competitive advantage of doing business in Indonesia, whereas for the employees a high contribution rate could reduce their purchasing power, which may affect the consumption level on the whole. Both these aspects would have a negative impact on the Indonesian economy.

The government also needs to consider the impact of the contribution amount for the Pension Program on participation rates. High contribution rates will lower the probability of participants from micro scale business to join this Pension Program, given their ability is very limited. Consequently, it will be more difficult for workers in this sector to receive pension benefits, although they are probably the ones who need these benefits the most.

4. Closing remarks

Indonesia is in the early stages of implementing a social security system. The BPJS Healthcare is aiming at the universal coverage of the national health insurance. The other four social security programs for workers will be the responsibility of the BPJS Labour, which is expected to be operationalized on July 1, 2015. As has been decided, the new social security system should start with all the existing yet fragmented social security programs offered by primarily different SOEs.

The institutional transformations of several SOEs into BPJS Healthcare and BPJS Labour require careful planning for several reasons. First, SOEs are subject to the State-Owned Enterprises' regulations. The government, as the ultimate shareholder, is represented by the Ministry of State-Owned Enterprises, appointed the entire Board of Directors and Commissioners through the Shareholders' Meeting. BPJS is different, and more complicated. The Board of Directors is appointed and dismissed by the President, while the Board of Trustees (acting as the Board of Commissioner) are submitted by the President to the House of Representatives for approval. Clearly, politics should not be the primary guiding factor to play in such appointments. This suggests a need for addressing governance issues concerning the BPJS. Second, the SOEs typically follow for-profit motives, while the BPJS is a not-for-profit organization. The organizational culture will require change, as under the BPJS the primary motive is service for participants.

Nevertheless, it is important to keep in mind the current existence of other different private insurance providers (be it on healthcare, pension, death benefits, or working accidents). The establishment of new social security programs should ensure that private providers can continue to exist offering different insurance schemes, on top of what is mandated by the BPJS-designed programs. That is important because some segments of the population may be willing and able to afford schemes involving greater premium and benefits. While the private providers may be in the business for profit, the BPJS should remain as not-for-profit organization.

One of the key areas impacting the extent of success in implementing the SJSN program, especially in long-term programs such as the Public Pensions and Old Age Savings, is the assets and liabilities management. If effectively managed, this aspect can help to accelerate universal coverage achievement in three dimensions, either directly or indirectly. The basic principle in the SJSN asset management regime is clearly stated in the SJSN Law and the BPJS Law that the asset management must be done in the best interest of the participants by considering aspects of liquidity, solvency, prudentiality, funds security, and adequate investment returns.

The BPJS Law also introduces the asset separation principle. It requires that the management of the assets of the BPJS (as the organizer of the program) and, on the other hand, the asset management of the Social Security Fund (whose assets arise largely from collection of contributions from participants and investment returns) be kept separate.

This is in contrast with asset management tasks performed by PT Askes and PT Jamsostek. With this principle, BPJS Healthcare manages two assets, BPJS Healthcare assets and Social Security Health Care Fund assets. Meanwhile, BPJS Labour manages five assets, BPJS Labour assets and four Social Security Employment Fund assets.

The sustainability of Indonesian social security programs would depend greatly on the ability of the system to collect insurance premiums from the participants. For BPJS Labour, that should be more straightforward since it is based on a worker's status. Nevertheless, the system must still be established and implemented with great caution to ensure compliance.

The BPJS Healthcare faces a much greater challenge. The PBI covers, currently, those belonging to the 35 percent of the population with the lowest incomes and the existing BPJS members (that have been migrated from the old system) who are from the upper half of income distribution in the country. The missing group is actually the middle class, primarily dominated by the informal workers and their families. This is another challenge for the sustainability of the social security system in Indonesia.

Note

1 Dependency ratio is an age-population ratio of those typically not in the labour force (the dependent part) and those typically in the labour force (the productive part). Here, we use the population younger than 15 or older than 64 as the dependent to the working-age population of 15–64.

References

BPS. (2013). *Indonesia population projection 2010–2035.* Jakarta, Indonesia: Badan Pusat Statistik.

BPJS Healthcare. (2013). *Roadmap of BPJS healthcare,* http://www.djsn.go.id/ROADMAP%20JKN_Edisi%20Lengkap_CD%20Version.pdf

BPJS Healthcare. (2014). *Membership status report.* Mimeo.

BPJS Labour. (2014). *Roadmap of BPJS labour,* http://www.djsn.go.id/FA-roadmap BPJS-digitalDistribution.pdf

Handra, H. & Dita, A. (2016). Pension system and its fiscal implications in Indonesia. In Mukul Asher & Fauziah Zen (Eds.). *Age Related Pension Expenditure and Fiscal Space,* pp. 104–136. Oxon, UK: Routledge.

Republic of Indonesia. (2004). Law 40/2004 on National Social Security System

Republic of Indonesia. (2011). Law 24/2011 on BPJS

WHO. (2008). *The world health report 2008: Primary health care now more than ever.* Geneva, Switzerland: WHO, http://www.who.int/whr/2008/whr08_en.pdf

World Bank. (2011). 2008 Again?. *Indonesia Economic Quarterly,* March 2011. Jakarta, Indonesia: World Bank.

7 Japan's public pension expenditure projections

When will the macro-economy indexation work?

Junichiro Takahata[1]

1. Introduction

Aging trends in the world economy have become more pronounced since the end of last century. This trend became obvious following a rapid reduction of the total fertility rate (TFR) of developed countries over the latter half of the 20th century. An aging population creates a dilemma for policy-makers with respect to the financial strain it imposes on the social security system that is financed as a pay-as-you-go system. In this chapter we focus on the case of Japan, where fertility has fallen from 5 to 1.3 over a span of 60 years, and consider how to keep the public pension system sustainable in terms of indexation. While Japan is clearly a developed economy, its experience of establishing and maintaining a social security system can be potentially useful to emerging economies that are currently in the process of establishing one.

Japan is one of the world's fastest aging countries. In 2012, the old-age dependency ratio stood at 39 percent (see Table 7.1). This is higher than the OECD average of 25 percent, and compares less favourably against other individual European countries, such as Germany and Italy, at 32 percent each. Figure 7.1 shows the population pyramid for Japan in 2011. It is clear that there are two peaks at 60–65, the so-called the baby-boomer generation, and at 35–40, i.e. their children.

With global aging taking on a pace previously unseen anywhere in the world, the experience of Japan in managing its pension system and reforms presents an interesting and natural case study to examine and for developing countries to draw inferences from.

Japan introduced a public pension system around 50 years ago, and since then the level of benefit payments for the retired has illustrated an increasing trend. Figure 7.2 shows the total amount of National Pension payments since the 1970s. However, a structural transformation had already begun in the domestic economy from the 1960s, when the rural young moved to urban areas for work opportunities. The rural regions thus largely comprised parents who were supported remotely by remittances from their children.

Table 7.1 Old-age dependency ratio in 2012

Japan	39%
Germany	32%
Italy	32%
France	27%
United Kingdom	26%
United States	20%
China	12%
India	8%
Indonesia	8%
World	12%

Source: World Bank's World Development Indicator:
http:/data.worldbank.org

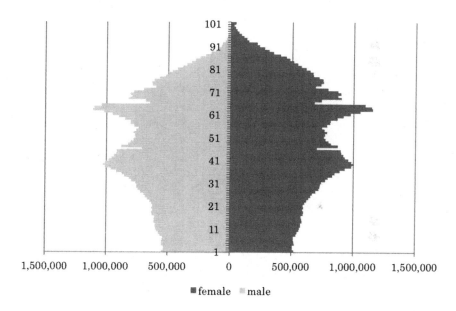

Figure 7.1 Japan population pyramid 2011

Figure 7.3 shows the relative magnitude of urbanization in Japan, where the three major cities of Tokyo, Osaka, and Aichi form more than 20 percent of the national population. Such changes might therefore also be happening in other emerging economies where the existing old-age dependency ratio is still low.

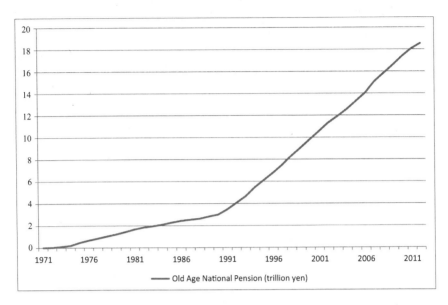

Figure 7.2 Historical trend of old age national pension expenditure

Source: MHLW website

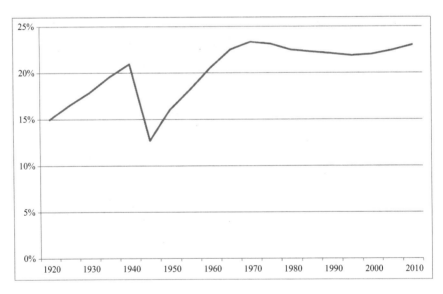

Figure 7.3 Urban population ratio in Japan

Note: The ratio is defined as people living in the 3 largest urban areas – Tokyo, Osaka, and Aichi – to the whole population in Japan.

Following the 2004 reforms, the government started releasing their methods and future projections for the public pension system. However, these were considered as being too optimistic for a public pension system managed under a "macro-economy indexation system" to work effectively.

The purpose of this chapter, therefore, is to modify some of these assumptions, discuss the indexation system in further detail, and present the revised projection results.

A common practice is that the models used to forecast pension expenditures explicitly take into account what is termed as the "limited balance system"[2] in the model. However, this chapter employs a simplified model which does not consider the adjustment period, only examining the effectiveness of macroeconomic indexation for sustainable pension expenditure to calculate the pension-expenditure-to-GDP ratio. This is because what is important is not only pension finance but also the whole public finance. Recently it has been settled that the benefit payment for the National Pension system is supported in half from the general account. Moreover, we will surely have a big increase in other social security expenditures, such as health insurance and long-term care. The limited balance system is a system where macro-economy indexation is executed only when the public pension system does not have enough reserves; that is, pension fund accumulation after a hundred years will be left for one-year benefit payments in order to maintain the public pension finance. Since not only is the sustainability of a public pension system important but also that of public finance itself, in this chapter we will consider a pension problem in an environment where the macro-economy indexation is a permanent system.

An aging population is simply the case where the number of young people in each succeeding generation is less than the previous. The literature on pension projections suggests that in such an environment indexation might not fully work if there is no growth or inflationary pressures in the economy. Hence, the use of a simple model which abstracts from other expenditure considerations of the government allows us to identify specifically the conditions under which macroeconomic indexation works, *ceteris paribus*, where the main variable we focus on is the pension-expenditure-to-GDP ratio.

The structure of the rest of this chapter is as follows: the history of Japan public pension system and its reform is introduced in Section 2. Section 3 reviews some of the literature pertaining to the government's pension expenditure projection, and presents and discusses it shortcomings. In Section 4, the assumptions that are used in this study are explained, and Section 5 shows our projection results. Section 6 concludes the chapter.

2. Public pensions in Japan

The public pension system in Japan developed gradually after the Second World War. The main impetus came in the 1960s when Japan experienced a high economic growth period, averaging annual growth rates of almost 10 percent. In that decade a significant amount of rural-urban migration of youth took place (See Figure 7.3), leaving the majority of the rural population to be elderly. As a result, it became necessary to have a social security system to support the elderly who did not make the migration and who likely had no other means of support apart from periodic remittances from their children.

The government thus introduced the National Pension system in 1961, where coverage was extended to people older than 50 year olds at that time. This group would become eligible for benefits under this scheme on reaching 70 years of age. Price indexation was introduced in 1973, which greatly expanded the amount of pension benefits given. This was executed on an annual basis but applied only when inflation exceeded 5 percent. Wage indexation was also introduced during this period to employees' pension systems. This indexation is not executed every year, but is executed every five years when fiscal projection is examined.

Following this change, social security expenditure, including the public pension system, started to grow greatly from around 1975. The total benefit amounts paid out by the Old Age National Pension system for 2000 and that of 2010 were 1.5 times and 2 times greater than that of 1990, respectively (see Figure 7.2).

The current pension system is composed primarily of three pillars, as shown in Figure 7.4: the basic pension (the first pillar), the wage proportional pension (the second pillar), and the funded pension (the third pillar). There are three types of working-age population in the first pillar: self-employed persons and others (Category I insured persons, totalling about 19 million), salaried workers of private sectors, government employees, and private school workers (Category II

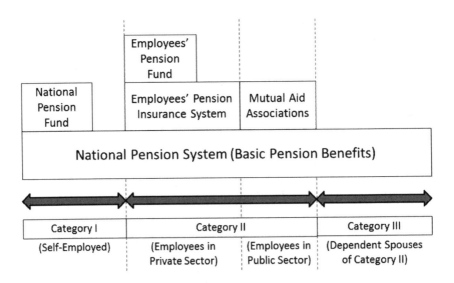

Figure 7.4 National pension system in Japan

Source: Reconstructed from the figure in the Website of Japan Pension Service; http://www. nenkin.go.jp/n/www/english/detail.jsp?id=38

insured persons, about 39 million), and dependent spouses of Category II insured persons (Category III insured persons, about 10 million).

The social security system is financed by a partially funded scheme. In the early stages of its establishment, the economic growth rate was higher than the rate of return from capital, as total fertility rate (TFR) remained at above the replacement ratio (see Figure 7.5), rendering the pay-as-you-go (PAYG) scheme as more preferable. As the economy developed over time however, TFR has dropped from 5 to around 1.3, and the return from capital became higher than the economic growth rate. As a result of reduced wage contributions arising from lower economic growth, fund balances have been decreasing, and the financial situation of the pension system has continually deteriorated.

However, to move from a partially funded, or PAYG, scheme to fully funded scheme, it is necessary for either the current generation to bear the financing burden or to issue debt, postponing it into the future – and both options appear almost identical from no reform. It will also be politically difficult to settle how the debt burden is to be shared among future generations.

2.1. Reforms before 2000

With the TFR falling over the past half century, several attempts at reform were attempted prior to the 2004 reforms to try remedy the state of finances in the pension system. These happened in 1985, 1994, and 2000.

At the onset, pension eligibility was set at age 60 for men and 55 for women. In the reform in 1985, it was decided that the eligibility age for

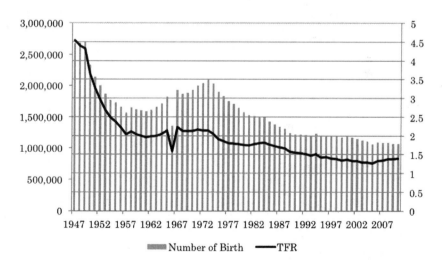

Figure 7.5 Trend of the number of births and TFR

Source: IPSS website

women should be raised by one year in every three years, starting from 1987, until it reached 60. Therefore, the eligibility age became 56 in 1987, 57 in 1990, and so forth. In 1999, the pension eligibility age for both sexes finally equalized at 60.

In the reform of 1994, the eligibility age for basic pensions was raised to 65, with a year increment implemented every three years until 2018. For men, this was reached in 2013. A 5-year lag was decided for women, with the increase to 65 only taking effect from 2018 on.

The reform of 2000 decided that the eligibility age for wage-proportional pension benefits was to be raised every three years from 2013. As such, it became 61 in 2013, 62 in 2016, etc., reaching 65 in 2025 for men. A similar 5-year gap was mandated for women so that it becomes 61 in 2018, 62 in 2021, and finally hitting 65 in 2030.

In addition to increasing the eligibility age, the pension tax rate has been raised stepwise many times over the decades (see Figure 7.6). Over the same period, the premium payment ratio, the ratio of people paying their pension premium, has dropped (see Figure 7.7). The Ministry of Health, Labour, and Welfare (MHLW) suggests that this fall may be attributed to the fact that (1) contributors might not be working, (2) contributors' income is too low to pay the premiums, or (3) contributors (especially the younger generations) are sceptical about the working and sustainability of the system.

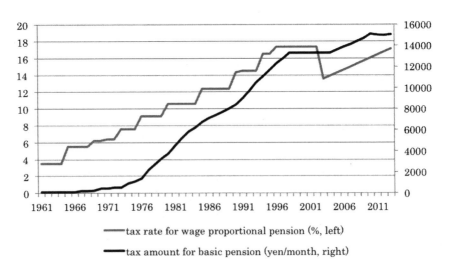

Figure 7.6 Trend of tax rate and amount 1961–2013

Note: From 2003, the tax base of the wage proportional pension came to include not only monthly salary but also bonus payments, and for this adjustment the rate looks decreased in this year. However, the actual tax amount was not reduced.

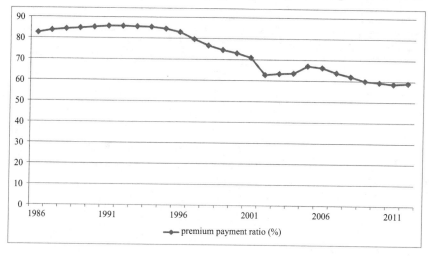

Figure 7.7 Premium payment ratio 1986–2012
Source: MHLW website

Price indexation was fully introduced in 1989. In 1994, an employee's pension was indexed to the level of disposable income instead of the general wage level. In 2000, pension for pensioners who have been already receiving pension was indexed to price level, which was indexed to disposable income before.

2.2. Reforms in 2004

The reforms enacted prior to 2004 left the impression that there will be an increasing pension burden coupled with reduced benefits. The 2004 reforms were undertaken in order to prevent such a situation from happening. In this reform, the pension tax rate and amount contributed were raised from 13.58 percent to 18.3 percent and to 16,900 yen (from 13,300 yen) per month at a gradual implementation schedule until 2017, after which it will be fixed with no further increases (see Figure 7.6 for the past contribution rate trend).

It should be noted that since the pension contribution rate will be fixed after 2017, a balanced pension financial account is maintained by cutting pension benefits or by pension reserves earning a higher rate of return. With respect to the latter option, the Government Pension Investment Fund (GPIF) started to manage the fund in 2001, after the government instituted a corporation reform of the pension fund management.

The fund amount stood at 123.92 trillion yen at the end of September 30, 2013. Around 75 percent of the portfolio is invested in domestic bonds and stocks, and another 20 percent or so is in international bonds and stocks. The rate of return for the 2012 fiscal year was 10.23 percent, which was the highest since 2001. Table 7.2 lists the historical rates of return. If the rate of return is to be higher, the pension reserve must have more risky assets.

Table 7.2 Previous GPIF's rate of return

Fiscal year	2001	02	03	04	05	06	07	08	09	10	11	12
Return (%)	−1.8	−5.4	8.4	3.4	9.9	3.7	−4.6	−7.6	7.9	−0.3	2.3	10.2

Source: GPIF website.

At the same time, the government started releasing more data and their projections for five-year intervals for the following 100 years with the 2004 reforms. These will be shown and discussed in the following section ("Government projection").

The "macro-economy indexation system" was also introduced with this reform. We will examine this in greater detail next.

2.3. Macro-economy indexation system

As mentioned, the level of pension benefits is indexed to the "macro-economy". What this means in turn is that the pension benefit is indexed to a revision rate which adjusts the pension benefit following the wage growth rate (for first-time pension recipients) and the inflation rate (for those already in receipt of pension benefits). This is supposed to take into account the comprehensive effects of both a decreasing younger generation population size and expanding longevity. It is represented in the following equations: for new pensioners,

$$revision\ rate = wage\ growth\ rate - slide\ adjustment\ rate, \qquad (7.1)$$

and for pensioners who received once ("old pensioners"),

$$revision\ rate = inflation\ rate - slide\ adjustment\ rate. \qquad (7.2)$$

Under this system, the revision rate is dependent on determining the slide adjustment rate. The slide adjustment rate is defined as the sum of the average growth rate of the number of contributors for the previous three years (about 0.6 percent in 2009) and the rate for expanding longevity (0.3 percent). According to this mechanism, when the inflation rate is 3 percent and the slide adjustment rate is 2 percent, the revision rate would be 3%–2%=1%.

However, when the price is not going up in an economy with deflation, the revision rate cannot be adjusted lower than the negative inflation rate. In Japan the price level has been slightly decreasing for 20 years. Therefore, such an adjustment has never worked effectively since the indexation system was introduced.

Furthermore, in principle, even when the inflation rate is negative the benefit level should be reduced at the same rate as the negative inflation rate. However, since the Japanese economy has been in a serious situation, the "special treatment" was introduced in 2004. In this treatment, initially introduced from

2000 to 2002, the benefit level is not revised when the economy is in deflation. Without this treatment, the benefit would be reduced by 1.7 percent based on the same level of deflation. In addition, the benefit is cut only when the price level becomes lower than the benchmark year, while the benefit is kept at the same level when the price level goes up. Currently, the benefit level is higher than the original level by 2.5 percent for such a treatment. For example, when the wage growth rate and inflation rate are 1% and the slide adjustment rate is 2%, the revision rate calculated from the formula is 1%–2%= –1%. However, since the revision rate cannot be a negative number when the growth rate is positive, the revision rate is 0% in this case. Moreover, when the wage growth rate and inflation rate are –1% and the slide adjustment rate is 2%, the revision rate calculated from the formula is –1%–2% = –3%. In this case, the revision rate will be –1% since it is not fair to the pensioners to keep a constant benefit level. Therefore, only when the growth rate is negative can the revision rate be negative in this system.

Figure 7.8 illustrates the four theoretically possible cases of adjustment. The first case is when wage growth rate is higher than inflation rate. In this case, the revision rate is the same as the previous formula. It should be noticed that even when either the wage growth rate or the inflation rate is negative this revision is executed. The other three cases refer to situations where the wage growth rate is lower than the inflation rate. In these cases the previous formula requires some modification before it can be applied.

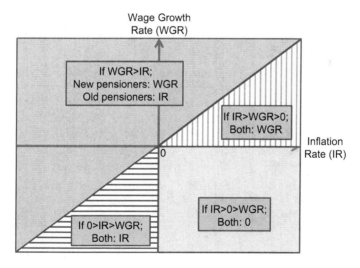

Figure 7.8 The revision rate for various cases

Edited by the author from the MHLW website. Note that the rate shown in the table is before subtracting the slide adjustment rate.

The second case is when both the wage growth rate and the inflation rate are positive. In this case even old pensioners have wage indexation, namely the revision rate is wage growth rate minus the slide adjustment rate both for new and old pensioners. The explanation for this rule by MHLW is that it is not fair for old pensioners to enjoy a higher revision rate than new pensioners.

The third case is when both wage growth and inflation rates are negative. In this case even new pensioners have inflation rates for adjustment, namely the revision rate is inflation rate minus the slide adjustment rate both for new and old pensioners. The rationale by MHLW is the same as before, but with the addendum that it is not valid to set a revision rate lower than the inflation rate.

The fourth case is where the inflation rate is positive but the wage growth rate is negative. In this case no adjustment occurs both for new and old pensioners. Namely, the revision rate is zero minus the slide adjustment rate.

This indexation is executed only before pension finance is balanced. This system is the so-called "limited balance system". If the pension reserve earns higher returns than expected, the "pension benefit adjustment period" will end earlier. According to the government projection in the 2009 fiscal inspection, this period will start in 2012, and end in 2038 for the National Pension and in 2019 for the Employees' Pension.

2.4. 2009 reforms

In 2009, the ruling government parties changed from the Liberal Democratic Party (LDP) and New Komeito coalition to the Democratic Party (DP), which remained in power until 2012. The new DP government introduced several reforms to the pension system. There are seven main pension reforms conducted by the government in this period: (1) a law enabling people to top-up previously unpaid premiums or to apply for an exemption; (2) a law enabling pension benefits to be payable after 10 years of enrolment (shortening from the previous 25-year requirement); (3) a law raising the tax subsidy rate of the National Pension to half of the whole expenditure of the National Pension System by 2014; (4) a law enlarging the number of workers who are eligible for wage proportional pension; (5) a law partially integrating the wage proportional pension for workers of the private and public sectors and private school workers; (6) a law cancelling the subsidized 2.5 percent pension benefit in the special treatment; and (7) a law supporting pensioners whose income is rather low and who cannot afford to pay the pension premium.

The first policy is only effective for two years, from October 1, 2012, to September 30, 2014, with the main beneficiaries being those who had lapsed in their pension contributions. The second policy, which provides incentive for workers who do not meet the previous 25-year requirement to resume their premium contributions, will be enacted in October 1, 2015. The fifth policy of integrating the three pension systems (for public servants of the central government, the local governments, and for workers of private schools) refers, in practice, to synchronizing and equalizing the pension tax rates of all three systems on October 1, 2015. The schedule of implementation for the sixth policy is for a 1 percent reduction of the benefit gap to take effect on October 1, 2013, and another 1 percent on April 1, 2014. The remaining 0.5 percent will be cut on April 1, 2015.

2.5. Recent reforms

At the end of 2012, the LDP and New Komeito won control of lower house and returned as the ruling party. Despite the increase in social security expenditure (see Figure 7.3) becoming a budgetary issue, the government chose instead to deal largely with issues of health and long-term care. There was no immediate consideration to revise (increase) the eligibility age for entitlement to pension benefits. Furthermore, the key policy debate at the current time of writing was on raising the rate of Value-Added Tax (VAT) to 8 percent in April 2014, and 10 percent in October 2015, up from the current tax rate of 5 percent (which was set in 1997).

It has been announced that the revenue from 1 percent out of the proposed 5 percent change in VAT will be used to improve social security services such as enlarged day care services for children or long-term care for the old, and the rest will be used to stabilize the public pension and health systems. Before 2004, one third of the National Pension expenditure was subsidized by revenue from the general account of the government's budget. In the 2004 reforms, it was decided to increase the expenditure share coming from the general account to half over 5 years. However, until the VAT increase is passed, the issue of fiscal resources will remain unsettled.

In addition to raising VAT, various tax reforms have also been implemented to enhance the fiscal space to support the aging population. For example, changes to the inheritance tax system will take effect from January 1, 2015. The tax rate will be kept at the same level, but the threshold will become 60 percent of the previous level: the sum of 30 million yen as the standard deduction and 6 million yen times the number of recipients, which was 50 million yen plus 10 million yen times recipient numbers before.

3. Government projection

3.1. Some literature

Thus far various pension projections with macro-economy indexation have already been examined in Japan. Kawase *et al.* (2007) considers a higher inflation rate case (2 percent) than the assumption of 1 percent used in government projections, holding wage growth rates unchanged for examining how inflation affects their original model based on Kawase *et al.* (2004). The study focuses on intergenerational equality and shows the ratio of lifetime benefits to contributions for each generation. They conclude that the health of public pension finances will be improved in the presence of a higher inflation rate.

Kitamura *et al.* (2006) focused on the relationship between the pension fund portfolio and the necessity for reform of the public pension system. In their study, "pension reserve degree" is considered explicitly, which is pension reserve divided by pension expenditure, but not on pension reserve itself, as an index for the soundness of pension finance. This index is also employed in the limited balance system. The study employs a pension model developed by Kitamura *et al.* (2006), which takes account of the 2004 pension reforms explicitly in the model. They found that under the current pension fund portfolio, the pension reserve degree will be very low in 2050, where a reform is required. Moreover, it is pointed out that when the rate of return from domestic investment drops, the portfolio will contain more risky asset in order to maintain the rate of return at the previous level, and the risk of having low benefits for future generations would be greater. They conclude that public pension design and pension fund portfolios are closely related and that it is necessary to reform altogether when the Government Pension Investment Fund (GPIF) alters the portfolio in future.

Fukao *et al.* (2007) also provides pension projection using the RIETI model, which is a dynamic stochastic general equilibrium model. They show that future interest rate in Japan will be lower, as the total fertility rate is lower. A lower TFR implies that labour becomes a scarce factor of production, thus raising its return (and thereby total contributions) while reducing that of capital. Together with the larger pool of funds for investment, this drives down the equilibrium return on capital (or the interest rate) further, resulting in a lower rate of return for the pension fund when the total fertility rate is low.

Ueda *et al.* (2011) conducts a simulation study where distributions of various pension-related figures, such as replacement ratio, pension benefit, and pension fund, are derived in a model developed by Ueda *et al.* (2010), with stochastic economic variables such as inflation rate and wage growth rate. They point out that the macro-economy indexation only works when the inflation rate or wage growth rate is positive enough to offset the "slide adjustment rate",[3] and derive the distribution of pension benefits for younger generations, which will be asymmetric in the sense that the benefits for future generations will be cut if growth rate is low. They conclude that the risk caused from stochastic fluctuation in the macro-economy burdens younger generations through the change in exit timing of a "pension benefit adjustment period".

Nakazawa *et al.* (2014) provides several quantitative analyses based on the model of Ueda *et al.* (2010), discussing that malfunctioning of macro-economy indexation which might happen when growth rate is low, deteriorating pension finance. In order to avoid such a pension finance problem, they examine several reform scenarios for increasing the pension eligibility age in Japan. They show the impacts of increasing the eligibility age on the pension replacement rate and benefit adjustment period, on the pension balance sheet, and on inter-generational equality.

3.2 Problems with the existing assumptions and projections

After the 2004 reforms, the government started to publish their evaluation results for five-year intervals of the basic pension and wage proportional pension expenditure scenarios for the private sector workforce. In this report, the benchmark assumptions of the price level growth rate was set at 1 percent, wage growth rate at 2.5 percent, and the rate of return from the pension fund at 4.1 percent. The calculation was based on the assumption of a fixed, premium payment ratio with various exemption ratios.

As GDP is not derived from the model used in this projection, there is no calculated pension-expenditure-to-GDP ratio. However, as the total amount of standard remuneration, i.e. the total wage amount for the tax base, is available, it is actually possible to have projection of GDP. Assuming that GDP is three times of the total standard remuneration from its historical trend, the future GDP trend can be derived up until 2105. The pension-expenditure-to-GDP ratio is illustrated in Figure 7.9.

Yet some of the assumptions used for this project do not correspond to reality. First, the wage growth rate is too high; it was assumed to 2.5 percent for the next hundred years in the benchmark calibration, but it was largely decreasing over the preceding 10 years to the formulation of the model (see Table 7.3). As a result, even if the future working age population decreases, total standard remuneration grows by three times in the model's calculations. If the average standard remuneration amount, dividing total standard remuneration by the working age population, is used instead, this figure increases by more than 10 times by 2105.

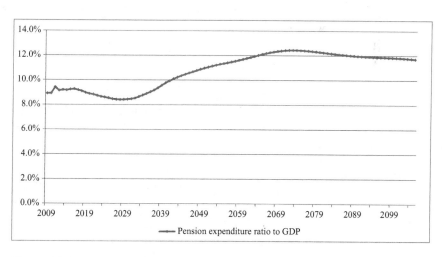

Figure 7.9 Pension expenditure ratio to GDP 2009–2105

Calculated by the author based on the pension expenditure provided by MHLW.

Table 7.3 Long-term assumptions on economic environment for Japan pension with historical economic trend

Year	Inflation Rate	Wage Growth Rate	Rate of Return
2003	−0.3	−0.6	–
2004	0.0	−0.2	–
2005	−0.3	−0.2	–
2006	0.3	−0.3	–
2007	0.0	−0.3	–
2008	1.4	−0.1	–
2009	−0.4	0.1	1.5
2010	0.2	3.4	1.8
2011	1.4	2.7	1.9
2012	1.5	2.8	2.0
2013	1.8	2.6	2.2
2014	2.2	2.7	2.6
2015	2.5	2.8	2.9
2016	1.0	2.5	3.4
2017	1.0	2.5	3.6
2018	1.0	2.5	3.9
2019	1.0	2.5	4.0
2020	1.0	2.5	4.1
2021	1.0	2.5	4.1

Source: MHLW website.

In the macro-economy indexation system, the expected decrease in the number of contributors will automatically be taken into account in the benefit calculations as spelt out in the previously mentioned formulas. However, this adjustment is effective only when the corresponding growth rate is sufficiently high to offset the slide adjustment rate. When the inflation rate (wage growth rate) is lower than the slide adjustment rate and the revision rate is 0, no revision is implemented. Similarly, when the wage growth rate is negative, no revision will occur. Therefore, revision occurs only when the difference between the two rates is positive, with the size of revision following accordingly. The government projections done in 2009 assumed a 2.5 percent wage growth and 1 percent inflation over the long term. Given what existing economic data suggests, it appears that pension finances were not seriously considered in the analysis.

A second major shortcoming of the report was the omission of the Mutual Aid Association, as shown in Figure 7.4. This is a wage proportional pension for public servant and private school workers, and was eliminated from the projection estimates. In 2011 there were 34.41 million workers in the Employees' Pension Insurance, while 4.42 million were in the Mutual Aid Association. This means that roughly 10 percent of wage proportional pension expenditure is missing from the projection calculations.

4. Some assumption modifications

For the purpose of this chapter, we assume that there are no drastic reforms or parameter changes affecting the existing pension system. We only assume and analyse the outcomes to several different scenarios under the existing system. The variables and data required to obtain the ratio of future pension expenditure to GDP are just inflation rate, economic growth rate, and some demographic numbers.

Required data on demographic projections for Japan are available from the National Institute of Population and Social Security Research (IPSS), which provides demographic projections for several scenarios for the next 100 years. We use these results spanning up to 2110, but our focus is primarily on the next 50 years, until 2060.

Figure 7.10 shows the total population trend in the future for 3 birth rate scenarios. In 2010, the total population is around 127 million, declining by

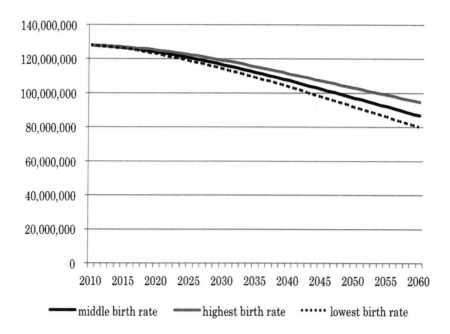

Figure 7.10 Total population

Calculated from the data provided by IPSS.

almost a third to 86 million in 2060. Even in a scenario with the highest birth rate, the total population would taper off at 94 million. It thus seems inevitable for a population decrease in Japan over the next 50 years. Figure 7.5 shows that the TFR in Japan has been below 1.5 for almost 20 years, and this low fertility rate exacerbates the decreasing population trend. The number of each age group population, 0–14, 15–64, and over 65 are shown in Figure 7.11. While the number of old people remains relatively constant for the next 50 years, the number of working age population decreases by almost half.

Following IMF (2011), it is possible to decompose the pension expenditure ratio into 5 factors:

$$\frac{PE}{GDP} = \frac{population\,65+}{population\,15-64} * \frac{pensioners}{population\,65+}$$
$$* \frac{average\,pension}{average\,wage} * \frac{population\,15-64}{workers} * \frac{compensation}{GDP} \qquad (7.3)$$

where PE stands for public pension expenditure. It is evident that the ratio depends largely on demographic variables from this equation. The variables that need to be calculated to forecast the pension expenditure ratio are pension expenditure and GDP.

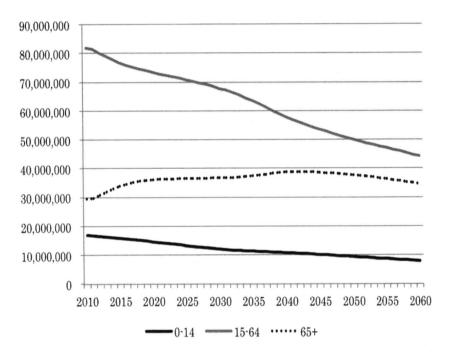

Figure 7.11 Demographic change for three groups

Calculated from the data provided by IPSS.

For the purpose of this projection, per capita GDP is calculated by dividing GDP at 2011, about 468 trillion yen, by productive population in the same year, 81.3 million people. The "per capita GDP for the working age population" is obtained as about 5.76 million yen, and no stochastic shocks are assumed. The following scenarios are hypothesized: per capita GDP is constant at the 2011 level for the baseline case (as Scenario 1); with 1 percent growth (Scenario 2); and with 2 percent growth (Scenario 3).[4] Total GDP is thus calculated as the product of "per capita GDP for working age population" and working age population. These estimates are shown in Figure 7.12, where even a 1 percent growth scenario still leads to a reduction in GDP in 2060. This is driven largely because the decrease in the productive population of Japan from 81.3 million in 2011 to 44.2 million in 2060.

Public pension expenditure is calculated as the product of per capita amount of public pension benefit and the number of people aged over 65. Per capita pension benefit for 2011 is calculated by dividing total pension expenditure, 52.2 trillion yen, by the number of people aged over 65 in the same year, 29.8 million people.

In this study, we assume that the wage rate grows at the same level as the price level for simplicity. The baseline calibration and projection is sets a zero percent growth for both wages and prices (Scenario 1), in line with the inflation and wage growth rates for the previous 20 years. The effects of a 1 percent growth (Scenario 2) and a 2 percent growth (Scenario 3) are examined as alternatives.

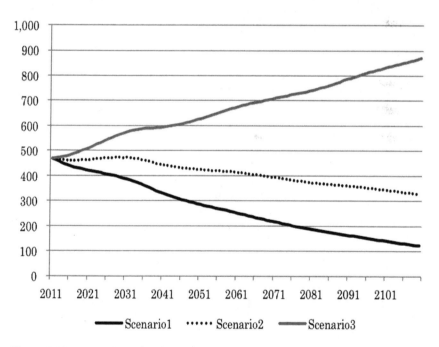

Figure 7.12 Future GDP for three scenarios: 2011–2110

Calculated by the author.

Since the macro-economy indexation system works effectively only when the economy is growing, the pension expenditure ratio to GDP varies widely among the above cases. The growth rate of contributors is shown in Figure 7.13.

As future population age group data is available annually, we consider two reform scenarios: increasing pension eligibility age to 67 (Scenario 4) and to 70 (Scenario 5) from 2010. Figure 7.14 shows the ratio of people aged 65

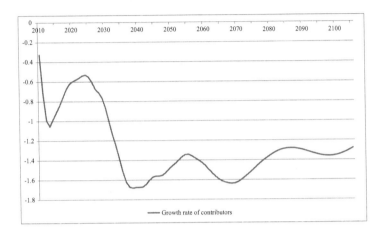

Figure 7.13 Growth rate of contributors: 2010–2105

Calculated from the data provided by IPSS.

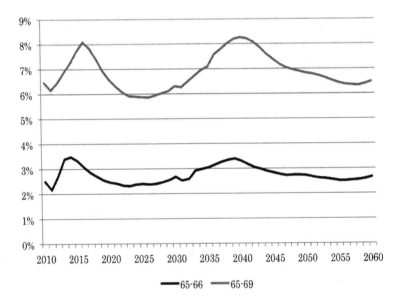

Figure 7.14 Ratio of 65–66- and 65–69-year-olds to the whole population

Calculated from the data provided by IPSS.

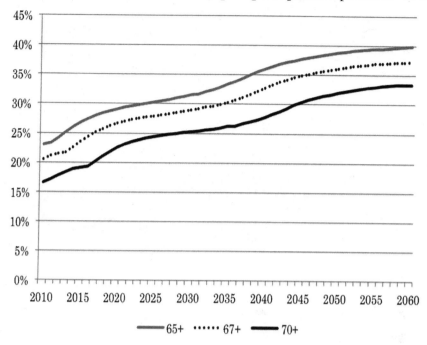

Figure 7.15 Old people ratio
Calculated from the data provided by IPSS.

to 66 at almost 3 percent, and 7 percent for the 65 to 69 age group in 2010. By raising the pension eligibility age in 2010, these are the two groups most directly affected, as they no longer receive benefits but will have to pay contributions instead. This effectively raises public pension balances at the time of implementation.

Figure 7.15 shows the ratios of people aged over 65, 67, and 70 to the whole population. The continual upward trend for all three age groups simply suggests that the OADR will fall continually, and this is liable to create problems for the financing of public pensions in future.

5. Projection results

Based on the assumptions set out in the previous section, the projection results are calculated and presented here. Figure 7.16 shows the projection results for pension-expenditure-to-GDP ratio. For the baseline case, this ratio is estimated to be 20.4 percent, almost double the ratio from 2010. This implies that a doubling of pension contributions/revenue will be necessary in 2040. This is an unprecedented situation for Japan, and there will be a need to consider

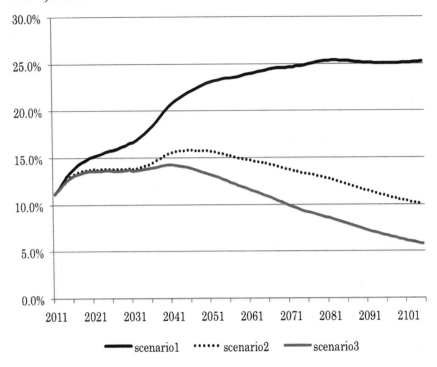

Figure 7.16 The ratio of pension expenditure to GDP: 2011–2110
Calculated by the author.

methods, including reducing public pensions or other expenditure, to create the necessary fiscal space if revenue collected is insufficient to meet expenditure.

For other scenarios, the pension expenditure to GDP ratio is lower. Assuming a growth rate of 1 percent, this will be 15.4 percent in 2040, 14.8 percent in 2060, and 10.0 percent in 2110. At 2 percent growth, the ratio is projected to be 14.8 percent in 2040, 11.7 percent in 2060, and 5.8 percent in 2110. The forecast for 2110 is even lower than the one in 2010.This is not only because the ability of the younger generation to pay pension contributions is high and that the pension liability becomes relatively small when the growth rate is high, but also because the macro-economy indexation can fully work when the growth rate is high enough to offset the slide adjustment rate. In Scenario 2, where the growth rate is 1 percent, these effects are weaker than those in Scenario 3, and thus the ratio will be higher.

Figure 7.17 shows how the indexation affects the revision rate for each respective growth rate. According to this figure, it will work fully when the growth

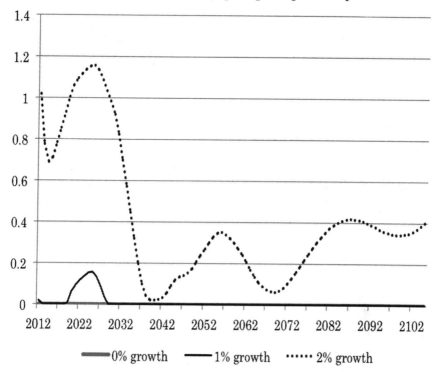

Figure 7.17 Pension revision rate (%) for three scenarios
Calculated by the author.

rate is 2 percent, while it does not work at all when there is no growth. It partially works when the growth rate is 1 percent.

Second, when the economy grows even at 1 percent, the macro-economy indexation works somehow and the pension-expenditure-to-GDP ratio greatly improves. As in Figure 7.17, the macro-economy indexation works effectively until around 2030, and there exists only a small difference between a 1 percent growth case and a 2 percent growth case. This is because the decreasing rate of the number of contributors will be mostly lower than 1 percent until around 2030, and after that the decrease rate will be greatly worse than 1 percent, almost 1.7 percent. Therefore, the difference between Scenarios 2 and 3 are mostly after 2030.

Now we turn to the projection results for the reform scenarios. Figure 7.18 shows the results for the two types of reforms: increasing the pension eligibility age to 67 and to 70, together with the baseline case. First, increasing the eligibility age to 67 (Scenario 4) reduces the pension expenditure ratio by almost 1 or 2 percent. A 3 or 4 percent reduction appears as the outcome when eligibility is raised to 70 (Scenario 5).

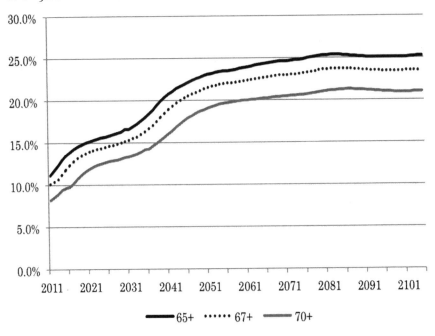

Figure 7.18 Pension GDP ratio when eligibility age is raised to 67 and 70
Calculated by the author.

More importantly, when the eligibility age is raised to 70, pension expenditure stands at approximately 20 percent of GDP. The alternative under a no-reform scenario projects a 25 percent expenditure-to-GDP ratio. This is clearly a heavy burden to the economy, making an increase in pension eligibility a seemingly viable policy choice in the future. It should be noted too that even with such a reform, the 20 percent expenditure-to-GDP ratio is still high compared to what Japan has historically experienced. As a digression, it may also be necessary, in view of such numbers, to explore and examine which socio-demographic groups may warrant support under a social security system.

As an exploratory analysis, the population pyramid (Figure 7.1) shows the existence of two humps in Japan's population development. There were two generations of baby boomers: the first between 1947 and 1949, and the second generation between 1972 and 1974. From the 2010s, the first generation will begin to retire and receive pension benefits that need to be financed. Figure 7.19 shows that by raising the eligibility age of this group to 70, pension contributions increase by almost 4 percent of GDP, which will clearly go a long way towards helping create the fiscal space necessary.

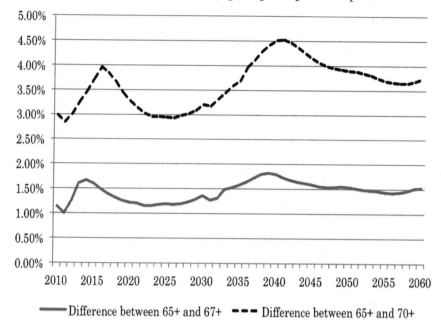

Figure 7.19 How much reform could improve pension finance
Calculated by the author.

6. Conclusion

This chapter focused on the use of a macro-economy indexation applied to pension benefit levels. We considered a pension system without the "limited balance" for Japan and performed some pension expenditure projections up until 2110. These were then compared with the official government projections done under a different set of simplifying assumptions. The government projection estimates place focus only when the macro-economy indexation functions effectively for the revision formula currently in use. However, it is clear that under low economic growth, which has been the case of Japan for an extended period now, its validity and realism is suspect.

In this study, the robustness of the revision rule attached to the macro-economy indexation is examined for several growth cases. It is shown that macro-economy indexation works effectively only when the economy grows at greater than 2 percent, high enough to exceed the "slide adjustment rate" inherent in the pension benefits revision rule. At 1 percent, indexation only works for several years. These results show clearly that there is room for improvement in using the current macro-economy indexation if pension sustainability is to be maintained.

It is already known that cutting pension levels is a politically difficult decision to undertake. This was observed from public reactions to the "special treatment" of pension benefits in the early 2000s. Yet when the number of working age population is decreasing, benefits must be adjusted according to maintain financial soundness of the system. The current system imposes a zero-lower bound adjustment, which curtails its ability to work as it was intended to, and this is likely to be the same in future with a high probability. It may thus be necessary to introduce an alternative type of indexation, where negative revision rates are allowed such that the revision rate formula responds better to the macro economy.

It is expected that the government expenditure will increase not only for public pension but also for health and long-term care, or for public assistance, placing a further strain on public finances in future. As expenditure capacity of the economy is limited, one way to ensure continued financial soundness of the pension system is to curtail pension expenditures in response to increases in government spending in other areas. In the case of Japan, the projection results in this chapter suggest that increasing the eligibility age may be an alternative policy to undertake as well. This may also be considered as a natural course of action to take, since the ratio of the working age to the entire population is continually decreasing.

For emerging economies in the process of establishing and their pension systems, there is a strong case to have an automatic indexation and benefit reduction mechanism in the design. The case of Japan demonstrates some of the robustness issues involved in incorporating such an index, and the difficulty of introducing and modifying one after the system is already established along with a tight pension budget

Notes

1 Address: Dokkyo University, 1–1, Gakuen-cho, Soka-shi, Saitama 340–0042 Japan, Phone/Fax: 81–48–942–6426; E-mail: jtakahat@gmail.com.
   This research was conducted as a part of the project for the Economic Research Institute for ASEAN and East Asia (ERIA) titled "Social Security System and Fiscal Policy in China, India, and Indonesia". The author is deeply indebted to the members of this project for their invaluable suggestions. The opinions expressed in this chapter are the sole responsibility of the author and do not reflect the views of the ERIA.
2 Pension benefit adjustment period is a period during which benefit payment is subject to the macro-economy indexation. Such an adjustment for the indexation occurs only when the pension system in the following 100 years will be balanced, and such a system is called "limited balance system".
3 See section titled "Public pensions in Japan" for more details.
4 In the government projection, GDP is not calculated. Instead, total standard remuneration is calculated, which is the tax base for wage-proportional pension.

References

Fukao, M., Hasumi, R., & Nakata, D. (2007). Declining fertility and aging of society, lifecycle, and public pension finance (In Japanese). Discussion Papers 07019, Research Institute of Economy, Trade and Industry (RIETI).

Horioka, C. Y., Suzuki, W., & Hatta, T. (2007). Aging, savings, and public pensions in Japan. *Asian Economic Policy Review* 2: 303–319.

IMF (International Monetary Fund). (2011). *The challenge of public pension reform in advanced and emerging economies.* Washington, DC: International Monetary Fund.

Kawase, A., Kitaura, Y., & Kimura, S. (2004). An impact of social security reform on public finance. *Osaka Economic Papers* 53: 108–126. (In Japanese).

Kawase, A., Kitaura Y., Kimura S. & Maekawa, S. (2007). Public pension reform of 2004 in Japan: Simulation analysis. *JCER Economic Journal* 56: 92–121. (In Japanese).

Kitamura, T., Nakashima, K., & Usuki, M. (2006). Risk analysis of pension reserve investment with macro economy indexation under the 2004 public pension reform. *Economic Analysis* 178: 23–52.

Nakazawa, M., Kageyama, N., Toba, T. & Takamura, M. (2014). Quantitative analysis on pension finance and pension eligibility age. KIER Discussion Paper Series 1313. (In Japanese).

Ueda, J., Teraji, Y., & Morita, S. (2010). Constructing model for relationship analyses of public pension and macro economy/public finance. KIER Discussion Paper Series 1008. (In Japanese).

Ueda, J., Mikami, Y., & Ishida, R. (2011). The influence of price and wage fluctuation on pension finance and pension asset distribution. KIER Discussion Paper Series 1108. (In Japanese).

Appendix

Table A3.1 Reform proposals in literature

Literature	Scenario	Method	Main Results
Oksanen, 2012	Baseline and 3 reform scenarios: Scenario 1: retirement age up by 5 years, contribution down to 20%, coverage increased Scenario 2: NDC reform with second pillar Scenario 3: NDC reform without second pillar	Demographic projection (urban, migrant, rural) System Simulation Model	Baseline: the system goes into red in 2013 and annual deficit exceeds 1% of GDP by 2030 Scenario 1: the system is manageable across the next two decades. Deficit increases dramatically afterwards. Scenario 2 and Scenario 3: annual balance can be reached. Scenario 3 is better than Scenario 2. Replacement ratio in both scenarios is lower than Scenario 1.
Sin, 2005	Baseline and 12 reform scenarios: Scenarios 1–4: projection assumptions under State Council Doc #26 Scenarios 5–9: projection assumptions under State Council Doc #42 Scenario 10: increasing retirement age to 65 Scenario 11: 100% price indexation from 2026 Scenario 12: gradual reduction in the contribution rate	World Bank, PROST Model	Baseline: the accumulated debt in 2075 is 95% of GDP in 2001. Scenarios 10, 11, 12: required contribution rate will be lower down. Three scenarios combined will lower the contribution rate to 17% in 2075.

(Continued)

180 *Appendix*

Table A3.1 (Continued)

Literature	Scenario	Method	Main Results
Wang, et al., 2004	Baseline and 3 sets experiments. The major experiments are: Experiment 2.4: multi-pillar system with government finances transition costs through VAT revenue Experiment 3.1: Experiment 2.4 combined with expanded coverage Experiment 3.2: Experiment 2.4 combined with higher retirement age	CGE Model	Baseline: Required contribution rate is 45% in 2030 Experiment 2.4: Required fiscal resources is 1.7% of GDP in 2005 to 0.8% of GDP in 2045 and decline thereafter. The reserves increase more rapidly when coverage is expanded and retirement age is raised. In Experiment 3.2, the system remains surplus.
Feldstein & Liebman, 2008	Separating legacy cost Reducing payroll tax rate Social pooling be redesigned by raising retirement age, reducing benefits Keep investment-based individual accounts	Not reported	An investment-based system can produce a benefit equal to 35% of a worker's final wage using a contribution rate of between 4% and 8% (depending on investment return)
Barr & Diamond, 2010	Notional defined contribution system (NDC)Extending coverageRaising retirement age	No simulation	NDC system is to have fiscal sustainability, giving workers more confidenceBenefits from individual accounts using interest rates based on quasi-actuarial principles.

Notes: The baseline scenario is referred to provisions of State Council Document #26 and #38.

Figure A3.1 shows the UN demographic projection, which generates slightly more population than we do in Figure 3.8. The urbanization rate provided by Figure A3.1 in 2050 is about 77 percent, while in our calculations the number is 80 percent. In this way we guarantee the robustness of the methodology used in the main text.

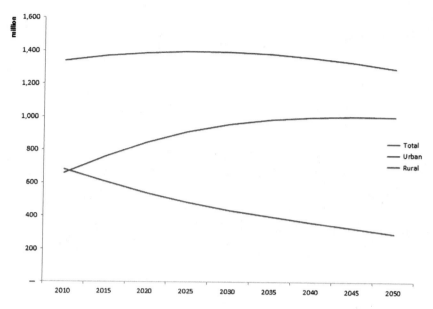

Figure A3.1 World population prospects from UN (2012 revision)
Source: http://esa.un.org/unpd/wup/DataQuery/

Table A3.2 Demographic structure (China)

Million	2005	2010	2015	2020	2025	2030	2035	2040	2045	2050
0–14	270	247	255	261	251	231	215	209	207	204
15–64	947	1000	1015	1004	1002	988	951	909	885	849
65+	101	114	132	168	196	235	282	317	322	331
total	1318	1360	1402	1433	1449	1453	1449	1436	1414	1385
Age structure %										
0–14	20.51	18.14	18.17	18.23	17.34	15.87	14.86	14.58	14.66	14.74
15–64	71.82	73.51	72.38	70.07	69.16	67.95	65.68	63.35	62.57	61.33
65+	7.67	8.35	9.45	11.70	13.50	16.18	19.46	22.06	22.77	23.92
total	100.00	100.00	100.00	100.00	100.00	100.00	100.00	100.00	100.00	100.00

Source: Population Division of the Department of Economic and Social Affairs of the United Nations Secretariat, World Population Prospects: The 2012 Revision, http://esa.un.org/unpd/wpp/index.htm (Medium variant)

Table A4.1 Annual return under NPS central government scheme

PFM	2008–09	2009–10	2010–11	2011–12	2012–13
SBI	17.36%	8.88%	8.05%	5.83%	12.75%
UTI	12.90%	9.27%	8.45%	5.60%	12.26%
LIC	10.02%	12.27%	8.30%	5.85%	12.06%
Average	13.43%	10.14%	8.27%	5.76%	12.35%
Wt. Avg.	13.84%	9.95%	8.25%	5.76%	12.39%

Source: http://financialservices.gov.in/pensionreforms/PRStatistics/NPS%20Returns.pdf

Table A4.2 Cumulative annual growth rate under NPS central government scheme

PFM	2009–10	2010–11	2011–12	2012–13
SBI	8.37%	9.88%	6.82%	13.01%
UTI	7.83%	11.34%	6.12%	13.22%
LIC	7.96%	10.77%	6.72%	12.75%
Average	8.05%	10.66%	6.55%	12.99%
Wt. Avg.	8.06%	10.64%	6.56%	13.00%

Table A5.1 Portfolio composition of Indonesia's pension funds investment (trillion IDR)

Year	Money Market*	Gov't Bond	Bond	Stock	Mutual Fund	Direct Investment	Real Estate	Debenture
1995	5.33		0.97	1.01	0.07	1.16	1.61	0.04
1997	8.83		1.40	1.06	0.23	1.82	1.97	0.13
1999	17.81		1.49	1.57	0.27	1.98	2.08	0.24
2001	23.82	0.03	3.24	1.59	0.36	2.32	2.38	0.40
2003	27.66	1.96	9.13	1.89	1.70	2.35	2.48	0.24
2005	18.16	16.01	15.81	4.24	1.81	2.71	2.77	0.58
2007	21.01	19.20	22.64	13.99	4.97	2.83	3.00	0.27
2009	23.83	29.74	25.99	16.00	5.41	3.51	3.48	0.11
2011	34.74	30.33	32.99	22.07	9.37	4.02	4.22	0.00

Source: Bappepam, 2012

* Money market comprises time deposits, on-call deposits, deposit certificates, and Bank Indonesia certificates

Box A5.1 Possible strategies for social pension design

Although social pension has not been discussed by the stakeholders at the moment, the unpatched ambiguous verse of the SJSN Law and the nature of its political economy will leave room to raise the issue of the provision of old-age security for the poor. These are several possible strategies that may help the Government of Indonesia in its provision:

- *Use more robust poverty measurement* while still taking regional disparities into account. With the current definition of the poverty line, individual poverty status is prone to change each month.
- *Develop comprehensive database with individual level data, which monitors social assistance benefits received from state, to minimize overlapping spending.* The existing electronic ID (e-KTP) database might be utilized for the expansion for such purposes. While the poverty status of an individual needs physical verification, inclusion error can at least be minimized when those with sum of social assistance benefits above the poverty line are excluded.
- *Hairline gaps of the poor and vulnerable calls for differentiation of state's pension programs for the uncovered population.* There needs to be two programs of state pension: with contribution, and non-contribution. If only a single program is provided (non-contribution to cover all the poor), the government may eventually bear unfunded full pension liabilities for a large proportion of the population at a time.
- *Non-contribution social pension should aim for the poorest of the uncovered poor.* The rest should be covered in different scheme with low contribution rates, nevertheless also subsidized by government.
- Some considerations for the system design:
  - *Different poverty lines will consequently result in different benefits across regions.* Social pension is the responsibility of the Central Government, and keeping it simple by using a single measurement will streamline the cost. Local Governments can be encouraged to deal with the regional disparities of the social pension benefit.
  - *On the other side, the social pension with contribution should take into account different income/expenditure levels of the participants.* Ideally, in the event of uncertainties, it must allow some degree of flexibility to switch contribution rates (followed by a switch in contribution subsidies and benefits to be received).
  - *To the possible extent, benefits and the contribution rates of the two plans should be designed to incorporate proper self-selection incentives.* Administrative costs to verify welfare status *vis-a-vis* eligibility of an individual might be larger than the benefits payment.

Name Index

Subject Index

Page numbers in *italics* refer to figures and tables.

private pension funds (DPLK),
   Indonesia 116–17
private sector programs: China 67; India
   78–80, 88–9, *91*; Indonesia 110–12,
   114–*15*
projection techniques: arithmetical
   method 6, 15, 17–20; dynamic
   general equilibrium method 6, 22–3;
   micro-simulation method 6, 20–2
prospective age 4
Provident Fund Regulatory and
   Development Authority (PFRDA) Bill
   90–1
Public Employee Pension system (PEP)
   36, *38–9*, 60
public expenditure 7
public pension systems: China 7–8,
   36–41, 49–57, 61–9; defined benefits
   (DB) 78; defined contributions (DC)
   78; fiscal sustainability 36–7; India
   78–94, 96, 98; Indonesia 104–6,
   111–14, 118–19, 131–3, 139–40,
   144, 146–50; Japan 152, 155–9,
   167–76; limitations of 117; lump sum
   payouts 112–13; notional defined
   contribution (NDC) 68; pay-as-
   you-go (PAYG) schemes 111–12;
   pension reforms 158; private sector
   78–80; public sector 78–*9*; reforms
   54–5, 67–8; regulation of 90–1. *See
   also* social security systems

Resident Pension 39
retirement financing: defined benefits
   (DB) 3; defined contributions
   (DC) 2–3; methods 2–3; state-
   intermediation of 3
retirement funding 2
retrospective age 4
rural migrant workers 39
rural-urban migration: agrarian
   economies 14; China 2, 41–50;
   effects of 14; old-age dependency
   ratio 48–50

SBI Pension Funds Private Limited 88
Sistem Jaminan Sosial Nasional. See
   SJSN Law of 2004 (Indonesia)
SJSN Law of 2004 (Indonesia) 10–11,
   104, 111, 117–19, 122–3, 132–3,
   137, 139–40, 148, 150, 183

Social Insurance Law (China) 39
social pension design 183
social security systems: challenges to
   105; expenditure projections 14–15;
   Indonesia 104–5, *111*, 117, 137, 139,
   144–6, 149–50; Japan 156–7; United
   States 23. *See also* public pension
   systems
Sovereign Wealth Funds (SWFs) 2, 65
State Civil Service *79*
state-owned enterprises (SOEs) 64–5, 111
static micro-simulation model 20
Swavalamban Scheme *80*, 88–90

Tabungan Hari Tua (THT) 112
total fertility rates (TFR): China 42;
   developed countries 152; European
   Union 27; India 75–6; Japan 28–9,
   157; projection of 29

UNDESA. *See* Population Division of
   the Department of Economic and
   Social Affairs of the United Nations
Union (Central) Government (India) 9
Union Civil Service Pension *79*
United States: budget balance
   projection 17; demographic
   projections 17; life expectancy 17;
   pension expenditure estimates 22–3
Urban and Local Bodies (ULBs) 97,
   100
urbanization 37, 50
Urban Old Age Dependency Ratio
   (OADR) 8
Urban Resident Pension scheme (URP)
   36, *38*–41, 51, 54
UTI Retirement Solutions Limited 88

Value-Added Tax (VAT): Indonesia 119;
   Japan 163
voluntary private pension funds:
   corporate participation 116;
   Indonesia 114–16

women: labor force participation 75, 77,
   110; life expectancy *30*, 75, 78
Workers Accident Program (Indonesia)
   147–8
World Economic Outlook (IMF) 23–4
World Population Prospects (United
   Nations) 24